Fresh Ways with
Terrines and Pâtés

COVER
Colourful rows of fresh vegetables provide a crisp counterpoint to smooth low-fat chicken and mushroom mousselines (recipe, page 91).

TIME-LIFE BOOKS

EUROPEAN EDITOR: Ellen Phillips
Design Director: Ed Skyner
Director of Editorial Resources: Louise Tulip
Chief Sub-Editor: Ilse Gray

LOST CIVILIZATIONS
HOW THINGS WORK
SYSTEM EARTH
LIBRARY OF CURIOUS AND
UNUSUAL FACTS
BUILDING BLOCKS
A CHILD'S FIRST LIBRARY OF LEARNING
VOYAGE THROUGH THE UNIVERSE
THE THIRD REICH
MYSTERIES OF THE UNKNOWN
TIME-LIFE HISTORY OF THE WORLD
FITNESS, HEALTH & NUTRITION
HEALTHY HOME COOKING
UNDERSTANDING COMPUTERS
THE ENCHANTED WORLD
LIBRARY OF NATIONS
PLANET EARTH
THE GOOD COOK
THE WORLD'S WILD PLACES

HEALTHY HOME COOKING

SERIES DIRECTOR: Jackie Matthews
Studio Stylist: Liz Hodgson

Editorial Staff for *Fresh Ways with Terrines and Pâtés:*
Editor: Frances Dixon
Researcher: Ellen Dupont
Designer: Mike Snell
Sub-Editors: Wendy Gibbons, Eugénie Romer

PICTURE DEPARTMENT
Administrator: Patricia Murray
Picture Co-ordinator: Amanda Hindley

EDITORIAL PRODUCTION
Chief: Maureen Kelly
Assistant: Samantha Hill
Editorial Department: Theresa John, Debra Lelliott

THE CONTRIBUTORS

JOANNA BLYTHMAN is a cook and recipe writer who owns a specialist food shop in Edinburgh. She contributes articles on cookery to a number of newspapers and trade periodicals.

SILVIJA DAVIDSON studied at Leith's School of Food and Wine and specializes in the development of recipes from Latvia and other international cuisines.

JOANNA FARROW, a home economist and recipe writer who contributes regularly to food magazines, is especially interested in decorative presentation of food. Her books include *Creative Cake Decorating* and *Novelty Cakes for Children.*

ANTHONY KWOK, originally a fashion designer from Hong Kong, has won several awards for his Orient-inspired style of cooking and was the *London Standard* Gastronomic Seafish Cook of 1986.

STEVEN WHEELER is a chef and the author of three books on desserts. He has also written a book about Seasonal English Cooking.

The following also contributed recipes to this volume:
Pat Alburey, Maddalena Bonino, Carole Clements, Jill Eggleton, Scott Ewing, Anne Gains, Sally Major, Colin Spencer, Susie Theodorou.

THE COOKS

The recipes in this book were cooked for photography by Pat Alburey, Allyson Birch, Jane Bird, Jill Eggleton, Anne Gains, Antony Kwok, Lesley Sendall, Jane Suthering, Rosemary Wadey, Steven Wheeler. *Studio Assistant:* Rita Walters.

CONSULTANT

PAT ALBUREY is a home economist with a wide experience of preparing foods for photography, teaching cookery and creating recipes. She has written a number of cookery books and she was the studio consultant for the Time-Life series *The Good Cook.* In addition to acting as the general consultant on this volume, she also created a number of the recipes.

NUTRITION CONSULTANT

PATRICIA JUDD trained as a dietician and worked in hospital practice before returning to university to obtain her MSc and PhD degrees. Since then she has lectured in Nutrition and Dietetics at London University.

Nutritional analyses for *Fresh Ways with Terrines and Pâtés* were derived from McCance and Widdowson's *The Composition of Food* by A. A. Paul and D. A. T. Southgate, and other current data.

This volume is one of a series of illustrated cookery books that emphasize the preparation of healthy dishes for today's weight-conscious, nutrition-minded eaters.

Fresh Ways with Terrines and Pâtés

BY

THE EDITORS OF TIME-LIFE BOOKS

TIME-LIFE BOOKS/AMSTERDAM

Contents

Terrine of Wild Rabbit with Mixed Lentils and Peas

Potted Pheasant with Chestnuts

*Terrine of Guinea Fowl,
Squabs and Quail with Wild Mushrooms*

4 Terrines for Dessert 111

Terrine of Prunes and Almonds

Fresh and Smoked Mackerel Pâté

3 Vegetables in Novel Guises 85

Two-Lentil Terrine

5 Microwaved Terrines and Pâtés 129

The New Terrines and Pâtés

The intriguing pâtés, terrines and galantines displayed in the windows of good delicatessens are often regretfully forsworn by today's health-conscious food lovers. When made in the conventional manner, these delicacies too often fall into the category of forbidden fruit: they are rich in pork fat, laden with salt, and packed with exquisite morsels of meat or seafood whose savour is exceeded only by their cholesterol count. The good news, however, is that consolation is at hand. A new style of cookery now renders such delights as these accessible even to those who wish to keep to a lighter, leaner diet.

Justifiably or not, a certain mystique surrounds the preparation of these dishes. Cooks debate, often heatedly, about their very names. To the purist, a pâté — French for a pie or pasty — is only entitled to that label if it is a savoury assemblage of ingredients presented in some form of pastry crust. A terrine, taking its name from the French *terre*, for earth, after the earthen-

ware vessel in which it was traditionally baked, is a loaf based on meat, fish or vegetables that have been cut into small pieces, or finely minced to form the mixture known as a forcemeat. Nevertheless, contemporary common usage has blurred the distinction between the two, and the terms pâté and terrine are now often used interchangeably for any spreadable, savoury paste. Indeed, even the old division between sweet and savoury is breaking down, as a rising generation of adventurous cooks use fruits, yogurt, low-fat white cheeses and chocolate to explore a hitherto little-known avenue — the dessert terrine.

Still more linguistic and culinary debate surrounds the galantine. Some culinary historians contend that the name is derived from an old French word for hen, and that the only true galantine is a boned, stuffed bird, poached in gelatinous stock, glazed with its own jelly, ornately decorated and served cold. A more liberal interpretation applies the term to other boned, stuffed meats and fishes. Some of these creations, in the hands of chefs with a penchant for showmanship, can take on an extravagant, even barbarous, splendour: a whole suckling pig, for instance, or the head of a boar, cleverly boned and stuffed to

keep its shape, sauced and painted with a gilded glaze. Yet the galantine also possesses a set of humbler cousins, devised in thrifty farmhouse kitchens: robust brawns and other jellied meats, such as parslied duck *(page 139)* or morsels of chicken in a lemon-tarragon aspic *(page 49)*.

Whatever names their admirers give them, all these dishes share one common characteristic: they are food for those who genuinely like to cook. They invite imaginative marriages of flavours and textures, encourage a free hand with the spice box, and offer generous rewards for those of experimental disposition. Of the 105 original recipes in this volume some, such as the broccoli and blue cheese pâté *(page 88)* or the mackerel pâté *(page 68)*, take little time to prepare; others, more complex, require a modicum of patience. But even the most elaborate are easily achieved by following a sequence of simple procedures that can be accomplished in advance, and in easy stages. The results amply repay the effort expended: these dishes look as wonderful as they taste, whether intended as the glamorous centrepiece of a formal buffet, or as the inviting mainstay of a rustic lunch, needing no other accompaniment than crusty bread, with a little cheese and fruit to follow.

A new approach to an old tradition

Any attempt to create pâtés and terrines that respect the contemporary preference for lighter, healthier eating has to begin by addressing the problem of fat. Traditional terrines and pâtés have always relied heavily on animal fats. Egg yolks, butter, cream and, most particularly, pork fat — minced, cubed, or cut into the sheets known as bards — play many roles: they bind and moisten, enhance flavour, produce a suavity of texture and, in some cases, act as a preservative. Indeed, to some cooks, the very notion of a low-fat pâté would be absurd.

The recipes in this volume have been designed to reduce fat content substantially, without making an unrealistic attempt to eliminate it altogether. Less emphasis is placed on pork and other fatty meats; more use is made of poultry, naturally lean game, fish and vegetables. When some form of enrichment or lubrication is necessary, alternative sources of more modest fat content are found. Streaky bacon, for instance, provides a leaner alternative to bards of pork fat for lining baking dishes and covering terrines; so, too, does caul, the pliable, lacy membrane that surrounds a pig's stomach. Wrapped round a mixture of highly spiced meat and vegetables to form a single large terrine *(page 25)*, caul will gradually melt in the oven's heat, basting the filling as it cooks, and crisping and browning into an attractive lattice pattern on the surface of the finished dish. Caul is available, fresh, dry-salted or frozen, from specialist butchers who manufacture their own sausages and pâtés.

Classic fish and vegetable terrines are often based on mousseline, an amalgam of cream and egg whites — sometimes further enriched with egg yolks and butter — blended with pounded fish or chicken. Yet the mousseline's delicate flavour and silken texture need not be renounced by the health-conscious: a lighter but highly satisfactory version can be made with low-fat soft cheese or yogurt, using only the whites of egg. Not only does this variant contain appreciably less fat, but it is also easier to handle: it is less prone to break or curdle, and does not need to be kept as cold as ordinary mousselines, which will often fall apart unless prepared over a bowl of ice.

Potted meats, poultry and seafood need even less fat. These simple, quickly made dishes are moistened instead with stock, fruit juice or yogurt. The marinated guinea-fowl on page 40, for instance, is packed in a reduction of its own aromatic cooking juices; the devilled crab on page 81 relies on yogurt.

Another approach to reducing fat content is to modify the doughs and pastries used for covering pâtés. The simple shortcrust that forms part of the beef and veal en croûte on page 16, for instance, uses polyunsaturated margarine instead of butter or lard to reduce the amount of saturated fat. A brioche dough, as used in the salmon coulibiaca on page 60, is a good low-fat alternative to classic puff paste with its heavy cargo of butter. The Healthy Home Cooking version calls for only two egg yolks instead of the usual seven per 500 grams (1 lb) of flour.

Raised savoury pies, a hallmark of old English cookery, are characterized by their sturdy hot-water crusts. Indeed, so robust is this casing that it was used in the 18th century as the packaging for a celebrated regional speciality known as Yorkshire Goose Pie. This delicacy consisted of a whole tongue embedded in forcemeat and enclosed within a boned chicken which, in turn, was placed inside a hollowed-out goose. The entire assemblage was then sealed into its hot-water crust and posted to distant friends as a gift for Christmas. The modern hot-water crust on page 36 may be less suitable for shipping across the Yorkshire moors in a horse-drawn coach, but it is considerably lower in

cholesterol than its prototype, and is again made with polyunsaturated margarine instead of lard.

Such substantial structures as these would seem to have little in common with fragile aspic glazes and the shimmering surfaces of galantines. Yet jelly, in its various forms, plays a part equal to that of pastry in covering, sealing and decorating terrines and pâtés. In brawns and other jellied preparations, such as the moulded rabbit and spring vegetables on page 30, jelly serves as the binding element that holds the other ingredients together. A topping of jellied glaze keeps terrines moist, while pastry-wrapped pâtés are often made with a layer of jellied stock interposed between filling and crust. For the sweet terrines that are the subject of Chapter 4, jelly is indispensable, both as binder and decoration. Indeed, it is only the imaginative use of gelatine that has made it possible to develop the new style of light dessert terrine, as typified by the exotic fruits in champagne jelly *(page 125)* or the gingered melon mousse *(page 119)*.

The starting point for any savoury jelly is a good, full-bodied and virtually fat-free stock *(page 10)*. Both meat and fish stocks derive their substance from the natural gelatine present in bones and flesh; vegetable stocks require the addition of powdered gelatine if they are to set. So, too, do sweet jellies, which are based on a fruit juice or purée.

An aspic is a brilliantly clear meat, fish or vegetable jelly that is produced by adding gelatine to stock and clarifying it. Even scrupulously skimmed and degreased stocks may be muddy; to clarify, or clear, them, egg whites and crushed egg shells are added, and the mixture is then boiled and strained *(page 12)*. For cooks in a hurry, packets of commercially prepared aspic are available, but they are far higher in salt, and will not produce the same purity of flavour or lightness of texture as an aspic prepared from home-made stock.

For the best results, jellies and aspics need to be given sufficient time to set, in cold conditions. The setting times indicated in this book are those required if the jelly is to be set in the refrigerator. However, it is also possible to set jellies in the freezer, or in a fairly cool room over a bowl of ice. In all cases, these mixtures will chill more rapidly if placed in metal containers. When assembling layered jellies in contrasting hues, such as the cassis, peach and raspberry layered pudding on page 124, it is essential to let each layer set thoroughly before adding the next, to avoid the risk of one colour seeping into another.

Tools and techniques

There was a time when every kitchen, whether of the grand hotel or of the farmhouse, had a sufficiency of helping hands. Those days are over; the modern cook relies on food processors and microwave ovens instead of kitchen maids and turn-spits. The

The Key to Better Eating

This book, like others in the Healthy Home Cooking series, addresses the concerns of today's weight-conscious, health-minded cooks with recipes developed within strict nutritional guidelines.

The chart on the right gives dietary guidelines for healthy men, women and children. Recommended figures vary from country to country, but the principles are the same everywhere. Here, the average daily amounts of calories and protein are taken from a report by the U.K. Department of Health and Social Security; the maximum advisable daily intake of fat is based on guidelines given by the National Advisory Committee on Nutrition Education (NACNE); guidelines for cholesterol and sodium are based on upper limits suggested by the World Health Organization.

The volumes in the Healthy Home Cooking series do not purport to be diet books, nor do they focus on health foods. Rather, the books express a commonsense approach to cooking that uses salt, sugar, cream, butter and oil in moderation while including other ingredients that also contribute flavour and satisfaction. The portions themselves are modest in size.

The recipes make few unusual demands. Naturally they call for fresh ingredients, offering substitutes should these be unavailable. (Only the original ingredient is calculated in the nutrient analysis, however.) Most of the ingredients can be found in any well-stocked supermarket; the occasional exceptions can be bought in speciality or ethnic food shops.

About cooking times

To help the cook plan ahead effectively, Healthy Home Cooking takes time into account in all its recipes. While recognizing that everyone cooks at a different speed, and that stoves and ovens may differ somewhat in their temperatures, the series provides approximate "working" and "total" times for every dish. Working time stands for the minutes actively spent on preparation; total time incudes unattended cooking time, as well as time devoted to marinating, steeping or soaking various ingredients. Because the recipes emphasize fresh foods, the dishes may take a bit longer to prepare than those that call for canned or packaged products, but the difference in flavour, and often in added nutritional value, should compensate for the little extra time involved.

Recommended Dietary Guidelines

		Average Daily Intake		Maximum Daily Intake			
		CALORIES	PROTEIN _grams_	CHOLESTEROL _milligrams_	TOTAL FAT _grams_	SATURATED FAT _grams_	SODIUM _milligrams_
Females	7-8	1900	47	300	80	32	2000*
	9-11	2050	51	300	77	35	2000
	12-17	2150	53	300	81	36	2000
	18-53	2150	54	300	81	36	2000
	54-74	1900	47	300	72	32	2000
Males	7-8	1980	49	300	80	33	2000
	9-11	2280	57	300	77	38	2000
	12-14	2640	66	300	99	44	2000
	15-17	2880	72	300	108	48	2000
	18-34	2900	72	300	109	48	2000
	35-64	2750	69	300	104	35	2000
	65-74	2400	60	300	91	40	2000

*(or 5g salt)

new style of cooking takes full advantage of this technology; mousselines, for instance, or layered terrines take minutes instead of the hours they once required.

One great advantage for the hard-pressed cook is that terrines and pâtés can often be assembled, cooked and served in the same container. Rectangular loaf tins or earthenware terrine dishes are classic, and easy to unmould, but not compulsory: oval or round containers, or a set of individual ramekins, are equally suitable. Often, the nature of the recipe will dictate the most appropriate serving dish. Earthenware is particularly suited to robust, country-style mixtures, while china heart-shapes or ramekins would be a happier choice for a delicate aspic or mousseline. In this book, loaf tins and terrines are specified according to their dimensions, moulds according to their capacity.

For pâtés with a crust, a hinged metal container, such as an eye-shaped mould or a cake tin with a removable base, makes a convenient receptacle. When using metal pans and dishes, however, be sure to use only non-reactive materials, such as stainless steel, that will not react chemically with vegetables, fruit and other ingredients to affect the colour or flavour of the finished dish. Copper and cast iron, in particular, are best avoided.

The gentle, even cooking required for most of these dishes is achieved most effectively in an easily improvised water bath, sometimes called a bain-marie. To assemble a water bath, set the filled terrine mould in a large, deep roasting pan or baking dish, place the pan in a preheated oven, and pour in enough boiling water to come about two thirds of the way up the side of the mould. As the terrine bakes, heat will circulate gently round it, allowing all parts of the mixture to cook at the same rate. Once cooked, many terrines — especially those without a pastry case — must be cooled to room temperature and chilled under weights to produce the desired firm, compact texture.

Pâtés that have been baked in a pastry-lined mould are not weighted. After baking, they are allowed to cool, then filled with gelatinous stock through a hole made in the top of the pastry, and chilled until the jelly sets. It is vital to check that the baked crust is perfectly intact before adding the stock, to prevent leaks that may ruin the whole composition. If the pastry does crack during baking or unmoulding, it is easily rescued: wrap the pâté in plastic film, gently pushing the sides of the crack together to seal the breach, and place the pie in the freezer for about 30 minutes, until it is well chilled but not frozen.

Chilling time for pâtés and terrines varies according to their contents. Meat terrines are often allowed to mature for a day or two to develop their flavours, although the relatively low fat content of the meat terrines in this volume precludes the longer keeping time allowed for traditional, high-fat preparations. Fish and vegetable terrines, however, are generally given only sufficient time to chill and set.

To be enjoyed at their best, terrines should not be served immediately upon removal from the refrigerator. Instead, they should be allowed to come up to a cool, rather than frigid, temperature. A large meat terrine may need about an hour at cool room temperature, while small, single-serving pâtés require only 15 or 20 minutes to take the chill off.

Galantines and other jellied preparations are best served cold, since prolonged exposure to warm room temperatures will melt their surfaces, ruining the decorative sheen that renders them so attractive. Unmoulding jellies without mishap requires care. The simplest procedure is to dip the base and sides of the mould in hot water for a few seconds, place a serving plate on top, invert the mould and plate together and lift off the mould. Swift though it is, this treatment has one drawback: the outer surface of the jelly will melt slightly upon contact with the heat. If an impeccably neat surface is required, another method is to invert the terrine on its serving plate and wrap the mould in hot towels, changing them as they cool, until the container lifts neatly away leaving the jelly intact. At times it may be necessary to run a knife or skewer along the sides of the jelly to prise it gently from its mould.

Those pâtés and terrines that look most dramatic in their uncut form should be brought to the table intact, and divided just before serving. Some very delicate mixtures, such as the pink trout mousse on page 60, are best served with a spoon. If you do wish to slice a terrine, use a very sharp knife for best results. Owners of electric carving knives may find these tools convenient for producing thin slices, but run the risk of marking the pâté's surface with the blade.

Delights for all occasions

Pâtés and terrines are not restricted to a single place on the menu. Because of their delicacy, fish and shellfish terrines are most often served as first courses, while those made with vegetables would be equally at home as starters, as side dishes to accompany a roast, or as main courses for a light lunch. Meat terrines and pâtés, because of their comparative richness and greater complexity of flavour, are, perhaps, less versatile. If they are to serve as a first course, the rest of the menu should be kept fairly light; many are substantial enough to provide the centrepiece of a lunch or light supper in their own right, supported by a selection of salads.

On the following pages are dishes to serve all purposes and seasons: lavishly decorated galantines for buffets, sophisticated terrines for intimate dinner parties, robust country-style pies and coarse pâtés for informal snacks and picnics. For the most elegant, a few salad leaves or a spoonful of carefully matched sauce are the most appropriate accompaniments. But for the great majority of these preparations, some form of bread is the traditional, and most welcome, partner. Crusty French loaves, dark ryes and wholemeal bread, all have their partisans. Mixtures of a softer, more delicate texture, liable to be overshadowed by too substantial a crust or crumb, are better spread on lighter, crisper bases such as Melba toast, warmed pitta, small muffins, rolls or protein-rich sesame sticks. A basket filled with a generous selection of breads and biscuits adds to the sense of occasion created by the appearance of a home-made terrine or pâté — heady with herbs and spices, too good to resist, as pleasing to the taste-buds as it is delightful to the eye.

Chili Peppers — a Cautionary Note

Both dried and fresh hot chili peppers should be handled with care. Their flesh and seeds contain volatile oils that can make skin tingle and cause eyes to burn. Rubber gloves offer protection — but the cook should still be careful not to touch the face, lips or eyes when working with chilies.

Soaking fresh chilies in cold, salted water for an hour will remove some of their fire. If canned chilies are substituted for fresh ones, they should be rinsed in cold water in order to eliminate as much of the brine used to preserve them as possible.

Stocks for Full Flavour

A good, well-flavoured stock adds moistness and flavour to terrines and pâtés, provides a poaching liquid for galantines and, when mixed with gelatine and clarified *(page 12)*, makes aspic. Producing good stock is a simple procedure. Recipes for five basic stocks appear on the right.

Stock comes from humble beginnings indeed — inexpensive cuts of meat, fish bones, or chicken wings and backs. Attention to details will reward you with a rich and limpid stock: any large fat deposits should be trimmed away beforehand; large bones, if they are to cede the treasured gelatine that gives body to a stock, should first be cracked. During cooking, skim off the scum that collects on top of the liquid to prevent it from clouding the stock. After its initial rapid cooking, a stock must not be allowed to return to a full boil during preparation; the turbulence would muddy the liquid. As a final cleansing, the stock should be strained through a fine sieve or a colander lined with muslin.

To prepare stock for storage, divide it among containers surrounded with iced water. Wait until the stock has cooled before covering the vessels, otherwise it may sour. Refrigerated in covered containers, any of these stocks will keep for up to three days. Because the fat on top of the stock will form a temporary seal, helping to keep it fresh, you need not degrease the stock *(box, opposite)* until shortly before you are ready to use it. To prolong the life of a refrigerated stock, first remove and discard the congealed fat, then boil the stock for 5 minutes; either freeze the stock or boil it again every two or three days. As always, cool the stock quickly, uncovered, before storing it once more.

Fish stock and vegetable stock may be frozen for two months; the other three may be frozen for as long as four months. Stock destined for the freezer must first be degreased, since frozen fat can turn rancid.

The recipes that follow yield differing amounts of stock. Brown stock, for example, is made from large bones, which require more water for cooking. But, like any stock, it freezes well, meaning an abundance is never too much.

Vegetable Stock

Makes about 2 litres (3½ pints)
Working time: about 25 minutes
Total time: about 1 hour and 30 minutes

4	sticks celery with leaves, cut into 2.5 cm (1 inch) pieces	4
4	carrots, scrubbed and cut into 2.5 cm (1 inch) pieces	4
4	large onions, coarsely chopped	4
3	large broccoli stems, coarsely chopped (optional)	3
1	medium turnip, peeled and cut into 1 cm (½ inch) cubes	1
6	garlic cloves, crushed	6
30 g	parsley leaves and stems, coarsely chopped	1 oz
10	black peppercorns	10
4	fresh thyme sprigs, or 1 tsp dried thyme	4
2	bay leaves	2

Put the celery, carrots, onions, broccoli if you are using it, turnip, garlic, parsley and peppercorns into a heavy stockpot. Pour in enough cold water to cover the contents by about 5 cm (2 inches). Bring the liquid to the boil over medium heat, skimming off any scum that rises to the surface. When the liquid reaches the boil, stir in the thyme and the bay leaves. Reduce the heat and let the stock simmer, undisturbed, for 1 hour.

Strain the stock into a large bowl, pressing down lightly on the vegetables to extract all their liquid. Discard the vegetables.

Chicken Stock

Makes about 2 litres (3½ pints)
Working time: about 20 minutes
Total time: about 3 hours

2 to 2.5 kg	uncooked chicken trimmings and bones (preferably wings, necks and backs), the bones cracked with a heavy knife	4 to 5 lb
2	carrots, cut into 1 cm (½ inch) thick rounds	2
2	sticks celery, cut into 2.5 cm (1 inch) pieces	2
2	large onions, halved, one half stuck with two cloves	2
2	fresh thyme sprigs, or ½ tsp dried thyme	2
1 or 2	bay leaves	1 or 2
10 to 15	parsley stalks	10 to 15
5	black peppercorns	5

Put the chicken trimmings and bones into a heavy stockpot; pour in enough water to cover them by about 5 cm (2 inches). Bring the liquid to the boil over medium heat, skimming off the scum that rises to the surface. Reduce the heat and simmer the liquid for 10 minutes, skimming and adding a little cold water to help precipitate the scum.

Add the vegetables, herbs and peppercorns, and submerge them in the liquid. If necessary, pour in enough additional water to cover the contents of the pot. Simmer the stock for 2 to 3 hours, skimming as necessary to remove the scum.

Strain the stock, discard the solids, and degrease the stock *(box, opposite)*.

EDITOR'S NOTE: *The chicken gizzard and heart may be added to the stock. Wings and necks — rich in natural gelatine — produce a particularly gelatinous stock, ideal for sauces and jellied dishes. Turkey, duck or goose stock may be prepared using the same basic recipe.*

Veal Stock

For a light veal stock, follow the chicken stock recipe, but substitute 2.5 kg (5 lb) of veal bones for the chicken trimmings and bones.

Fish Stock

Makes about 2 litres (3½ pints)
Working time: about 15 minutes
Total time: about 40 minutes

1 kg	lean-fish bones, fins and tails discarded, the bones rinsed well and cut into large pieces	2 lb
2	onions, thinly sliced	2
2	sticks celery, chopped	2
1	carrot, thinly sliced	1
½ litre	dry white wine	16 fl oz
2 tbsp	fresh lemon juice	2 tbsp
1	leek, trimmed, split, washed thoroughly to remove all grit, and sliced (optional)	1
3	garlic cloves, crushed (optional)	3
10	parsley stalks	10
4	fresh thyme sprigs, or 1 tsp dried thyme	4
1	bay leaf	1
5	black peppercorns	5

Put the fish bones, onions, celery, carrot, wine, lemon juice, 2 litres (3½ pints) of cold water, and the leek and garlic, if you are using them, in a large, non-reactive stockpot. Bring the liquid to the boil over medium heat, then reduce the heat to maintain a strong simmer. Skim off all the scum that rises to the surface.

Add the parsley, thyme, bay leaf and peppercorns, and simmer the stock gently for a further 20 minutes.

Strain the stock; allow the solids to drain thoroughly before discarding them. If necessary, degrease the stock (box, right).

EDITOR'S NOTE: *Because the bones from oilier fish produce a strong flavour, be sure to use only the bones from lean fish. Sole, plaice, turbot and other flat fish are best. Do not include the fish skin; it could discolour the stock.*

Brown Stock

Makes about 3 litres (5 pints)
Working time: about 40 minutes
Total time: about 5 hours and 30 minutes

1.5 kg	veal breast (or veal shin or beef shin meat), cut into 7.5 cm (3 inch) pieces	3 lb
1.5 kg	uncooked veal or beef bones, cracked	3 lb
2	onions, quartered	2
2	sticks celery, chopped	2
2	carrots, sliced	2
3	unpeeled garlic cloves, crushed	3
8	black peppercorns	8
3	cloves	3
2 tsp	fresh thyme, or ½ tsp dried thyme	2 tsp
1	bay leaf	1

Preheat the oven to 220°C (425°F or Mark 7). Place the meat, bones, onions, celery and carrots in a large roasting pan and roast them until they are well browned — about 1 hour.

Transfer the contents of the roasting pan to a large stockpot. Pour ½ litre (16 fl oz) of water into the roasting pan; with a spatula, scrape up the browned bits from the bottom of the pan. Pour the liquid into the pot.

Add the garlic, peppercorns and cloves. Pour in enough water to cover the contents of the pot by about 7.5 cm (3 inches). Bring the liquid to the boil, then reduce the heat to maintain a simmer and skim any impurities from the surface. Add the thyme and bay leaf, then simmer the stock very gently for 4 hours, skimming occasionally during the process.

Strain the stock; allow the solids to drain thoroughly into the stock before discarding them. Degrease the stock (box, right).

EDITOR'S NOTE: *Thoroughly browning the meat, bones and vegetables should produce a stock with a rich mahogany colour. If your stock does not seem dark enough, cook 1 tablespoon of tomato paste in a small pan over medium heat, stirring constantly, until it darkens — about 3 minutes. Add this to the stock about 1 hour before the end of the cooking time.*

Any combination of meat and bones may be used to make the stock; ideally, the meat and bones together should weigh about 3 kg (6 lb). Ask your butcher to crack the bones.

Degreasing Stocks

An essential step in making stocks as healthy as they can be is degreasing, or removing the fat from the surface of the liquid. Stock must always be degreased before it is used in a recipe, frozen, or transformed into aspic.

The easiest and most effective degreasing method is to refrigerate the finished stock, then lift the congealed layer of fat from its surface. To inhibit bacterial growth, a hot stock should be cooled quickly in small containers surrounded by ice cubes, then covered and refrigerated. The fat may then be spooned off. So that the stock will not sour, it should be covered and refrigerated only when it has cooled.

For a completely fat-free stock, lightly draw an ice cube across the cold stock's surface; the fat will cling to the cube. Alternatively, blot up any remaining fat with paper towels: lay a corner or strip of towel directly on the fat, then immediately lift away the towel. Continue this process, always using a dry section of towel, to rid the surface of every drop of fat.

Crystal-Clear Aspic

Aspic is the clear jelly that is used to glaze many terrines and galantines, to bind the elements in brawn and other jellied preparations, and to fill the gap between pastry and filling in traditional pâtés. It is derived from stock, set with gelatine and clarified — cleared of its impurities — with egg whites and shells.

Aspic may be made from any type of stock but in this book, vegetable stock, usually the easiest to prepare, is always used. A recipe for vegetable aspic is given on the right, and the techniques for making it are shown below. The gelatine may be omitted if you wish simply to clarify a stock rather than to set it. But note that if you subsequently add gelatine to clarified stock, the liquid will become cloudy again.

Making Aspic

1 *SCALDING THE EQUIPMENT. Fill a large pan with cold water and place a wire whisk, metal sieve and length of muslin in the pan. Bring the water to the boil. Remove the scalded items from the pan, then pour the boiling water into a large bowl, to scald that too. Empty the bowl. Wring out as much water as possible from the muslin. Line the sieve with a double layer of the muslin and set it over the bowl.*

2 *ADDING THE INGREDIENTS. Pour the cold stock into the pan. Add the gelatine to the stock, then add the clarification ingredients — the egg whites and shells, and the vinegar. Set the pan over medium heat.*

3 *FORMING THE RAFT. Using the scalded whisk, whisk the gelatine, clarification ingredients and stock together thoroughly. In a few minutes, the egg whites will float to the surface of the stock, forming a thick, foamy layer known as the raft. Remove the whisk from the pan and bring the mixture to the boil.*

4 *COMPLETING THE CLARIFICATION. When the raft rises to the rim of the pan, set the pan aside and leave the foam to settle for a minute or so. Boil up the stock twice more, then leave the foam to stand for 5 minutes. Without breaking up the raft, carefully pour the clarified aspic through the muslin-lined sieve into the bowl. When cool, it will set to a clear jelly.*

Vegetable Aspic

Makes about 90 cl (1½ pints)
Working time: about 45 minutes
Total time: about 2 hours and 45 minutes

250 g	carrots, sliced	8 oz
250 g	leeks, sliced	8 oz
2	onions, finely chopped	2
4	sticks celery, sliced	4
10	parsley sprigs	10
1	rosemary sprig	1
1	thyme sprig	1
4	garlic cloves, unpeeled	4
½ tsp	salt	½ tsp
8	black peppercorns	8
45 g	powdered gelatine	1½ oz
2	eggs, whites and washed shells only	2
1 tbsp	red wine vinegar	1 tbsp

Put the carrots, leeks, onions, celery, parsley, rosemary, thyme, garlic, salt and peppercorns into a large saucepan with 1.75 litres (3 pints) of cold water. Bring the water to the boil, then reduce the heat and partially cover the saucepan with a lid. Simmer gently for about 2 hours, or until the liquid is reduced by half.

Strain the stock through a nylon sieve into a large bowl; discard the vegetables. Measure the stock, and make it up to 90 cl (1½ pints) with water, if necessary. Allow the stock to cool.

Scald a wire whisk, a large metal sieve and a length of muslin in a saucepan of boiling water (opposite page, Step 1). Line the sieve with a double layer of muslin and place it over the bowl.

Pour the cold stock back into the saucepan and add the gelatine, egg whites and shells, and vinegar. With the scalded whisk, whisk the stock over medium heat until the egg whites form a thick foam on the surface. Stop whisking, then bring the mixture to the boil so that the foam rises to the top of the saucepan — do not allow it to boil over. Remove the saucepan from the heat and allow the foam to settle back down. Repeat this process twice more, then allow the mixture to stand for 5 minutes.

Very gently and carefully pour the aspic through the lined sieve, without allowing the foam floating on top of the liquid to break up. Leave the aspic to cool. Once it has cooled, it will assume a firm jelly-like consistency.

EDITOR'S NOTE: *Vegetable aspic may be kept in the refrigerator for a few days, ready to be used when needed. Once set, it can be quickly melted again by placing the bowl over a saucepan of hot water.*

Dissolving Gelatine

Gelatine is a vital element in many of the fish, vegetable and sweet terrines made in this book. Although it is available as both leaves and powder, the powdered variety is more generally available and has been used throughout this volume. Leaf gelatine may, however, be substituted if you wish.

To ensure a smooth and lump-free final result, gelatine should be softened in a little cold liquid: powdered gelatine requires only 2 minutes, leaf gelatine some 30 minutes. The gelatine is then melted over gentle heat (below). Make sure the mixture does not boil, or the gelatine's setting power will be reduced.

Softening and Melting Gelatine

1 SOFTENING THE GELATINE. Place the liquid, as specified in the recipe, in a heatproof bowl. Sprinkle the gelatine lightly and evenly over the surface of the liquid (above, left). Leave it for 2 minutes, to allow the gelatine granules to soften and swell (above, right).

2 MELTING THE GRANULES. Set the bowl over a saucepan of gently simmering water. Using a metal spoon, stir the mixture constantly for about 3 minutes, or until the gelatine granules have completely dissolved (above, left). Check the mixture by lifting a spoonful of the gelatine solution out of the bowl and allowing it to trickle back: the liquid should be completely clear and there should be no grainy deposits remaining in the spoon (above, right).

1 *Shimmering aspic encases a flavoursome combination of lean marinated pork and wild mushrooms (recipe, page 25).*

Reinterpreting the Classics

In the best traditions of peasant cookery, almost any type of meat or poultry found its way into pâtés and terrines. Miscellaneous portions of farm-reared pigs and rabbits, fowl long past the laying stage and game brought home by the hunter were transformed into brawns, herb-flecked terrines and crépinettes, savoury pies, puddings and potted meats.

The once lovingly fattened pig may now be bred for greater leanness, the quail and venison as likely to be farmed as caught in the wild, but meat terrines and pâtés are still as varied and as versatile as ever. Some of the recipes in this chapter remain close to their rustic origins: the herbed pork and veal terrine on page 22 is not unlike one that might have been produced in any farmhouse kitchen. Others, such as the layered terrine of mixed game birds and wild mushrooms embedded in a Madeira-flavoured jelly *(page 38)*, reflect a more sophisticated, contemporary style.

But all of these dishes demonstrate a departure from tradition in their reliance on a relatively small proportion of fat. Pork, beef and lamb are not rejected outright, but only lean cuts are used, and then only when scrupulously freed of fat. Greater emphasis is placed on meats that are naturally lean: game birds, rabbit, venison and veal are especially suitable. Poultry is usually skinned, with all visible fat cut away.

The recipes employ diverse means of providing the succulence that fat would have lent: many include a layer of vegetables, some are served with a sauce. For a number, the ingredients are marinated in an aromatic infusion of wine, spirits, fruit juices and spices. Meats should be marinated in the refrigerator, or in a cool larder, loosely covered to allow air to circulate. Game, such as venison, will benefit from up to 48 hours in marinade; other meats, and poultry, are best steeped for no more than half that time.

Undeniably, many of the recipes in this chapter call for a long list of ingredients and a considerable number of necessary steps. Yet meat terrines and pâtés are ideally suited for advance preparation; their production can be divided into easy stages and accomplished well ahead of time. An interval of a day or so between cooking and serving will only enhance the complex flavours of the dish.

Moreover, the product of your labours can very often be successfully frozen for a future occasion. The traditional, densely textured type of meat terrine freezes well — either whole or cut in slices — but do not attempt to freeze any that are bound with jelly. Where an aspic topping is called for, this can be added at a later stage, after the terrine has been thawed. Pâtés encased in a pie crust are best not frozen because the pastry tends to become soggy when thawed.

Beef and Veal en Croûte

Serves 16 as a main course
Working time: about 1 hour and 15 minutes
Total time: about 2 hours and 50 minutes

Calories **220**
Protein **20g**
Cholesterol **65mg**
Total fat **11g**
Saturated fat **3g**
Sodium **280mg**

½ tbsp	virgin olive oil	½ tbsp
1	large onion, finely chopped	1
500 g	lean veal, trimmed of fat and connective tissue, cut into cubes	1 lb
60 g	fresh white breadcrumbs	2 oz
3 tbsp	chopped parsley	3 tbsp
150 g	polyunsaturated margarine	5 oz
30 g	skinned pistachio nuts	1 oz
1	egg white, beaten	1
1 ¼ tsp	salt	1 ¼ tsp
	freshly ground black pepper	
500 g	rump steak, trimmed of fat and connective tissue, very finely chopped	1 lb
45 g	dried ceps, soaked for 20 minutes in tepid water, drained and chopped	1 ½ oz
250 g	plain flour	8 oz
2	eggs	2

Heat the oil in a frying pan over medium heat. Add the onion and cook it gently for 6 to 8 minutes, until softened but not browned. Remove the pan from the heat and allow the onion to cool for 5 minutes.

Meanwhile, process the veal in a food processor until it is finely minced. Transfer it to a bowl. Add the onions to the veal, together with the breadcrumbs, parsley, 30 g (1 oz) of the margarine, the pistachio nuts, beaten egg white, ¼ teaspoon of the salt and

some black pepper. Mix the ingredients together well and set them aside. Put the steak in a bowl and thoroughly mix in the chopped ceps, ¼ teaspoon of the salt and some black pepper.

Lay a 38 by 30 cm (15 by 12 inch) sheet of plastic film flat on the work surface. Spread out the beef mixture to form a 30 by 20 cm (12 by 8 inch) rectangle on top of the plastic film. Form the veal mixture into a 30 cm (12 inch) long sausage shape, and place it along the centre of the steak. With the aid of the plastic film, wrap the steak round the veal to enclose it completely and form a neat roll. Cover the roll with the plastic film and put it on to a flat tray. Chill the roll in the refrigerator while you make the pastry.

Preheat the oven to 220°C (425°F or Mark 7). Lightly grease a baking sheet. Sift the flour and the remaining salt into a mixing bowl, then rub in the remaining margarine until the mixture resembles fine breadcrumbs. Make a well in the centre of the mixture. Beat one of the eggs with 1 tablespoon of cold water, pour it into the well and, using a round-bladed knife, mix it in to form a dough. Knead the dough lightly on a floured surface, until it is smooth.

Roll out the pastry to form a 50 by 30 cm (20 by 12 inch) rectangle. Carefully remove the plastic film from the chilled meat roll and place the roll in the centre of the pastry. Cut a 7.5 cm (3 inch) square from each corner of the pastry.

In a small bowl, beat the remaining egg. Lift the two short ends of the pastry up and over the meat, then brush them with a little of the beaten egg. Lift one of the long sides up and over the meat and brush it with the egg. Bring the remaining long side up and over the meat to enclose it completely. Press the pastry joins firmly together to seal them.

Place the meat roll on the baking sheet, with the joins underneath. Re-knead and re-roll the pastry trimmings to form a long rectangle. Cut out two 45 by 1 cm (18 by ½ inch) strips from the pastry. Brush the roll with beaten egg. Decorate it with the pastry strips and brush the strips with egg. Make three evenly spaced holes in the top of the pastry.

Bake the roll until the pastry is golden-brown — about 30 to 35 minutes. Allow it to stand for 1 hour before serving, to make slicing easier. Serve the roll warm or cold, cut into slices.

SUGGESTED ACCOMPANIMENT: *broccoli and cauliflower florets.*

Tomato Sirloin Loaf

Serves 8 as a main course
Working time: about 20 minutes
Total time: about 8 hours (includes chilling)

Calories **285**
Protein **27g**
Cholesterol **50mg**
Total fat **12g**
Saturated fat **4g**
Sodium **300mg**

2 tbsp	virgin olive oil	2 tbsp
2	onions, finely chopped	2
400 g	canned plum tomatoes, chopped	14 oz
1 tbsp	fresh oregano, or 1 tsp dried oregano	1 tbsp
1 tsp	lightly crushed fennel seeds	1 tsp
¼ tsp	salt	¼ tsp
	freshly ground black pepper	
750 g	beef sirloin, trimmed of fat and minced	1½ lb
3	garlic cloves, finely chopped	3
30 g	parsley, chopped	1 oz
1 tsp	Tabasco sauce	1 tsp
2 tsp	Worcester sauce	2 tsp
175 g	dry breadcrumbs	6 oz
3	egg whites	3

Heat 1 tablespoon of the oil in a heavy saucepan over medium-low heat. Add half of the onion, stir, then cover the pan and cook the onion until it has softened — about 5 minutes. Add the tomatoes,

oregano, fennel seeds, salt and a little pepper. Simmer the tomato sauce uncovered, stirring occasionally, until it has reduced to about 30 cl (½ pint) — about 40 minutes. Press the sauce through a sieve.

Preheat the oven to 180°C (350°F or Mark 4). Brush a 20 by 12 by 7.5 cm (8 by 5 by 3 inch) loaf tin with some of the remaining olive oil.

Put the sirloin in a bowl with the tomato sauce. Mix in the garlic, the remaining onion, the parsley, Tabasco sauce, Worcester sauce and plenty of freshly ground black pepper. Add the breadcrumbs and mix well. Finally, add the egg whites and blend them thoroughly into the mixture with your hands.

Form the mixture into a smooth fat sausage shape and lay it in the tin, pressing it down firmly on all sides. Brush the top of the loaf with the remaining olive oil, then cover it with foil. Bake the loaf until it is cooked through and a skewer inserted into the middle is hot to the touch when withdrawn — about 1 hour.

Leave the loaf to cool to room temperature — about 2 hours — then chill it in the refrigerator for at least 4 hours before serving.

SUGGESTED ACCOMPANIMENTS: *boiled new potatoes; steamed asparagus spears.*

Smooth Potted Beef

Serves 12 as a first course
Working time: about 40 minutes
Total time: about 8 hours (includes chilling)

Calories **160**
Protein **30g**
Cholesterol **60mg**
Total fat **4g**
Saturated fat **2g**
Sodium **115mg**

1.5 kg	topside of beef	3 lb
¾ tsp	salt	¾ tsp
½ tsp	grated nutmeg	½ tsp
1½ tsp	ground allspice	1½ tsp
30 cl	unsalted veal stock (recipe, page 10)	½ pint
1 tsp	powdered gelatine	1 tsp
	fresh thyme or parsley sprigs, for garnish	

Preheat the oven to 200°C (400°F or Mark 6). Put the beef into a roasting pan and sprinkle it evenly with ¼ teaspoon of the salt. Roast the beef for 15 minutes, then reduce the oven temperature to 180°C (350°F or Mark 4) and continue roasting the meat for about 1¾ hours, basting it frequently, until it is well done. Transfer the beef to a plate, cover it loosely with foil and allow it to cool. Pour the pan juices into a bowl, allow them to cool for 30 minutes, then put them into the refrigerator until the fat rises to the surface and solidifies — about 2 hours. Remove the juices from the refrigerator and discard the layer of fat.

Cut away all fat from the roast beef, then cut the meat into small chunks. Put the chunks into a food processor and process them until the meat is finely minced. Add the nutmeg and allspice, the remaining salt, the roasting juices and 17.5 cl (6 fl oz) of the veal stock. Process the mixture to a smooth paste.

Spoon the beef paste into a serving dish. Press the paste down firmly, levelling and smoothing the top. Refrigerate the potted beef for 1 hour.

Meanwhile, dissolve the gelatine in 2 tablespoons of water (page 13). Quickly stir the dissolved gelatine into the remaining veal stock. Chill the stock until it begins to thicken, but is not yet set — about 30 minutes.

Pour the thickened stock evenly over the potted beef, then garnish it with the thyme or parsley sprigs. Refrigerate the potted beef for a further 2 to 3 hours, until it is well chilled.

SUGGESTED ACCOMPANIMENT: *triangles of hot toast.*

Three Tongues Terrine Perfumed with Chinese Five Spices

Serves 20 as a first course
Working time: about 1 hour and 30 minutes
Total time: about 20 hours (includes soaking and chilling)

Calories **185**
Protein **14g**
Cholesterol **80mg**
Total fat **13g**
Saturated fat **3g**
Sodium **440mg**

1	calf's tongue (about 1.25 kg/2½ lb)	1
2	pig's tongues (about 140 g/4½ oz each)	2
4	lamb's tongues (about 75 g/2½ oz each)	4
1	calf's foot, quartered	1
60 cl	dry white wine	1 pint
3	large garlic cloves, unpeeled	3
1½	cinnamon sticks	1½
4	slices Chinese liquorice root, or two sticks liquorice root (optional)	4
½ tsp	Sichuan pepper	½ tsp
8	cloves	8
2	star anise pods	2
5 cm	piece fresh ginger root, unpeeled, cut into four or five slices	2 inch
2	carrots, each cut into four or five rounds	2
1	onion, quartered	1
3 tsp	salt	3 tsp
1 tsp	light brown sugar	1 tsp
Caper sauce		
450 g	low-fat fromage frais	15 oz
2 tsp	Dijon mustard	2 tsp
4	spring onions, finely chopped	4
6	small pickled gherkins, finely chopped	6
1	small sweet yellow pepper, skinned (page 90) seeded, deribbed and finely diced	1
1	small sweet red pepper, skinned (page 90) seeded, deribbed and finely diced	1
2 tsp	capers, rinsed and finely chopped	2 tsp
½ tsp	salt	½ tsp
	freshly ground black pepper	

Trim any visible fat and cartilage from the tongues and scrub them well. Soak the tongues in several changes of water for about 4 hours, to draw out the blood. Put the tongues and the calf's foot in a large pan of cold, fresh water and bring it to the boil. Rinse the tongues and foot under cold water and wash out the pan.

Return the tongues and foot to the pan and pour the wine over them. Add the garlic, cinnamon and liquorice root, if you are using it; then add the Sichuan pepper, cloves, star anise, ginger, carrots, onion, salt and sugar. Pour in enough cold water to cover all the ingredients. Bring the liquid to the boil, skim the liquid and reduce the heat to very low. Cover the pan and leave the tongues and the calf's foot to simmer very slowly for 1 hour.

Using a slotted spoon, remove the pig's and lamb's tongues from the pan; continue to simmer the calf's tongue and foot. Peel off and discard the skins of the pig's and lamb's tongues. Return the peeled tongues to the pan for a further 30 minutes, or until they are soft. Test them with a skewer: they should be of an almost melting consistency. Put the pig's and lamb's tongues in a dish. Take several spoonfuls of stock from the pan and pour it over the tongues to keep them moist. Cover the dish and set it aside.

Simmer the calf's tongue and foot for a further 30 minutes. Remove the tongue, peel it and return it to the pan. Continue to simmer the calf's tongue and foot for another 45 to 60 minutes, until the tongue is very soft when tested with a skewer.

Remove the calf's tongue and calf's foot from the pan and set them aside; cover the tongue to prevent it from darkening and hardening through exposure to the air. Strain 60 cl (1 pint) of the stock into another saucepan. Degrease the strained stock *(page 11)*, reduce it over high heat by two thirds, then set it aside.

When the calf's tongue is cool enough to handle, cut it into 1 cm (½ inch) thick slices; reserve enough neat slices to form two layers in a 20 by 11 by 7.5 cm (8 by 4½ by 3 inch) terrine or loaf tin. Dice the rest of the calf's tongue. Cut the lamb's tongues into slightly smaller dice than the calf's tongue. Neaten the pig's tongues to fit the terrine when laid end to end and dice

any trimmings. Remove the white, gelatinous tendons from the calf's foot and dice them finely; discard the rest of the foot. Mix the diced meats together.

Line the base of the terrine or loaf tin with half of the reserved calf's tongue slices. Spread a layer of the mixed diced meat over the calf's tongue, place the whole pig's tongues along the centre of the terrine, then arrange the rest of the diced meat along the sides and on the top. Lay the remaining slices of calf's tongue over this. Pour the warm reduced stock into the terrine to cover the meat. Cover the terrine loosely with plastic film and set it aside for 1 hour, while it cools and begins to set.

Weight the terrine with a 1 kg (2 lb) weight *(below)*, then chill it for at least 12 hours before serving. To make the caper sauce, blend all the sauce ingredients together in a large bowl. Serve the terrine cut into very thin slices, accompanied by the sauce.

Weighting a Terrine

Some cooked terrines benefit from being pressed under weights to form a cohesive mass that will make slicing easier and neater. Too heavy a weight, however, would force out the terrine's juices and make it dry. The amount of weight required for terrines in this book is given in each recipe. Place the weights — scale weights or unopened tins — on a wooden board cut to fit inside the rim of the terrine and sanded smooth. Alternatively, stiff cardboard can be substituted; but it must be wrapped in plastic film or aluminium foil to keep it dry, and it will not last as long as wood.

Raised Veal and Ham Pie

MAKE THIS PIE A DAY IN ADVANCE AND CHILL IT OVERNIGHT
TO ALLOW THE STOCK TO SET THOROUGHLY AND THE
FLAVOURS TO MATURE.

Serves 12 as a main course
Working time: about 1 hour
Total time: about 14 hours
(includes chilling)

Calories **300**
Protein **26g**
Cholesterol **100mg**
Total fat **11g**
Saturated fat **3g**
Sodium **445mg**

1 kg	lean leg of veal, trimmed of fat and connective tissue, cut into 1 cm (½ inch) cubes	2 lb
250 g	smoked gammon, trimmed of fat and connective tissue, cut into 1 cm (½ inch) cubes	8 oz
8	spring onions (about 125 g/4 oz), chopped	8
4 tbsp	chopped parsley	4 tbsp
2	hard-boiled eggs, chopped	2
17.5 cl	unsalted veal stock (recipe, page 10)	6 fl oz
½ tsp	salt	½ tsp
	freshly ground black pepper	
1 ½ tsp	powdered gelatine	1 ½ tsp
Hot-water crust pastry		
350 g	plain flour	12 oz
¼ tsp	salt	¼ tsp
1	egg yolk	1
90 g	polyunsaturated margarine	3 oz
1	egg, beaten, for glazing	1

Put the veal and gammon in a bowl, together with the spring onions, parsley, chopped eggs and 3 tablespoons of the veal stock. Season with the salt and some black pepper. Mix the ingredients well together,

then set them aside while you make the pastry.

Sift the flour and salt into a mixing bowl and make a well in the centre. Put the egg yolk into the well. In a saucepan, gently heat the margarine with 12.5 cl (4 fl oz) of cold water, until the margarine has melted. Increase the heat and bring the liquid to a rolling boil. Immediately pour the hot liquid into the well in the flour, stirring with a round-bladed knife at the same time, to mix the ingredients to a soft dough. Knead the dough on a lightly floured surface until smooth.

Preheat the oven to 200°C (425°F or Mark 7). Thoroughly grease a round springform tin, 20 cm (8 inches) in diameter, at least 7.5 cm (3 inches) deep.

Cut off one third of the pastry, wrap it in plastic film and set it aside. Roll out the remaining pastry to a large round, about 33 cm (13 inches) in diameter. Line the greased tin with the pastry, pressing it firmly over the base and up the sides, allowing a little excess pastry to overhang the edge.

Fill the lined tin with the veal and gammon mixture. Roll out the reserved pastry to a round large enough to cover the pie. Brush the overhanging pastry edges with a little cold water, then set the pastry lid in position. Press the edges firmly together to seal them. Using a pair of kitchen scissors, trim the pastry to neaten the edges.

With the tip of a small knife, lightly score the join all round the pie. Then press the back of the blade into the join at intervals to create a scalloped effect. Make three evenly spaced holes in the top of the pie.

Re-roll the pastry trimmings and cut out leaves, or other shapes, to decorate the pie. Brush the top of the pie with some of the beaten egg, then decorate the pie with the pastry shapes. Brush the decorations with a little more egg. Reserve the remaining egg.

Place the pie on a baking sheet and bake it for 20 minutes, then reduce the oven temperature to 190°C (375°F or Mark 5). Continue cooking for 1½ hours.

Remove the pie from the oven and carefully release and remove the outside of the tin. Brush the sides of the pie with the reserved beaten egg, then return it to the oven to continue cooking for 10 to 15 minutes, until it is golden-brown all over. Allow the pie to cool for 1 hour, then refrigerate it for 2 to 3 hours until cold.

Dissolve the gelatine in 3 tablespoons of water following the method on page 13. Quickly stir the gelatine into the remaining veal stock. Using a funnel, carefully pour the stock into the pie through the holes in the top. Refrigerate the pie overnight. Before serving, remove the pie from the base of the tin.

SUGGESTED ACCOMPANIMENTS: *boiled potatoes; grated carrot salad.*

Pork and Duck Terrine with Cranberries

Serves 12 as a main course
Working time: about 1 hour
Total time: about 36 hours (includes marinating and chilling)

Calories **220**
Protein **25g**
Cholesterol **105mg**
Total fat **10g**
Saturated fat **4g**
Sodium **415mg**

500 g	boneless duck breasts, skinned, trimmed of all fat and connective tissue	1 lb
4 tbsp	brandy	4 tbsp
½ tsp	green peppercorns, rinsed and crushed	½ tsp
1	cinnamon stick, broken into three pieces	1
500 g	pork fillet, minced or finely chopped	1 lb
60 g	fresh wholemeal breadcrumbs	2 oz
1	small egg, beaten	1
1 tsp	ground cinnamon	1 tsp
½ tsp	salt	½ tsp
	freshly ground black pepper	
150 g	green streaky bacon rashers, rind removed	5 oz
60 g	whole fresh, or thawed frozen cranberries, rinsed and dried	2 oz

Cut the duck breasts into 5 mm (¼ inch) thick slices, then cut the slices into thin, 2.5 cm (1 inch) long strips. Place the strips in a bowl. Pour the brandy into a small pan and add the peppercorns and cinnamon. Warm the mixture very gently until hot but not boiling. Allow this marinade to cool until tepid, then pour it over the duck. Cover the bowl and leave the duck to marinate in the refrigerator for about 6 hours.

After this time, discard the cinnamon pieces from the marinade. Drain the strips of duck on paper towels and pat them dry. Place the chopped pork fillet in a bowl and pour the marinade over it. Lightly mix the wholemeal breadcrumbs with the beaten egg, ground cinnamon, salt and some pepper. Add the breadcrumbs to the pork and stir well to combine.

Preheat the oven to 180°C (350°F or Mark 4).

Lay the bacon rashers on a board and, using the back of a heavy kitchen knife, stretch them as thinly as possible. Line an 18 by 8.5 by 6 cm (7 by 3½ by 2½ inch) loaf tin with the bacon rashers; lay the rashers across the tin with their ends overhanging the rim. Press one third of the pork mixture into the bottom of the tin. Place half of the duck strips over the pork, then scatter the cranberries over the strips. Press half of the remaining pork over the duck strips and cranberries and repeat the layers, finishing with a layer of pork. Fold the ends of the bacon rashers over the terrine and cover it tightly with a lid.

Stand the tin in a large roasting pan or dish. Pour boiling water into the roasting pan to come two thirds of the way up the outside of the tin. Bake the terrine until a skewer inserted into the centre of the terrine feels hot to the touch — 1¼ to 1½ hours. Weight the terrine with a 500 g (1 lb) weight *(page 19)* and leave it to cool to room temperature — about 1 hour. Put the terrine in the refrigerator and chill it for 24 hours.

Just before serving, pour off the excess juices. Turn out the terrine on to a board and cut it into slices.

SUGGESTED ACCOMPANIMENT: *a salad of orange slices, fennel and watercress.*

Herbed Pork and Veal Terrine

Serves 10 as a main course
Working time: about 1 hour
Total time: about 14 hours (includes marinating and chilling)

Calories **200**
Protein **29g**
Cholesterol **60mg**
Total fat **7g**
Saturated fat **3g**
Sodium **290mg**

750 g	pork tenderloin, trimmed of fat and connective tissue, two thirds cut into 2.5 cm (1 inch) cubes, one third cut into 1 cm (½ inch) cubes	1½ lb
150 g	lean veal, trimmed of fat and connective tissue, cut into 2.5 cm (1 inch) cubes	5 oz
4 tbsp	brandy	4 tbsp
4 tbsp	dry white wine	4 tbsp
1 tbsp	chopped fresh thyme	1 tbsp
	freshly ground black pepper	
125 g	fresh spinach, washed and stemmed	4 oz
175 g	cooked long-grain rice (about 50 g/2 oz raw weight)	6 oz
1½ tsp	cut fresh chives	1½ tsp
1½ tsp	chopped fresh marjoram	1½ tsp
¼ tsp	chopped fresh rosemary	¼ tsp
1½ tbsp	chopped parsley	1½ tbsp
2	large garlic cloves, finely chopped	2
90 g	onion, finely chopped	3 oz
2	egg whites	2
½ tsp	dried oregano	½ tsp
½ tsp	dried thyme	½ tsp
½ tsp	grated nutmeg	½ tsp
¼ tsp	ground allspice	¼ tsp
125 g	lean ham, cut into 5 mm (¼ inch) cubes	4 oz
2	thin rashers green streaky bacon, rind removed	2
1	bay leaf, plus one bay leaf for garnish (optional)	1

Place all the pork and veal cubes in a shallow dish, keeping the small cubes separate from the large ones. In a small bowl, mix the brandy, the wine, half of the fresh thyme and a little black pepper. Pour the liquid evenly over the meat cubes. Cover the dish and leave the meat to marinate for about 4 hours.

Blanch the spinach in a large saucepan of boiling water for 1 minute. Drain the spinach, refresh it under cold running water, drain it again, then squeeze all the moisture from the leaves. Chop the spinach in a food processor, add the rice and process until the rice is reduced to tiny particles. Add the remaining fresh thyme, the chives, marjoram, rosemary and parsley, and continue processing until the mixture is well combined. Transfer it to a mixing bowl.

In a small non-stick frying pan, sweat the garlic and onion over low heat until soft — about 5 minutes — then add them to the rice mixture.

Drain the marinade from the meat and add it to the rice mixture, together with the small cubes of pork.

Place half of the large pork cubes and half of the veal cubes in the food processor with an ice cube. Pulse the processor until the meat is coarsely chopped, then add one egg white and purée the mixture until it is smooth. Add the purée to the rice mixture. Process the remaining meat cubes into a purée in the same way, adding the dried oregano and thyme, the grated nutmeg, ground allspice, some more pepper and another ice cube. Add the ham cubes and process briefly to break them into smaller pieces and to mix them in, but do not purée the ham. Add all the purée to the rice mixture and mix well by hand or with a wooden spoon, removing any filaments of connective tissue.

Preheat the oven to 180°C (350°F or Mark 4).

Lay the bacon rashers flat on a board and stretch them as thinly as possible with the flat blade of a knife. Line the bottom of a 22 by 10 by 6 cm (9 by 4 by 2½ inch)

terrine or loaf tin with the bacon. Pack the meat and rice mixture firmly into the terrine, spooning it in a little at a time and pressing down firmly with the back of the spoon. Place a bay leaf on top and cover with a lid or foil. Stand the terrine in a deep roasting tin and pour in hot water to come half way up its sides. Bake the terrine until a skewer inserted into the middle feels hot to the touch when removed — about 1½ hours. Remove the terrine from the oven, allow it to cool to room temperature — about 3 hours — then chill it in the refrigerator for at least 4 hours before serving. Remove the bay leaf and turn the terrine out on to a serving dish. Garnish it with a fresh bay leaf, if desired.

EDITOR'S NOTE: *The terrine may be kept in the refrigerator for up to two days. If you have a large-capacity food processor, all the meat can be processed at once.*

Rosemary and Pork Brawn

MAKE THIS DISH TWO DAYS IN ADVANCE AND CHILL IT TO ALLOW THE FLAVOURS TO DEVELOP FULLY.

Serves 10 as a main course
Working time: about 45 minutes
Total time: about 2 days (includes chilling)

Calories **200**
Protein **32g**
Cholesterol **70mg**
Total fat **7g**
Saturated fat **3g**
Sodium **135mg**

1.5 kg	lean pork shoulder, trimmed of fat and connective tissue	3 lb
2	pig's trotters, washed and split	2
15 cl	dry white wine	¼ pint
1	small onion, quartered	1
1	garlic clove, finely chopped	1
1	small carrot, cut into four	1
1	celery stick, cut into four	1
7	rosemary sprigs	7
4	lemons, juice only	4
12.5 cl	white wine vinegar	4 fl oz
1 tbsp	powdered gelatine	1 tbsp
¼ tsp	salt	¼ tsp
	white pepper	
1	fresh hot chili pepper, seeded and cut into thin strips (caution, page 9)	1

Place the pork shoulder and trotters in a large, heavy-bottomed saucepan, together with the white wine, onion, garlic, carrot, celery and one of the rosemary sprigs. Add 60 cl (1 pint) of water and bring the liquid gently to the boil, skimming the surface frequently to remove any scum. Reduce the heat, cover the pan and simmer for 2 hours, until the pork is tender.

Remove the pork shoulder from the saucepan, and set it aside. Strain the stock through a muslin-lined sieve, discarding the vegetables and trotters. Return the stock to the pan, add the lemon juice and wine vinegar, and bring it back to the boil. Boil the stock until it has reduced by half. Cool the reduced stock. Chill it in the refrigerator for 3 to 4 hours, then discard the fat that has risen to the surface.

Put 3 tablespoons of the degreased stock in a small bowl and sprinkle the gelatine over it. Dissolve the gelatine following the method on page 13. Warm the rest of the stock. Add the salt and pepper, then stir in the dissolved gelatine. Leave the stock to cool.

Cut the pork into bite-sized cubes and place them in a 1.25 litre (2 pint) round dish, scattering the strips of chili pepper among the cubes. Pour the cooled stock over the meat and immerse the remaining rosemary sprigs in it. Cover the dish and set it aside until it has cooled completely — about 1 hour. Chill it in the refrigerator for about 2 days before serving.

EDITOR'S NOTE: *If you do not have a heavy meat cleaver with which to split the trotters, you can ask the butcher to split them for you. If pig's trotters are unavailable, double the amount of gelatine in the recipe.*

Gamey Pork Terrine

THE PORK IN THIS RECIPE IS TREATED WITH A LONG
MARINATION TO GIVE IT AN INTENSE GAMEY FLAVOUR.
FOR AN EVEN RICHER FLAVOUR, BOAR MAY BE
SUBSTITUTED FOR PORK.

Serves 12 as a main course
Working time: about 1 hour
Total time: about 2 days (includes marinating)

Calories **175**
Protein **26g**
Cholesterol **60mg**
Total fat **6g**
Saturated fat **3g**
Sodium **160mg**

1.25 kg	lean pork loin, trimmed of fat (30 g/1 oz of soft fat reserved), rubbed all over with 1 tbsp of coarse salt and left in the refrigerator for 6 to 12 hours	2½ lb
30 g	dried ceps or other wild mushrooms, soaked for 20 minutes in tepid water	1 oz
500 g	Swiss chard, leaves and 125 g (4 oz) of the stems	1 lb
1	garlic clove	1
½ tsp	salt	½ tsp
6	juniper berries, toasted for 45 seconds under the grill and crushed	6
⅛ tsp	ground allspice	⅛ tsp
	freshly ground black pepper	
75 g	caul, soaked for 15 minutes in warm water and 1 tsp of malt vinegar	2½ oz
15 cl	vegetable aspic (recipe, page 13), melted (optional)	¼ pint
Red wine marinade		
35 cl	red wine	12 fl oz
1 tbsp	red wine vinegar	1 tbsp
1 tbsp	virgin olive oil	1 tbsp
1	onion, sliced	1
1	large garlic clove	1
6	juniper berries	6
6	black peppercorns	6
4	allspice berries	4
2	cloves	2
1	blade of mace	1
1	cinnamon stick	1

First prepare the marinade. Pour the red wine, wine vinegar and oil into a non-reactive saucepan. Add the onion, garlic, juniper berries, peppercorns, allspice berries, cloves, mace and cinnamon stick. Slowly bring the liquid to the boil, then remove the pan from the heat and allow the liquid to cool. Rinse the meat under cold running water to remove the salt and exuded juices, and pat it dry with paper towels. Place the meat in a large bowl and pour the marinade over it. Cover the dish and put it in the refrigerator for 36 hours, turning the meat from time to time.

Rinse the soaked mushrooms to remove any grit, drain them well, then chop them roughly. Cook the Swiss chard stems in boiling water for 3 minutes. Add the leaves, and cook for a further 2 minutes. Drain the chard, refresh it under cold running water, and drain it again. Squeeze both leaves and stems in muslin to extract all the water, then finely chop them separately.

Preheat the oven to 180°C (350°F or Mark 4). Reserving 1 tablespoon of the marinade, drain the meat, then dry it on paper towels. Cut the meat and the reserved fat into 5 mm (¼ inch) cubes. Mix the cubes with the mushrooms, chopped chard leaves and stems and the tablespoon of marinade. Crush the garlic clove with the salt, and add it to the meat mixture, together with the toasted juniper berries, ground allspice and some freshly ground black pepper. Mix the ingredients thoroughly, and form the mixture into an oval shape that will fit into a 90 cl (1½ pint) terrine.

Drain the caul thoroughly and stretch it out as thinly as possible on a sheet of plastic film. Lay a second sheet of plastic film over the stretched caul, and flatten it with a rolling pin. Remove the top piece of plastic film. Place the moulded meat mixture on top of the caul and wrap it up, cutting away any excess caul. Put the parcel into the terrine with the join underneath. Cover the terrine with a lid.

Place the terrine in a large ovenproof dish or roasting tin. Pour in boiling water to come two thirds of the way up the side of the terrine. Bake the terrine until it is cooked through and a skewer inserted in the middle feels hot to the touch — about 1 hour. Remove the terrine from the oven, leave it to cool — about 2 hours — then chill it for at least 4 hours.

If you wish, pour the melted aspic over the terrine and chill it again for at least 2 hours before serving.

SUGGESTED ACCOMPANIMENTS: *crusty wholemeal bread; mushroom salad.*

EDITOR'S NOTE: *If you are making this terrine with boar, marinate it for 12 hours only.*

Liver and Fruit Pâté

THIS SMOOTH, LIGHT PÂTÉ, IDEAL FOR SPREADING ON BREAD OR TOAST, IS MADE TWO DAYS IN ADVANCE TO ALLOW THE FLAVOURS TO DEVELOP FULLY. THE LIVER IN THE PÂTÉ IS A RICH SOURCE OF VITAMINS, BUT ALSO HAS A RELATIVELY HIGH CHOLESTEROL CONTENT.

Serves 16 as a first course
Working time: about 40 minutes
Total time: about 3 days (includes chilling)

Calories **150**
Protein **10g**
Cholesterol **110mg**
Total fat **6g**
Saturated fat **2g**
Sodium **435mg**

125 g	dried apricots, chopped	4 oz
125 g	stoned prunes, chopped	4 oz
4	oranges, juice only	4
2 tbsp	virgin olive oil	2 tbsp
2	large onions, finely chopped	2
500 g	pig's liver, sliced	1 lb
90 g	thin rashers green streaky bacon, rinds removed, chopped	3 oz
2	large cooking apples, peeled, cored and roughly chopped	2
2 tbsp	chopped fresh thyme	2 tbsp
2 tbsp	chopped flat-leaf parsley	2 tbsp
125 g	fresh brown breadcrumbs	4 oz
1	lemon, juice only	1
2	eggs, beaten	2
1 tbsp	green peppercorns, rinsed and coarsely crushed	1 tbsp

Place the apricots and prunes in a bowl. Pour in the orange juice, and leave the fruit to soak for at least 2 hours, or overnight.

Heat the oil in a large saucepan over medium heat. Add the onions and cook them until they are transparent — about 5 minutes. Add the liver and chopped bacon, and cook them, stirring occasionally, until the liver is evenly browned — about 10 minutes. Mix in the apple, thyme and parsley, and cook for a further 2 to 3 minutes. Remove the pan from the heat, allow the mixture to cool slightly, then transfer it to a food processor or blender. Add the breadcrumbs, lemon juice and eggs, and process the ingredients to a smooth pâté. Turn the pâté into a bowl, then stir in the prunes and apricots with any unabsorbed orange juice. Add the green peppercorns, and mix lightly.

Preheat the oven to 180°C (350°F or Mark 4). Line a 22 by 10 by 6 cm (9 by 4 by 2½ inch) terrine or loaf tin with parchment paper. Spoon the pâté into the prepared terrine, pressing it down with the back of the spoon. Cover the terrine tightly with a lid or foil. Place the terrine in a large roasting pan or dish and pour in boiling water to come two thirds of the way up the side of the tin. Bake the pâté until it is firm to the touch — about 1½ hours. Leave the pâté to cool — about 1 hour — then weight it with a 500 g (1 lb) weight *(page 19)*. Chill the pâté for at least 8 hours or overnight. Remove the weight, cover the pâté and leave it in the refrigerator for two more days before serving. Turn out the pâté and serve it cut into slices.

SUGGESTED ACCOMPANIMENT: *crusty bread rolls.*

EDITOR'S NOTE: *Because the pâté is soft, a very sharp knife is essential for cutting thin slices.*

Mediterranean Lamb Wrapped in Vine Leaves

Serves 6 as a main course
Working time: about 45 minutes
Total time: about 9 hours (includes cooling and chilling)

Calories **210**
Protein **27g**
Cholesterol **65mg**
Total fat **9g**
Saturated fat **4g**
Sodium **210mg**

750 g	aubergines, trimmed	1 ½ lb
4	garlic cloves, thinly sliced	4
1 tbsp	virgin olive oil	1 tbsp
125 g	fresh vine leaves, blanched for 1 minute in boiling water, rinsed, drained well and dried	4 oz
30 g	dry-packed sun-dried tomatoes, soaked in hot water to cover for 15 minutes, drained, squeezed dry and roughly chopped	1 oz
1 tbsp	tomato paste	1 tbsp
1 tsp	red wine vinegar	1 tsp
500 g	lean lamb, minced	1 lb
1 tsp	ground cumin	1 tsp
½ tsp	salt	½ tsp
	freshly ground black pepper	

Preheat the oven to 190°C (375°F or Mark 5).

Make slits in the aubergine skins large enough to hold the garlic slices. Insert the garlic slivers into the skins. Roast the aubergines until they are cooked through and soft — 30 to 40 minutes. Set the aubergines aside to cool. Reduce the oven temperature to 180°C (350°F or Mark 4).

Lightly brush a 20 by 6 by 6 cm (8 by 2½ by 2½ inch) terrine or loaf tin with a little of the olive oil and line it with the vine leaves, vein side out. Overlap the vine leaves so that there are no gaps, and allow some of the leaves to overhang the container's edges so that they can be folded over later to enclose the filling.

In a large bowl, mix the chopped sun-dried tomatoes with the tomato paste, most of the remaining oil and the vinegar. Stir in the minced lamb.

Remove the garlic slivers from the cooked aubergines and press them through a small sieve or garlic press. Scrape the aubergine flesh away from the skin and purée the flesh in a food processor. Add the garlic pulp to the purée, together with the lamb mixture, cumin, salt and some pepper, and process until the ingredients are well mixed. Spoon the mixture into the lined terrine, pressing it down with the back of the spoon. Fold the overhanging vine leaves over the contents of the terrine. Brush the exposed side of the vine leaves with the remaining olive oil and cover the terrine with a lid or foil.

Bake the terrine until it is firm to the touch and a skewer inserted in the middle is hot when removed — about 50 minutes. Weight the top of the terrine with a 500 g (1 lb) weight *(page 19)* and allow it to cool to room temperature — about 2 hours. Chill the terrine for at least 4 hours. About 30 minutes before serving, remove the terrine from the refrigerator and allow it to come to room temperature. Drain off any excess juices, then turn out the terrine and slice it.

SUGGESTED ACCOMPANIMENTS: *spinach salad; cherry tomatoes and flat-leaf parsley.*

EDITOR'S NOTE: *Preserved vine leaves may be used if fresh leaves are not available. Wash them in cold water to rid them of excess salt, then drain them thoroughly on a folded tea towel. They do not require blanching. If sun-dried tomatoes are unavailable, increase the quantity of tomato paste to two tablespoons and add to the minced lamb two ripe tomatoes, skinned, seeded, chopped and drained.*

Terrine of Wild Rabbit with Mixed Lentils and Peas

WILD RABBITS, WHICH ARE SMALLER THAN DOMESTICATED
RABBITS, ARE CALLED FOR IN THIS RECIPE TO PROVIDE TWO
SADDLES THE CORRECT SIZE FOR LINING THE TERRINE.

Serves 8 as a main course
Working time: about 2 hours
Total time: about 20 hours (includes marinating and chilling)

Calories **285**
Protein **33g**
Cholesterol **70mg**
Total fat **9g**
Saturated fat **4g**
Sodium **75mg**

2	wild rabbits, jointed, bones removed and reserved. Saddle section, to include rib cage flaps, intact	2
1 tbsp	cognac, Armagnac or brandy	1 tbsp
2½	onions, two quartered, the half onion finely chopped	2½
2	celery sticks, sliced	2
1	carrot, sliced	1
3 tsp	fresh thyme, or ¾ tsp dried thyme	3 tsp
3½	garlic cloves, three unpeeled and crushed, the half clove finely chopped	3½
8	black peppercorns	8
1	bay leaf	1
2 tbsp	low-fat fromage frais	2 tbsp
¾ tsp	salt	¾ tsp
	freshly ground black pepper	
⅛ tsp	powdered saffron or turmeric	⅛ tsp
8	dried morels, soaked for 20 minutes in tepid water, drained and rinsed well, stalks removed	8
1 tsp	finely cut chives	1 tsp
1 tsp	finely chopped parsley	1 tsp
60 g	yellow split peas, picked over and rinsed	2 oz
60 g	green lentils, picked over and rinsed	2 oz
1 tsp	virgin olive oil	1 tsp
45 g	fresh mushrooms, wiped clean and finely chopped	1½ oz
30 g	fresh breadcrumbs	1 oz
10 g	piece of caul, softened in acidulated water for 10 minutes	⅓ oz
4	spinach leaves, blanched and drained, central ribs removed	4
4 tsp	powdered gelatine	4 tsp
1	egg, white and washed shell only	1
1 tsp	red wine vinegar	1 tsp

Trim the rabbit saddles to fit an 18 by 10 by 5 cm (7 by 4 by 2 inch) terrine; the fillets will line the bottom and the rib cage flaps will line the sides and extend over the filling. Flatten the flaps slightly between two sheets of plastic film, using a meat mallet or rolling pin. Rub the cognac into the saddles. Place them in a shallow dish, cover them and leave them in the refrigerator for 8 hours or overnight, to allow the flavour to develop.

Meanwhile, make a rabbit stock. Half fill a pot with water and bring it to the boil. Reserve the meat from two hind legs; add the remaining meat and bones to the water, and blanch them for 2 minutes to cleanse

them. Drain the meat and bones in a colander, discarding the liquid. Rinse the meat and bones under cold running water and return them to the pot. Add the quartered onions, the celery and the carrot. Pour in enough water to cover the contents of the pot by about 5 cm (2 inches), and bring the water to the boil over medium heat. Reduce the heat to maintain a simmer and skim any impurities from the surface. Add 1 teaspoon of the thyme, the crushed garlic, peppercorns and bay leaf, and simmer the stock very gently for 4 hours, skimming occasionally. Strain the stock into a large bowl; allow the solids to drain thoroughly before discarding them. Degrease the stock (box, page 11). Put 8 tablespoons of the stock into a small pan and reduce it by half. Set it aside and reserve 35 cl (12 fl oz) of the remaining stock separately.

While the stock is simmering, mince or finely chop the reserved leg meat. Wrap one third in plastic film and place it in the refrigerator. Beat the fromage frais, ¼ teaspoon of the salt and some pepper into the remaining minced meat to form a paste. Put the paste in the refrigerator to chill for 10 minutes. Transfer 3 tablespoons of the chilled paste to a small bowl and blend in the saffron or turmeric to turn it a bright yellow colour. Stuff the morels with this spiced paste. Mix the chives and parsley into the rest of the paste and spread it into a 16 by 7.5 cm (6½ by 3 inch) rectangle on a sheet of plastic film. Lay the stuffed morels along the centre of the rectangle and, with the help of the plastic film, roll the herbed paste round the mushrooms to form a sausage. Wrap the sausage in the plastic film and place it in the refrigerator for at least 20 minutes, until it is firm.

Put the split peas into a large pan of water and bring them to the boil. Reduce the heat and simmer the peas for 5 minutes; add the green lentils and simmer them for a further 15 minutes. Drain the split peas and lentils in a sieve, refresh them under cold running water and drain them again. In a frying pan, heat the oil over medium heat and brown the chopped onion lightly. Add the chopped garlic and fresh mushrooms and fry them gently until the mixture is quite dry — 7 to 10 minutes. Add the lentils and split peas, stir for 1 to 2 minutes to dry the mixture a little, then transfer it to a mixing bowl to cool slightly. Mix the reserved minced rabbit, the breadcrumbs, the remaining 2 teaspoons of thyme, the reduced stock, half of the remaining salt and some black pepper into the pea and lentil mixture. Cover the bowl and set the filling aside.

Preheat the oven to 230°C (450°F or Mark 8). Drain the caul and line the terrine with it, leaving enough overhanging to wrap over the filling. Put the rabbit saddles in the terrine, placing the fillets along the bottom and lining the sides with the flaps. Season with the remaining salt and some pepper. Spread half of the lentil and pea mixture in the terrine. Remove the plastic film from the rabbit sausage and wrap it in the spinach leaves. Place the sausage along the centre of the terrine and cover it with the remaining lentil and pea mixture. Fold the saddle flaps over the filling, then wrap the excess caul over the flaps.

Bake the terrine for 20 minutes. Remove it from the oven and cover it with a double thickness of foil. Reduce the oven temperature to 190°C (375°F or Mark 5). Set the terrine in a large roasting pan and add hot water to come two thirds up the side of the terrine; bake the terrine for a further 40 minutes. Turn off the heat and leave the terrine in the oven for 15 minutes.

Remove the terrine from the oven and discard the foil. Pour off and reserve any cooking juices. Turn out the stuffed rabbit saddles onto a plate. Deglaze the terrine with some of the reserved rabbit stock, strain this back into the stock with the cooking juices, and set the stock aside. Clean the terrine and replace the saddles in it, then cover it loosely with plastic film. Weight the terrine with a 2 kg (4 lb) weight *(page 19)*. Put the weighted terrine in the refrigerator to chill and press for 8 to 12 hours.

Meanwhile, using the powdered gelatine, the egg white and shell and the vinegar, convert the reserved rabbit stock into aspic, following the method on page 12. Pour the aspic over the terrine and return it to the refrigerator for a further 2 to 3 hours, until set. Serve the terrine cut into slices.

SUGGESTED ACCOMPANIMENT: *baby leeks vinaigrette.*

Rabbit Mould with Young Peas and Asparagus

Serves 6 as a main course
Working time: about 1 hour and 30 minutes
Total time: about 24 hours (includes marinating and chilling)

Calories **245**
Protein **39g**
Cholesterol **70mg**
Total fat **8g**
Saturated fat **3g**
Sodium **190mg**

1	rabbit (about 1.25 kg/2½ lb), jointed, trimmed of fat and membrane, offal discarded	1
1.25 litres	unsalted vegetable stock (recipe, page 10)	2 pints
½ tsp	salt	½ tsp
60 g	powdered gelatine	2 oz
3	eggs, whites and washed shells only	3
2 tbsp	vinegar	2 tbsp
175 g	fresh peas, shelled, or 60 g (2 oz) frozen peas, thawed	6 oz
60 g	thin asparagus	2 oz
3	young lavender sprigs	3
1 tbsp	lavender or thyme flowers (optional)	1 tbsp
Wine and herb marinade		
15 cl	dry white wine	¼ pint
1	bay leaf	1
1 tbsp	fresh thyme leaves	1 tbsp
1	lavender sprig, including flowers if in season	1

First prepare the marinade. In a small saucepan, briefly warm the wine, bay leaf, thyme leaves and lavender sprig over low heat, then leave the mixture to cool. Place the rabbit in a large bowl and pour the cooled marinade over it. Cover the dish and leave the rabbit to marinate in the refrigerator for 12 to 24 hours, turning the pieces of rabbit occasionally.

Place the rabbit and the marinade in a large non-reactive saucepan or fireproof casserole. Pour in half of the vegetable stock and bring it slowly to the boil, skimming the surface. Reduce the heat, cover the casserole and gently simmer the rabbit until it is tender and falling off the bone — about 2½ hours. Check the level of the liquid occasionally during cooking, and add more hot vegetable stock or boiling water to keep the rabbit covered by liquid.

Remove the pan from the heat. Leave the rabbit to cool to room temperature in its cooking liquid — about 1 hour — then remove the meat with a slotted spoon. Bone the rabbit as neatly as possible, separating the chunks of meat from the smaller trimmings.

Strain the cooking liquid through a nylon sieve into a large bowl; discard the bay leaf, thyme leaves and lavender. Add any remaining vegetable stock or enough water to make the liquid up to 1.25 litres (2 pints), and season it with the salt. Using the powdered gelatine, egg whites and shells and the vinegar, convert the stock into aspic following the method on page 12. Let the aspic cool to room temperature.

Meanwhile, blanch the peas and asparagus separately in rapidly boiling water, until just tender — about 2 minutes each. Refresh them under cold running water and drain them.

Pour a little of the cooled aspic into a 1.25 litre (2 pint) flat-bottomed charlotte mould, to a depth of 1 cm (½ inch). Chill this in the refrigerator until it is set — about 15 minutes. Arrange the peas in a single layer over the set aspic, reserving any that remain, and spoon a little more aspic over them to cover. Chill the aspic as before. Arrange half of the rabbit chunks to form a layer in the mould, and encircle the meat with half of the lavender sprigs, adding half of the lavender or thyme flowers, if you are using them. Spoon over a little more liquid aspic to cover the rabbit and chill the mould again until the aspic is set — about 15 minutes. Pile half of the smaller pieces of rabbit in the centre of the mould and surround them with half of the asparagus tips. Cover with a little more aspic and chill until set — about 15 minutes. Continue layering the remaining rabbit chunks and smaller pieces in this way, adding any remaining peas to the final layer. Chill the completed mould for at least 4 hours.

To serve the mould, dip the dish into hot water for about 5 seconds, then invert it on to a serving plate and shake free the contents.

SUGGESTED ACCOMPANIMENTS: *wholegrain mustard; wholemeal bread; green salad.*

EDITOR'S NOTE: *Chicken may be substituted for the rabbit in this recipe. The bird should be jointed and skinned, then cooked for just 1½ hours. If asparagus is not available, very fine green beans may be used instead.*

Terrine of Rabbit with Prunes and Green Peppercorns

Serves 8 as a main course
Working time: about 1 hour
Total time: about 7 hours (includes cooling and chilling)

Calories **285**
Protein **25g**
Cholesterol **70mg**
Total fat **15g**
Saturated fat **4g**
Sodium **440mg**

1	rabbit (about 1 kg/2 lb), boned, fillets left whole, liver reserved	1
½ tsp	salt	½ tsp
	freshly ground black pepper	
½ tsp	safflower oil	½ tsp
2	shallots, finely chopped	2
1 tbsp	raspberry vinegar	1 tbsp
1 tbsp	green peppercorns, rinsed and dried	1 tbsp
2	egg whites	2
45 g	low-fat fromage frais	1½ oz
1 tsp	fresh thyme or ¼ tsp dried thyme	1 tsp
1 tsp	fresh marjoram or ¼ tsp dried marjoram	1 tsp
⅛ tsp	ground allspice	⅛ tsp
30 g	shelled walnuts, finely chopped	1 oz
60 g	large stoned prunes, soaked for 20 minutes in hot water	2 oz
90 g	burghul, soaked for 10 minutes in 15 cl (¼ pint) water	3 oz
150 g	rashers streaky bacon, rinds removed	5 oz
30 g	shelled pistachio nuts	1 oz

Remove and discard the thin membrane which encloses each rabbit fillet. Divide each fillet lengthwise into one long and one short strip (the fillet tapers, so the division is a natural one). Trim the two short strips to even thicknesses. Season the strips of meat with half of the salt and plenty of pepper.

In a heavy frying pan, heat the oil over high heat, add the two long and two short strips of rabbit and cook them rapidly, turning once, until evenly sealed — about 20 to 30 seconds. Transfer the strips to a plate and reduce the heat to medium. Add the liver to the oil remaining in the pan and cook for 1 minute, turning once. Transfer the liver to the plate. Add the shallots to the pan and cook them gently until they are soft but not browned — about 2 minutes. Stir in the raspberry vinegar and green peppercorns, then remove the pan from the heat and leave the shallot mixture to cool in the pan.

In a food processor, process the remaining raw rabbit meat into a smooth paste — about 2 to 3 minutes. Add the egg whites and *fromage frais*, a little at a time, processing the ingredients between each addition. Add the cooked liver, thyme, marjoram, allspice, the remaining salt and some pepper, and process for a few seconds more, until the liver is finely chopped and the ingredients are well mixed.

Combine 1 tablespoon of the rabbit mixture with the chopped walnuts. Thoroughly drain the prunes and fill them with the walnut mixture. Set the stuffed prunes aside. Stir the cooled shallot mixture and the soaked burghul into the remaining rabbit mixture and mix well.

Preheat the oven to 180°C (350°F or Mark 4). Lay the bacon rashers flat on a board and stretch them as thinly as possible with the back of a knife. Line a 20 by 11 by 6 cm (8 by 4½ by 2½ inch) terrine or loaf tin with the bacon rashers, laying them across the terrine with ▶

the ends overhanging the rim. Spoon a quarter of the rabbit mixture into the bottom of the bacon-lined terrine. Press the mixture down with the back of the spoon, hollowing a channel down the middle. Place one of the long rabbit strips in the channel and arrange a row of pistachios on either side of it.

Top this layer with a third of the remaining rabbit mixture, spreading it evenly. Lay the prunes in a neat row down the middle of the terrine. Spoon half of the remaining rabbit mixture on top and spread it evenly. Lay the remaining long strip of rabbit on top, to one side of the terrine; lay the two short strips of rabbit, end to end, down the other side. Arrange a row of pistachios between them. Cover the rabbit strips with the remaining rabbit mixture, pressing it down lightly. Fold the loose ends of the bacon over the filling.

Cover the terrine tightly and stand it in a roasting pan or large ovenproof dish. Pour boiling water into the pan to come two thirds of the way up the side of the terrine. Cook the terrine until a skewer inserted in the middle feels hot to the touch when withdrawn — about 1 hour. When the terrine is cooked, remove the cover and weight it down with a 500 g (1 lb) weight *(page 19)*. Leave the terrine to cool for about 1 hour, then chill it for at least 4 hours.

To serve, turn out the terrine on to a serving platter and cut it into slices.

SUGGESTED ACCOMPANIMENTS: *crusty bread; mixed salad.*

EDITOR'S NOTE: *The cooked terrine will keep in the refrigerator for up to 10 days.*

Venison and Apricot Terrine

Serves 6 as a main course
Working time: about 1 hour
Total time: about 2 days (includes marinating)

Calories **495**
Protein **41g**
Cholesterol **60mg**
Total fat **13g**
Saturated fat **3g**
Sodium **505mg**

850 g	venison, sliced along the grain into 1 cm (½ inch) thick slices	1 ¾ lb
125 g	dried apricots	4 oz
6 tbsp	red wine	6 tbsp
200 g	round-grain brown rice, rinsed under cold running water	7 oz
8	large green cabbage leaves	8
1 tsp	virgin olive oil	1 tsp
1	onion, finely chopped	1
1	garlic clove, finely chopped	1
45 g	pine-nuts	1 ½ oz
6	rashers green streaky bacon (about 60 g/2 oz)	6
½ tsp	salt	½ tsp
	freshly ground black pepper	
1	egg white	1
60 g	fresh brown breadcrumbs	2 oz
1 tbsp	fresh rosemary leaves, plus six sprigs fresh rosemary, for garnish	1 tbsp
Red wine marinade		
1 tsp	virgin olive oil	1 tsp
1	stick celery, chopped	1
1	small carrot, chopped	1
1	small onion, chopped	1
1	garlic clove, crushed	1
8	black peppercorns, crushed	8
4	cloves	4
1½ tsp	chopped fresh ginger root	1½ tsp
12.5 cl	red wine	4 fl oz
1½ tbsp	balsamic vinegar, or 1 tbsp red wine vinegar mixed with ¼ tsp honey	1½ tbsp
1 tbsp	brandy	1 tbsp

To make the marinade, heat the oil in a heavy-bottomed pan over medium heat. Add the celery, carrot, onion and garlic, and sweat them until they are lightly browned — about 10 minutes. Add the peppercorns, cloves, ginger, wine and vinegar, and bring the liquid to the boil. Remove the pan from the heat, cover it and leave the ingredients to infuse and cool — about 1 hour. Put the venison in a large non-reactive bowl. Stir the brandy into the cooled marinade and pour it over the meat. Leave the meat to marinate in the refrigerator for about 48 hours, turning it several times.

Place the dried apricots in a heatproof bowl. Warm the red wine in a small pan, then pour it over the apricots. Cover the bowl and set it aside for at least 1 hour, until the apricots are plumped up.

Put the rinsed rice in a heavy-bottomed saucepan with 30 cl (½ pint) of water, and bring the water to the boil. Boil the rice for 2 minutes, skimming the surface of the liquid several times. Reduce the heat, cover the pan and simmer the rice for 15 minutes. Remove the saucepan from the heat and leave the rice to steam, covered, for a further 15 minutes. Remove the lid from the pan, and set the rice aside to cool.

Meanwhile, cut each cabbage leaf in half and discard the tough centre rib. Blanch the leaves in boiling water for 1 minute, refresh them under cold running water and drain them on paper towels. Heat the oil in a frying pan over low heat, add the onion and garlic, and sweat them gently for 3 minutes, until they start to colour. Add the pine-nuts, and fry until both the nuts and the onions are golden-brown — about 5 minutes. Stir the contents of the pan into the rice.

Line a 21 by 11 by 6 cm (8½ by 4½ by 2½ inch) terrine or loaf tin with six of the cabbage leaves, using a double layer on the base and leaving a 6 cm (2½ inch) overhang at the top. Stretch the bacon with the back of a knife so that each rasher is the length of the terrine. Drain the apricots and cut each one in half. Using a slotted spoon, remove the venison from the marinade. Pat it dry on paper towels and season it with ¼ teaspoon of the salt and some black pepper.

Lightly whisk the egg white together with the remaining ¼ teaspoon of salt, then stir it into the rice mixture. Add the breadcrumbs, rosemary leaves and some pepper, and mix the ingredients well together.

Preheat the oven to 180°C (350°F or Mark 4). Lay one third of the venison in the base of the terrine and place two bacon rashers lengthwise on top. Spread one quarter of the rice mixture over the bacon and venison. Arrange half of the apricots in two lengthwise rows on top of the rice, then add another quarter of the rice mixture, spreading it evenly. Repeat this sequence of layers, completing the terrine with a layer of venison topped with bacon. (The filling will be higher than the sides of the terrine.) Cover the bacon with the remaining two cabbage leaves and fold the overhanging cabbage leaves over them. Cover the terrine with a double thickness of foil.

Stand the terrine in a roasting pan, and pour in boil-ing water to come two thirds of the way up the side of the terrine. Cover the roasting pan with a large sheet of foil, and bake the terrine in the oven for 1¼ hours, until a skewer inserted in the middle of the terrine feels hot to the touch when withdrawn. Remove the terrine from the oven, and discard the foil coverings. Invert the terrine, still in its mould, on a sloping board and cover it with foil to help keep it warm. Place a 1 kg (2 lb) weight on top of the terrine's base and leave it to firm and drain for 30 minutes.

Unmould the terrine on to a platter and serve it cut into slices, garnished with the sprigs of rosemary.

SUGGESTED ACCOMPANIMENTS: *redcurrant jelly; a warm salad of broccoli, cauliflower and lettuce.*

EDITOR'S NOTE: *Rump steak can be successfully substituted for venison in this recipe.*

Lining a Loaf Tin

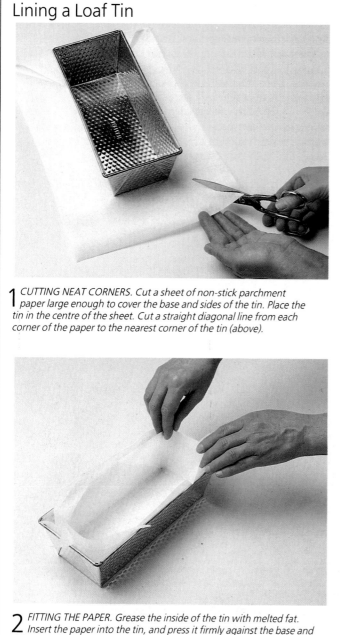

1 CUTTING NEAT CORNERS. Cut a sheet of non-stick parchment paper large enough to cover the base and sides of the tin. Place the tin in the centre of the sheet. Cut a straight diagonal line from each corner of the paper to the nearest corner of the tin (above).

2 FITTING THE PAPER. Grease the inside of the tin with melted fat. Insert the paper into the tin, and press it firmly against the base and sides. Overlap the corner flaps, lightly greasing their undersides so that the pairs of flaps adhere and lie flat.

Chicken and Rabbit Terrine with Wholegrain Mustard

Serves 20 as a first course
Working time: about 30 minutes
Total time: about 7 hours and 30 minutes (includes chilling)

Calories **100**
Protein **17g**
Cholesterol **45mg**
Total fat **3g**
Saturated fat **1g**
Sodium **180mg**

2	saddles of rabbit, meat removed from the bone to yield four fillets	2
2 tbsp	dry white wine	2 tbsp
4 tbsp	wholegrain mustard	4 tbsp
1 kg	boneless chicken breasts, skinned	2 lb
4	shallots, or ½ small onion	4
2 tsp	salt	2 tsp
	freshly ground black pepper	
3	egg whites	3

Place the rabbit fillets in a shallow dish. Mix the wine with 1½ teaspoons of the mustard and pour it over the rabbit. Turn the rabbit to coat it evenly, and set it aside to marinate for 30 minutes. Meanwhile, mince the chicken breasts by hand or in a food processor, with the shallots or onion half. Add 4½ teaspoons of the remaining mustard, the salt and some pepper to the minced chicken, and mix well.

Preheat the oven to 180°C (350°F or Mark 4). Drain the rabbit fillets on paper towels. Pour the remaining marinade into the chicken mixture, and mix well. Whisk the egg whites until they stand in very soft peaks, then lightly stir them into the chicken mixture.

Line a terrine or loaf tin measuring 18 by 8.5 by 6 cm (7 by 3½ by 2½ inches) with non-stick parchment paper (left).

Spoon half of the chicken mixture into the prepared terrine and press it down evenly but lightly with the back of the spoon. Lay the rabbit fillets on top of the chicken mixture. Cover the rabbit with the remaining chicken mixture, again pressing it down evenly with the back of the spoon. Spread the remaining 2 tablespoons of mustard over the top.

Cover the terrine with a piece of non-stick parchment paper or foil, and stand it in a large roasting pan or dish. Pour enough boiling water into the pan to come two thirds of the way up the side of the terrine. Bake the terrine until a skewer inserted into the middle feels hot to the touch when removed — about 1½ hours. Allow the terrine to cool — about 1 hour — then chill it for at least 4 hours. Turn out the terrine on to a platter, and serve it cut into slices.

SUGGESTED ACCOMPANIMENT: crusty bread.

Terrine of Pigeon and Veal

Serves 20 as a first course
Working time: about 25 minutes
Total time: about 14 hours (includes marinating and chilling)

Calories **95**
Protein **14g**
Cholesterol **40mg**
Total fat **3g**
Saturated fat **1g**
Sodium **130mg**

4	pigeon breasts, skinned	4
6 tbsp	dry Madeira	6 tbsp
1 tbsp	balsamic vinegar, or 2 tsp red wine vinegar mixed with ¼ tsp honey	1 tbsp
1 kg	minced veal	2 lb
60 g	fine fresh white breadcrumbs	2 oz
1 tbsp	finely chopped parsley	1 tbsp
1 tbsp	juniper berries	1 tbsp
2 tsp	salt	2 tsp
	freshly ground black pepper	
4	egg whites	4
2	bay leaves	2

Place the pigeon breasts in a shallow dish and pour 4 tablespoons of the Madeira and the balsamic vinegar over them. Cover the dish and leave the breasts to marinate overnight in the refrigerator.

Preheat the oven to 180°C (350°F or Mark 4). Combine the veal, breadcrumbs, parsley and remaining Madeira in a bowl. Reserving a few juniper berries for garnish, crush the remainder and add them to the veal mixture. Season with the salt and some black pepper. Whisk the egg whites until they stand in soft peaks, then lightly stir them into the veal mixture.

Place about a third of the veal mixture in a 1.5 litre (2½ pint) oval terrine and press it down evenly in the bottom of the dish. Lay two of the pigeon breasts on top of the veal mixture. Spoon another third of the veal mixture over the pigeon, spreading it in an even layer. Lay the remaining pigeon breasts in the terrine and top them with a final layer of veal. Pour any remaining marinade from the pigeon breasts over the terrine.

Place the bay leaves and the reserved juniper berries on top of the veal mixture. Cover the terrine closely with foil and stand the dish in a large roasting pan or dish. Pour boiling water into the roasting pan to come two thirds of the way up the side of the terrine. Bake the terrine until a skewer inserted into the middle of the terrine feels hot to the touch when withdrawn — about 2 hours. Leave the terrine to cool — about 1 hour — then chill it in the refrigerator for at least 2 hours, or overnight, before serving.

Lining an Eye-Shaped Mould with Pastry

1 *POSITIONING THE PASTRY. Roll up a pastry strip and carefully unroll it inside the mould to line the sides and the base. Keep the top pastry edge at least 4 cm (1½ inches) above the rim of the mould.*

2 *SEALING THE JOINS. Press the dough firmly against the sides and into the angles of the mould. Close and smooth out the seam in the base of the mould.*

Raised Pigeon Pie

THIS MODERN RAISED PIE IS MADE WITH A MINIMUM OF FAT WHILE RETAINING THE SHAPE, SATISFYING TEXTURE AND FLAVOUR OF TRADITIONAL FARE. MAKE THE PIE A DAY IN ADVANCE AND CHILL IT OVERNIGHT TO ALLOW THE FLAVOURS TO BLEND AND DEVELOP.

Serves 12 as a main course
Working time: about 1 hour and 30 minutes
Total time: about 18 hours (includes chilling)

Calories **365**
Protein **31g**
Cholesterol **105mg**
Total fat **16g**
Saturated fat **5g**
Sodium **330mg**

3	pigeon squabs (about 250 g/8 oz each)	3
2	onions, one quartered, one very finely chopped	2
2	garlic cloves, one unpeeled, one peeled and finely chopped	2
1	bay leaf	1
8	black peppercorns	8
1	fresh thyme sprig	1
1½ tsp	virgin olive oil	1½ tsp
750 g	veal escalopes, trimmed of fat and connective tissue	1½ lb
2 tsp	dried mixed herbs	2 tsp
1 tsp	salt	1 tsp
	freshly ground black pepper	
	ground allspice	
250 g	rump steak, trimmed of all fat and connective tissue, cut into 1 cm (½ inch) thick strips	8 oz
4 tsp	powdered gelatine	4 tsp
Hot-water crust pastry		
350 g	plain flour	12 oz
¼ tsp	salt	¼ tsp
1	egg yolk	1
125 g	polyunsaturated margarine	4 oz
1	egg, beaten, for glaze	1

Using a small, sharp knife, remove the breasts from each pigeon squab, then remove the skin from the breasts. Set the breasts aside. Put the carcasses into a large saucepan and pour in enough cold water just to cover them. Bring the liquid slowly to the boil, then reduce the heat to low. Skim off the scum from the surface of the liquid and add the quartered onion, the unpeeled garlic clove, the bay leaf, peppercorns and thyme sprig. Partially cover the saucepan, and simmer gently for 2 hours to make a pigeon stock.

Heat the olive oil in a frying pan over medium heat. Add the chopped onion and cook gently until it is softened but not browned — 6 to 8 minutes. Remove the pan from the heat and allow the onion to cool.

Cut the veal into small pieces, put them in a food processor and process them until the meat is very finely minced. Add the softened onion, chopped garlic, dried mixed herbs, ½ teaspoon of the salt and some black pepper. Process until the ingredients are evenly blended. Set the veal mixture aside.

Preheat the oven to 220°C (425°F or Mark 7). Thoroughly grease a 21 by 12 by 10 cm (8½ by 5 by 4 inch) eye-shaped raised pie mould.

To make the pastry, sift the flour and salt into a mixing bowl and make a well in the centre. Add the egg yolk. Put the margarine into a saucepan with 12.5 cl (4 fl oz) of cold water. Heat gently until the margarine melts. Bring the liquid to the boil. Immediately pour the boiling liquid into the well in the flour, stirring with a round-bladed knife at the same time, to incorporate the egg yolk and flour into a soft dough. Knead the dough on a lightly floured surface until smooth.

Cut off one third of the pastry, wrap it in plastic film

and set it aside. Roll the remaining pastry into a strip measuring about 52 by 15 cm (21 by 6 inches) and use it to line the greased pie mould (box, opposite).

Spoon the veal mixture into the pastry-lined mould, pressing it against the bottom and sides of the pastry with the back of the spoon to leave a hollow centre. Put two of the pigeon breasts in the bottom of the hollow. Season them with a little of the remaining salt, some freshly ground black pepper and the allspice. Place half of the rump steak strips on top of the pigeon breasts, and season as before. Repeat with the remaining pigeon breasts and steak strips, ending with a layer of pigeon breasts. Sprinkle 3 tablespoons of the pigeon stock over the filling.

Roll out the reserved pastry to an oval shape large enough to cover the pie. Brush the overhanging edges with water, then place the pastry lid in position on top of the pie. Press the edges firmly together to seal them. Using kitchen scissors, trim the edge of the pastry to neaten it, then pinch the edge between forefinger and thumb all round the pie to create a decorative edge. Lightly knead and re-roll the trimmings, and cut out leaf shapes to decorate the top of the pie.

Brush the pie with a little beaten egg, and make three evenly spaced holes in the top. Decorate the pie with the pastry leaves and brush them with a little more egg; reserve the remaining egg.

Place the pie on a baking sheet. Bake it for 20 minutes, then reduce the oven temperature to 190°C (375°F or Mark 5) and continue cooking for 1½ hours. Check that the top of the pie does not become too brown during cooking; if necessary, cover it loosely with a piece of foil. Remove the pie from the oven and very carefully remove the outside of the mould. Brush the sides of the pie with the reserved egg. Return it to the oven for 10 to 15 minutes, until the sides are golden-brown. Allow the pie to cool for 1 hour, then chill it for about 3 hours.

Meanwhile, degrease the remaining pigeon stock (page 11) and boil it until it is reduced to 45 cl (¾ pint) — 15 to 20 minutes. Dissolve the gelatine in 3 tablespoons of water, following the instructions on page 13. Add the dissolved gelatine to the reduced stock, and stir well. Leave the stock until it is cold but not set — about 40 minutes.

Using a funnel, carefully pour the stock into the pie through the three holes in the pastry lid. Refrigerate the pie overnight. Before serving, remove the pie from the base of the mould and transfer it to a plate.

EDITOR'S NOTE: *The pie will keep well in the refrigerator for up to four days.*

Terrine of Guinea Fowl, Squabs and Quail with Wild Mushrooms

Serves 8 as a first course
Working time: about 1 hour and 45 minutes
Total time: about 16 hours (includes marinating and chilling)

Calories **115**
Protein **14g**
Cholesterol **25mg**
Total fat **3g**
Saturated fat **trace**
Sodium **190mg**

1	guinea fowl (about 1 kg/2 lb)	1
2	pigeon squabs (about 250 g/8 oz each)	2
2	quail (about 250 g/8 oz total weight)	2
30 g	dried shiitake mushrooms	1 oz
30 g	dried morels	1 oz
30 g	dried horn of plenty mushrooms or wood ear mushrooms	1 oz
125 g	fresh chanterelle, or girolle, mushrooms, wiped clean	4 oz
125 g	fresh oyster mushrooms, wiped clean	4 oz
2	onions, quartered	2
2	sticks celery, chopped	2
2	carrots, sliced	2
3	unpeeled garlic cloves, crushed	3
8	black peppercorns	8
3	cloves	3
2 tsp	fresh thyme, or ½ tsp dried thyme	2 tsp
1	bay leaf	1
4	very ripe tomatoes, or 225 g (7½ oz) canned tomatoes	4
15 g	dried ceps	½ oz
¾ tsp	salt	¾ tsp
3 tbsp	Madeira	3 tbsp
20 cl	dry white wine	7 fl oz
15 cl	unsalted chicken stock (recipe, page 10)	¼ pint
2 cm	piece fresh ginger root, thinly sliced	¾ inch
1	egg, white and washed shell only	1
1 tbsp	red wine vinegar	1 tbsp
4 tsp	powdered gelatine	4 tsp
8	small bunches of mustard and cress or fresh herbs, for garnish	8
Madeira marinade		
½ tsp	black peppercorns	½ tsp
2	bay leaves	2
2 cm	piece fresh ginger root, peeled	¾ inch
1	garlic clove	1
3 tbsp	Madeira	3 tbsp

Remove the breasts from the guinea fowl, squabs and quail; reserve the carcasses. Skin the breasts of each bird, trimming away any fat and sinew, and flatten them a little with a mallet or rolling pin. Place the fillets in a single layer in a large, shallow dish.

To make the Madeira marinade, use a pestle and mortar to pound the peppercorns, bay leaves, ginger and garlic together into a rough paste, then mix in the Madeira. Pour the marinade over the breasts, and cover the dish. Leave the meat to marinate in the refrigerator for about 8 hours, turning it over several times during this period.

Soak the dried mushrooms in tepid water for 20 minutes, until they are soft; soak the shiitake mushrooms separately, since the other mushrooms are usually very gritty. Remove the mushrooms and squeeze them dry over their soaking bowls, then rinse them in several changes of cold water. Strain the mushroom-soaking liquids through a muslin-lined sieve into a small bowl; cover the bowl and set it aside. Trim away any tough stalks from the reconstituted dried mushrooms and the chanterelle and oyster mushrooms, reserving 60 g (2 oz) of the trimmings. Cover the mushrooms and put them in the refrigerator to chill until required.

Meanwhile, prepare the stock for the game aspic. Preheat the oven to 220°C (425°F or Mark 7). Remove and discard the skin and fat from the carcasses, and reserve the legs from the guinea fowl for another recipe. Place the bird carcasses in a large roasting pan, together with the onions, celery and carrots. Roast the carcasses and vegetables until they are well browned — about 1 hour. Turn off the oven. Transfer the contents of the roasting pan to a large pot. Pour ½ litre (16 fl oz) of water into the roasting pan and, using a spatula, scrape up the deposits from the bottom of the pan. Pour the liquid into the pot and add the garlic, peppercorns, cloves, thyme and bay leaf. Pour in enough water to cover the contents of the pot by about 5 cm (2 inches). Bring the liquid to the boil; reduce the heat to maintain a simmer and skim any impurities from the surface. Simmer the stock very gently for about 30 minutes. Add the tomatoes, dried ceps, reserved mushroom trimmings and mushroom-soaking liquid. Simmer the stock for a further 2½ hours, skimming it occasionally. Strain the stock; allow the solids to drain thoroughly into the stock before discarding them. Degrease the stock (box, page 11).

Preheat the oven to 240°C (475°F or Mark 9). Remove the breast fillets from their marinade and wipe them dry. Strain the marinade through a muslin-lined sieve into the game stock. In a non-stick frying pan, sear the breasts over medium heat, allowing 3 minutes on each side for the guinea fowl, 2 minutes on each side for the squabs and 1 minute on each side for the quail. Place the seared breasts in an oven-proof dish, season them with ¼ teaspoon of the salt and sprinkle on 1 tablespoon of the Madeira. Cover the dish with foil and cook the breasts in the oven for 3 minutes, then turn off the heat. Set the oven door slightly ajar and leave the meat to rest in the warm oven for another 10 minutes. Remove the dish from the oven and set it aside for the breasts to cool. (The squab breasts should still be pink.)

Cut the guinea fowl and squab breasts into 1 cm (½ inch) wide strips along the grain; leave the quail breasts whole. Place the meat in a dish, cover it and chill it in the refrigerator until required. Strain the cooking juices into the game stock. Bring the game stock to a simmer, add the reconstituted dried mushrooms and poach them for 20 minutes.

Meanwhile, mix the white wine with the chicken stock in a small saucepan, add the ginger and bring the liquid to a simmer. Add the fresh mushrooms and poach them for 5 minutes. (They would discolour if poached in the game stock.) Using a slotted spoon, remove the mushrooms from the stocks, drain them on paper towels, and place them in a dish. Cover the dish and place it in the refrigerator. Strain the chicken stock into the game stock.

Reduce the stock to about 90 cl (1½ pints). Using the egg white, egg shell and vinegar, convert the stock into aspic following the instructions on page 12. While the aspic is still hot, stir in the remaining salt and Madeira. Set the aspic aside to cool — about 1 hour.

Carefully ladle a thin layer of the cooled aspic into a 90 cl (1½ pint) terrine, and refrigerate it for 15 minutes until it is set. Set aside some of the better looking mushrooms for garnish. Arrange the quail breasts on the aspic, in a row along the centre of the terrine, and place the morels on either side. Pour on sufficient aspic to half cover them, and return the terrine to the refrigerator to partially set — about 15 minutes. Pour on more aspic to cover the quail breasts and morels completely. Repeat this process with the remaining ingredients in the following order: girolles, strips of squab, oyster mushrooms, horn of plenty mushrooms, strips of guinea fowl, and finally shiitake mushrooms. Chill the terrine for 2 to 3 hours.

Serve the terrine sliced, garnished with the reserved mushrooms and with small bunches of mustard and cress or fresh herbs.

EDITOR'S NOTE: *The bird breasts can be marinated overnight and the game stock prepared in advance.*

Potted Guinea Fowl with Caramelized Apples

Serves 4 as a main course
Working time: about 1 hour and 15 minutes
Total time: about 30 hours (includes marinating and cooling)

Calories **325**
Protein **27g**
Cholesterol **55mg**
Total fat **10g**
Saturated fat **3g**
Sodium **275mg**

1 kg	guinea fowl	2¼ lb
17.5 cl	plus 1 tsp calvados	6 fl oz
12	black peppercorns, crushed	12
1	blade of mace, crushed	1
1	shallot, halved	1
1	large garlic clove, finely chopped	1
1	leek, white part only, washed and split	1
1	carrot, sliced	1
1	stick celery, sliced	1
1	fresh bouquet garni	1
60 cl	unsalted chicken stock (recipe, page 10) or water	1 pint
2	firm dessert apples, peeled, cored and halved horizontally	2
½ tsp	salt	½ tsp
¼ tsp	ground mace	¼ tsp
5 tsp	clear honey	5 tsp
30 g	skinned, shelled hazelnuts, toasted	1 oz

Joint the guinea fowl, removing as much skin and fat as possible, and place it in a bowl. Sprinkle 15 cl (¼ pint) of the calvados, the crushed peppercorns and the crushed blade of mace over the joints. Cover the bowl and leave the guinea fowl to marinate in the refrigerator for 24 hours, turning the joints occasionally.

At the end of this time, put the shallot, garlic, leek, carrot, celery and bouquet garni in a large heavy-bottomed saucepan or fireproof casserole. Pour in the stock or water and bring it to the boil, skimming the liquid. Reduce the heat and add the guinea fowl joints and the marinade to the pan. Bring the liquid back to the boil, skim it again, then gently simmer the guinea fowl, partly covered, for 15 minutes. Add the apples, and simmer for a further 30 minutes; check the liquid from time to time and, if necessary, top it up with more boiling stock or boiling water to just cover the fruit.

Remove the apples with a slotted spoon and set them aside. Check the guinea fowl: the meat should be almost falling off the bones. If any of the meat is not tender, simmer the joints for a further 10 to 15 minutes. Using a slotted spoon, remove the guinea fowl from the pan and place the joints in a deep bowl. Strain the cooking liquid through a fine sieve over the guinea fowl, pressing down hard on the vegetables to extract all their juices. Leave the guinea fowl to cool in the liquid — about 1 hour.

When the guinea fowl has cooled, remove it from the cooking liquid. Skim off and discard any fat from the surface, then pour the liquid into a saucepan and boil it hard until it is reduced to 17.5 cl (6 fl oz). Meanwhile, cut all the meat from the bones. Shred the most tender meat with two forks and set it aside. Place the rest of the meat, the salt, the ground mace, the teaspoon of calvados, 2 teaspoons of the honey and all but 4 tablespoons of the reduced cooking liquid in a food processor, and process until smooth. Stir the shredded meat and the hazelnuts into the processed mixture, then pack it into a 60 cl (1 pint) serving dish and chill it briefly — about 30 minutes.

Just before serving the guinea fowl, caramelize the apples. Pour the reserved reduced cooking liquid into a non-reactive saucepan. Add the remaining calvados, the remaining honey and the poached apples to the saucepan. Simmer the contents gently for about 10 minutes, turning the apples once, until the liquid has turned into a golden caramel glaze coating the apples. Immediately remove the pan from the heat; cooking the caramel any longer will darken it.

Serve the potted guinea fowl, scooped on to individual plates, with the hot caramelized apples.

SUGGESTED ACCOMPANIMENTS: *French bread; mixed green salad leaves.*

EDITOR'S NOTE: *.To toast hazelnuts, place them on a baking sheet, and put the sheet in a preheated 180°C (350°F or Mark 4) oven for 10 minutes.*

Duck Pâté with Orange and Juniper

CHINESE DRIED CITRUS PEEL HAS A UNIQUE, RICH FLAVOUR
AND IS OFTEN USED IN DUCK AND BEEF DISHES. IT IS
AVAILABLE FROM CHINESE GROCERIES.

Serves 10 as a first course
Working time: about 1 hour and 30 minutes
Total time: about 16 hours (includes marinating and chilling)

Calories **155**
Protein **17g**
Cholesterol **55mg**
Total fat **6g**
Saturated fat **2g**
Sodium **95mg**

½ tsp	coarse salt	½ tsp
¼ tsp	sugar	¼ tsp
½ tsp	coarsely ground black pepper	½ tsp
4	duck legs and thighs, skinned and boned	4
1 tbsp	virgin olive oil	1 tbsp
300 g	lean pork, trimmed of fat and connective tissue, cut into large cubes	10 oz
1	large garlic clove, chopped	1
4	shallots, chopped	4
2 tbsp	brandy	2 tbsp
30 cl	red wine	½ pint
1	orange, juice only	1
20 cl	unsalted chicken stock (recipe, page 10)	7 fl oz
¼ tsp	salt	¼ tsp
10	juniper berries	10
10	black peppercorns	10
¼	Chinese dried citrus peel, or ¼ fresh tangerine or Seville orange peel	¼
3	bay leaves	3
8 cl	vegetable aspic (recipe, page 10), melted (optional)	3 oz

Combine the coarse salt, sugar and black pepper on a plate and coat the duck meat evenly with this mixture. Cover the duck and leave it to marinate in the refrigerator for at least 8 hours or up to 24 hours.

Wipe the duck clean with a damp cloth, pat it dry with paper towels and cut it into large cubes. Preheat the oven to 150°C (300°F or Mark 2).

Heat the olive oil in a large frying pan over medium heat, add the duck and pork cubes and brown the meat in the oil for about 5 minutes. Using a slotted spoon, remove the meat from the pan and set it aside in an ovenproof dish. Sweat the garlic and shallots gently in the pan until they are lightly browned. Warm the brandy in a small saucepan, add it to the onions and garlic, and set it alight. When the flame dies down, add the red wine and cook, scraping the pan with a spatula, until the liquid has reduced slightly. Add the orange juice and continue to cook until the liquid has reduced by a quarter.

Add the chicken stock to the frying pan. Bring the liquid to the boil and add the salt, then pour the contents of the pan over the duck and pork cubes. Sprinkle the juniper berries and black peppercorns evenly over the meat, tuck the dried citrus peel into the middle, and cover the dish tightly. Cook the duck and ▶

pork in the oven for 2½ hours.

Remove the dish from the oven and set it aside to cool, still covered, for about 30 minutes. Using a slotted spoon, remove the cooled meat from the cooking juices. Strain the cooking juices through a sieve into a measuring jug. You should have about 17.5 cl (6 fl oz) of liquid: if you have less, add a little stock; if you have more, reduce the liquid by boiling. Reserve a few of the juniper berries for garnish, and discard the rest of the spices in the sieve.

Separate the pork from the duck (the duck is the darker meat) and purée the pork in a food processor with the strained cooking juices. Transfer the pork purée to a mixing bowl. Using two forks, shred the duck and mix it into the pork purée. Pack the mixture into an earthenware pot and leave it in the refrigerator for 3 hours, or until it is set.

Decorate the top of the pâté with the reserved juniper berries and the bay leaves then, if you like, carefully spoon vegetable aspic over the top, to a depth of about 5 mm (¼ inch). Put the pâté in the refrigerator and chill it for at least 30 to 40 minutes, or until the aspic has set.

SUGGESTED ACCOMPANIMENT: *thin fingers of wholemeal toast.*

EDITOR'S NOTE: *The pâté will benefit from being left in the refrigerator for up to four days before serving so that the flavour can mature.*

Potted Pheasant with Chestnuts

Serves 6 as a first course
Working time: about 40 minutes
Total time: about 4 hours (includes cooling)

Calories **245**
Protein **25g**
Cholesterol **55mg**
Total fat **12g**
Saturated fat **3g**
Sodium **125mg**

½ tsp	safflower oil	½ tsp
2	rashers lean green bacon, rinds removed, roughly chopped	2
1	onion, sliced	1
2	garlic cloves, thinly sliced	2
2	sticks celery, sliced	2
1	small carrot, sliced	1
1	pheasant (about 750 g/1½ lb)	1
6	juniper berries, crushed	6
30 cl	red wine	½ pint
30 cl	unsalted vegetable or chicken stock (recipes, page 10)	½ pint
125 g	unsweetened chestnut purée	4 oz
½	orange, juice and grated rind	½
⅛ tsp	salt	⅛ tsp
	freshly ground black pepper	
30 g	polyunsaturated margarine	1 oz
	fresh bay leaves, for garnish (optional)	
	juniper berries, for garnish (optional)	
	orange slices, for garnish (optional)	

Preheat the oven to 180°C (350°F or Mark 4).

Heat the oil in a heavy frying pan, add the bacon and sauté it for about 2 minutes. Add the onion, garlic, celery and carrot, and sauté for a further 5 minutes, until the onion is transparent. Remove the pan from the heat and spoon half of the vegetable mixture into a casserole that will hold the pheasant snugly. Place the pheasant, breast down, in the casserole, then spoon the remaining vegetable mixture over the top and round the sides of the bird. Sprinkle the crushed juniper berries into the casserole. Pour in the red wine and enough vegetable or chicken stock to come two thirds of the way up the side of the bird.

Cover the casserole and bake the pheasant until it is tender and the juices run clear when a skewer is inserted in a thigh — about 2 hours. Allow the pheasant to cool in the cooking liquid. When the bird is cool enough to handle, lift it out of the casserole; reserve the cooking liquid. Remove the meat from the bones and chop it finely, discarding the skin.

Put the chestnut purée in a food processor or blender, together with the orange rind and juice, the salt, some pepper and 6 cl (2 fl oz) of the pheasant-cooking liquid (save the remaining cooking liquid for a soup). Blend the mixture until it is smooth. In a large bowl, beat the margarine with a wooden spoon until it is soft and creamy. Gradually mix in the chestnut purée, together with the chopped pheasant.

Divide the mixture among six individual small pots or ramekin dishes. Serve the potted pheasant at room temperature, garnished, if you like, with bay leaves, juniper berries and a slice of orange.

SUGGESTED ACCOMPANIMENT: *wholemeal bread.*

EDITOR'S NOTE: *To make the chestnut purée for this recipe from fresh chestnuts, slit about 125 g (4 oz) of chestnuts down one side, parboil them for about 10 minutes, then shell and peel them. Simmer the chestnuts in water for about 20 minutes, until they are tender. Drain and sieve them.*

125 g	fresh wholemeal breadcrumbs	4 oz
1	egg, beaten	1

Turkey and Pheasant Galantine

Serves 14 as a main course
Working time: about 2 hours and 20 minutes
Total time: about 1 day (includes chilling)

Calories **250**
Protein **40g**
Cholesterol **105mg**
Total fat **10g**
Saturated fat **3g**
Sodium **220mg**

1	oven-ready turkey, (about 3 kg/7 lb), boned (opposite), bones reserved	1
1	oven-ready pheasant, (about 1 kg/2½ lb), boned (opposite), shot removed, bones reserved	1
1	onion, sliced	1
½	lemon, sliced	½
1	bay leaf	1
5	parsley sprigs	5
10	black peppercorns	10
250 g	low-fat fromage frais	8 oz
¾ litre	vegetable aspic (recipe, page 13), melted	1¼ pint
	cucumber peel, cut into strips and diamond shapes, for garnish	
½	sweet red pepper, skinned (page 90), seeded, and cut into petal shapes using an aspic cutter, for garnish	½
1	black olive, for garnish	1
Mushroom stuffing		
1 tbsp	safflower oil	1 tbsp
1	onion, finely chopped	1
1	garlic clove, finely chopped	1
250 g	mushrooms, wiped clean and chopped	8 oz
½ tsp	salt	½ tsp
	freshly ground black pepper	
¼ tsp	ground coriander	¼ tsp
1 tbsp	cut chives	1 tbsp
1½ tbsp	chopped parsley	1½ tbsp

Put the turkey bones and pheasant bones into a large saucepan, pour in water to cover them, and bring the water to the boil, skimming off any scum that rises to the surface. Add the sliced onion to the pan. Reduce the heat, cover the saucepan and simmer for 1 hour, stirring the stock occasionally.

Meanwhile, prepare the mushroom stuffing. Heat the oil in a heavy frying pan, add the chopped onion and garlic, and cook gently over medium heat until the onion is soft — about 5 minutes. Add the mushrooms and continue to cook until they too have softened — 2 to 3 minutes. Using a slotted spoon, transfer the onions, garlic and mushrooms to a bowl. Mix in the salt, a little black pepper, the ground coriander, chives, parsley and breadcrumbs, then stir in the beaten egg to bind the stuffing together.

Lay the pheasant flat on the work surface, skin side down, and spoon the mushroom stuffing along the centre of the bird. Fold the sides of the pheasant over and around the stuffing. Lay the turkey flat on the work surface, skin side down. Carefully place the stuffed pheasant centrally on the turkey. Bring the sides of the turkey over the pheasant to enclose it completely. Using a trussing needle, sew up the join with string, leaving long ends of string for easy removal. Mould the turkey into a handsome shape; it will set in this shape when cooked. Wrap the galantine in a large piece of muslin, tying it securely at both ends with string.

Preheat the oven to 170°C (325°F or Mark 3). Stand the galantine on a long, double-thickness strip of foil, and use the foil to lower it into a large, fireproof casserole. Add the sliced lemon, bay leaf, parsley sprigs and peppercorns. Remove the bones from the stock and discard them, then strain sufficient stock into the casserole through a muslin-lined sieve to cover the galantine. Bring the stock slowly to the boil over medium heat. Cover the casserole tightly and cook it in the oven for 2 hours. Remove the casserole from the oven and leave the galantine to cool in the stock — about 3 hours. Carefully lift the cooled galantine out of the casserole, using the strip of foil, and let it drain well on a rack set over a tray. Put the galantine in the refrigerator and chill it overnight.

For the coating, combine the *fromage frais* and 30 cl (½ pint) of the vegetable aspic, and chill the mixture until the sauce is well thickened but not quite set — about 30 minutes. Remove the muslin and the string from the galantine and stand it on a wire rack set over a tray or large plate. Spoon and brush a layer of the sauce all over the turkey, then chill it until the sauce has set — about 20 minutes.

Collect the sauce which has dripped on the tray, place it in a basin and set it over a saucepan of simmering water to melt. Stir the sauce to remove any lumps, then chill it until it begins to set. Coat the galantine with a second layer of sauce. Set the galantine on the rack over a clean tray, and chill it in the refrigerator for a further 30 minutes.

Dip the cucumber-peel and red-pepper shapes and the olive in the remaining vegetable aspic and use them to decorate the sauce-coated galantine. Chill the galantine for 15 minutes, and chill the aspic until it is thick, but not set. Pour the aspic over the galantine to glaze it. Return the galantine to the refrigerator for 1 hour, until the aspic is completely set.

Place the galantine on a serving dish. Scrape the aspic on the bottom of the tray on to a piece of dampened greaseproof paper, and chop it with a wet knife. Garnish the galantine with the chopped vegetable aspic, and serve it sliced straight downwards to reveal the layers of turkey, pheasant and stuffing.

Boning a Bird for a Galantine

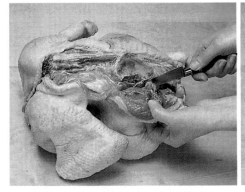

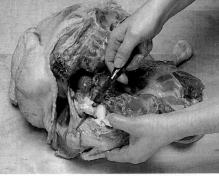

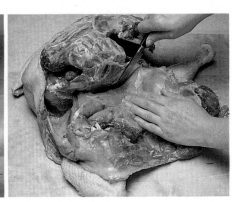

1 CUTTING THE BIRD OPEN. Place the chilled bird (here, a turkey) breast down on a wooden cutting board, drumsticks facing you. Using a boning knife or a small, strong, sharp knife, make a long slit from the neck to the tail, cutting through the skin to expose the long upper ridge of the backbone. Cut off the tail if it is still attached. With the knife blade held firmly against one side of the backbone, begin freeing the meat from that side of the bird. Using your other hand to lift away the skin and flesh, cut and scrape beneath the oyster-shaped morsel of meat (above) and round and down the outside of the collarbone.

2 SEVERING THE WING AND THIGH JOINTS. Working on the same side of the bird, pull the wing away from the breast. Cut round the base of the wing and through the joint to dislocate the wing. Cut about one third of the way down the rib bones, working along the length of the carcass until you encounter the thigh joint. To locate the thigh socket, grasp the end of the drumstick and pull the leg towards you. Cut away the meat and cartilage round the joint. Sever the joint by cutting round the ball where it joins the socket.

3 FREEING THE SIDES. Continue cutting downwards to detach the leg, being careful not to slice through the bottom layer of breast skin. Cut the skin and flesh from round the neck and collarbone, so that the back meat comes away from the carcass. Pressing the blade of the knife against the rib cage and then the breastbone, cut and scrape away the breast (above). Take care not to pierce the skin (that would allow filling to escape later), and stop when you reach the ridge of the breastbone. Repeat Steps 1, 2 and 3 on the other side of the bird.

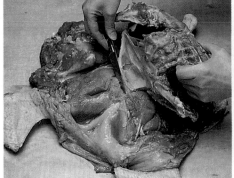

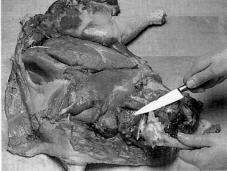

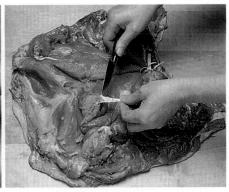

4 DETACHING THE CARCASS. Scrape away the flesh on either side of the breastbone to expose the ridge and tip of the breastbone. Lift the carcass with one hand. Then, starting at the tip of the breastbone, free the carcass by cutting just beneath the entire breastbone ridge and through the cartilage with the knife (above). Be careful not to puncture the skin; there is no flesh between the skin and the bone at this point. Cut off the wing tips at the first joint.

5 REMOVING THE LEG AND WING BONES. Starting at the detached end of one of the thigh bones, cut into the flesh on either side of the bone along its length. Scrape away the flesh from the sides and detached end of the bone. Holding the thigh bone with one hand, scrape down its length to expose the joint, and continue scraping down the length of the drumstick (above). Remove the leg. Repeat the process to remove the other thighbone and drumstick, then remove the wing bones in the same way.

6 OPENING OUT THE BONED BIRD. Remove the white tendon from the thick ends of the breast meat by slicing through the flesh on either side of the tendon. Remove the leg tendons in the same way. Carefully trim off any excess fat and membrane. Refrigerate the bird until required.

Chicken Galantine with a Herbed Veal and Vegetable Stuffing

THIS RECIPE FOR AN ELEGANT PARTY DISH USES FRESH YOUNG
VEGETABLES COMBINED WITH VEAL FOR ITS STUFFING.

Serves 10 as a main course
Working time: about 2 hours
Total time: about 12 hours (includes chilling)

Calories **140**
Protein **22g**
Cholesterol **50mg**
Total fat **4g**
Saturated fat **2g**
Sodium **90mg**

1.5 kg	oven-ready chicken	3 lb
½ tsp	salt	½ tsp
	freshly ground black pepper	
5 tbsp	Madeira	5 tbsp
60 g	young carrots, whole if tiny, otherwise cut into strips	2 oz
60 g	baby sweetcorn, trimmed if necessary	2 oz
½	leek, cleaned thoroughly, cut into 1.5 cm (½ inch) chunks	½
60 g	young turnip or kohlrabi, cut into matchstick-sized pieces	2 oz
60 g	young parsnips, cut into strips	2 oz
350 g	minced lean veal	12 oz
3 tbsp	finely chopped parsley, plus two parsley sprigs	3 tbsp
3 tbsp	finely chopped chervil	3 tbsp
6	fresh tarragon sprigs, leaves of four finely chopped	6
2 litres	unsalted veal stock (recipe, page 10)	3½ pints
3 tsp	powdered gelatine	3 tsp
150 g	low-fat fromage frais	5 oz

*fresh herb leaves, such as chervil,
flat-leaf parsley or chives, for garnish*

Bone the chicken, leaving the legs and wings intact, but cutting off the wing tips with a sharp knife *(page 45, Steps 1, 2, 3 and 4)*. Lay the boned chicken flat on the work surface, skin side down, and sprinkle the flesh with half of the salt, plenty of black pepper and 1 tablespoon of the Madeira.

Bring a large pan of water to the boil. Blanch the carrots and sweetcorn for 3 minutes, then add the leeks, turnips or kohlrabi and the parsnips, and boil for a further minute. Drain the vegetables, refresh them under cold running water, then drain them again.

Combine the veal with the finely chopped parsley, chervil and chopped tarragon, 1 tablespoon of the Madeira, the remaining salt and some pepper. Spread half of this mixture over the chicken flesh. Place the cooked vegetables lengthwise down the middle of the chicken, arranging them so that they lie in four or five rows stacked on top of each other from neck to tail; the vegetables should be arranged so that each slice of the galantine will contain a variety. Pack the remaining veal mixture over and around the vegetables. Bring the sides of the bird over the stuffing and, using a trussing needle, sew up the join with string, leaving a long end to ensure easy removal when the galantine is cooked. Mould the chicken to resemble the original shape of the bird; it will set in this shape when cooked.

Wrap the galantine in a large piece of muslin measuring about 60 by 45 cm (24 by 18 inches), tying it securely at both ends with string. Pour the veal stock into a fireproof casserole or saucepan large enough to hold the wrapped chicken. Add the tarragon and parsley sprigs to the stock and bring it to the boil. Lower the chicken into the stock and bring it back to the boil, then reduce the heat and gently simmer the chicken, partly covered, for 45 minutes. Carefully turn the chicken over in the stock and continue to simmer it for a further 30 minutes.

Remove the casserole from the heat, cover it tightly, and leave the chicken in its hot liquid for a further 30 minutes. Then remove the chicken, allow it to cool to room temperature — 1½ to 2 hours — and place it, still wrapped, in a baking tin or dish. Cover it with plastic film and chill it in the refrigerator for 6 hours.

Skim the fat off the surface of the stock. Pour the stock through a muslin-lined sieve into a saucepan, bring it to the boil, and boil it hard until it is reduced in volume to ¾ litre (1¼ pints). Set it aside to cool.

Unwrap the chilled chicken and carefully remove all of its skin. Remove and discard the string. Place a long, double-thickness strip of greaseproof paper or foil, about 10 cm (4 inches) wide, on a wire rack set over a baking sheet, and stand the chicken on it.

Dissolve 2 teaspoons of the gelatine in 2 tablespoons of the remaining Madeira *(page 13)*. Stir the dissolved gelatine into 15 cl (¼ pint) of the reduced cooking stock. Put the *fromage frais* into a bowl, then gradually stir in the stock, making sure the sauce is thoroughly blended. Chill the sauce until it is just beginning to set — about 10 minutes — then spoon it over the chicken to coat it evenly, including the leg and wing tips; work quickly as the sauce sets rapidly. Garnish the chicken with the fresh herb leaves, pressing them lightly into the sauce coating.

Dissolve the remaining gelatine in the remaining Madeira *(page 13)*, then stir it into 5 tablespoons of the remaining reduced stock, and chill the mixture until it is just beginning to set — about 10 minutes. Carefully pour this aspic over the galantine. Transfer the galantine to a serving platter, using the strip of greaseproof paper to lift it, and chill it for at least 1 hour, or up to 24 hours, before carving. The leg and wing joints may be removed and served separately.

EDITOR'S NOTE: *The remaining reduced stock may be chilled in the refrigerator until firm — at least 1 hour — then chopped and served as a garnish.*

Potted Turkey

Serves 4 as a first course
Working time: about 45 minutes
Total time: about 3 hours (includes chilling)

Calories **175**
Protein **19g**
Cholesterol **65mg**
Total fat **6g**
Saturated fat **2g**
Sodium **110mg**

500 g	boneless turkey breast, skinned and cut into 2.5 cm (1 inch) cubes	1 lb
1	onion, one half coarsely chopped, the other half finely chopped	1
1	bay leaf	1
2	lemon slices	2
¼ tsp	salt	¼ tsp
	freshly ground black pepper	
15 g	unsalted butter	½ oz
1	garlic clove, finely chopped	1
¼ tsp	ground allspice	¼ tsp
2 tbsp	dry sherry	2 tbsp
3 tbsp	plain low-fat yogurt	3 tbsp
25 cl	vegetable aspic (recipe, page 10), melted	8 fl oz
	dill sprig, for garnish	

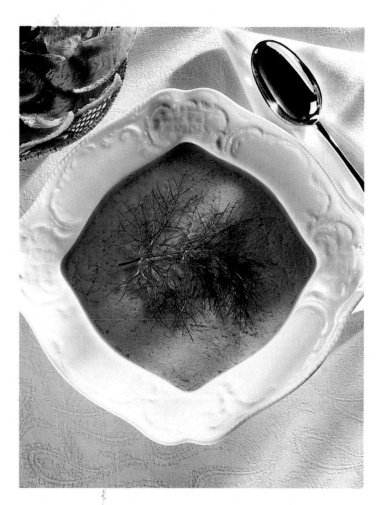

Place the turkey in a heavy-bottomed saucepan with the coarsely chopped onion, the bay leaf, lemon slices, half of the salt and a little black pepper. Pour 30 cl (½ pint) of water into the pan and bring it to the boil. Reduce the heat, cover the pan and simmer gently until the turkey is tender — about 20 minutes. Leave the turkey to cool in its cooking liquid for about 20 minutes. Using a slotted spoon, remove the turkey from the pan and set it aside. Boil the cooking liquid until it is reduced to about 1½ tablespoons, then strain it; discard the onion, bay leaf and lemon slices.

Melt the butter in a small frying pan over medium heat, add the finely chopped onion and garlic, and fry them until soft but not browned — about 3 minutes. Place the turkey, fried onion and garlic in a food processor and process until they are smooth. Transfer the turkey mixture to a bowl. Add the strained turkey-cooking liquid together with the allspice, sherry, yogurt, the remaining salt and plenty of pepper. Mix well; the mixture should be stiff but spreadable. Press the turkey mixture into a large serving bowl and chill it in the refrigerator for about 1 hour.

Allow the melted vegetable aspic to cool until it is just beginning to thicken, then spoon it over the turkey. Set the dill sprig into the aspic. Chill the potted turkey until the aspic has set — about 20 minutes.

SUGGESTED ACCOMPANIMENT: *toast, crackers or crusty bread.*

⅛ tsp	sugar	⅛ tsp
30 cl	plain low-fat yogurt	½ pint

Place the chicken breasts in a shallow baking dish and sprinkle the grated lemon rind and garlic over them. Set the chicken aside, covered, to marinate for 30 minutes to 1 hour. Meanwhile, preheat the oven to 200°C (400°F or Mark 6). When the chicken is ready, pour the white wine over the breasts, add the tarragon sprigs and cover the dish. Bake the chicken in the oven until it is tender — 25 to 30 minutes. Allow the chicken to cool, still covered, in its cooking liquid.

Place the asparagus spears in a steamer and steam them for 15 to 20 minutes, until they are tender. Drain the spears, refresh them under cold running water and drain them again. Cut the top 5 cm (2 inches) from the spears and set them aside. Thinly slice the stalks and set them aside separately.

Ladle a little of the vegetable aspic into a 25 by 11 by 7.5 cm (10 by 4½ by 3 inch) loaf tin to cover the bottom by 5 mm (¼ inch). Arrange the asparagus tips in an even layer across the bottom of the tin, alternating the direction of the tips. Pour in enough vegetable aspic just to cover the asparagus tips, and chill it until it is set — about 15 minutes.

Drain the chicken (reserve the cooking liquid for another use) and cut it into 5 cm by 5 mm (2 by ¼ inch) matchsticks. Position a chicken matchstick on each asparagus tip. Mix the chopped tarragon, chives and parsley together and sprinkle a third of the mixed herbs over the chicken matchsticks. Cover this layer with more of the vegetable aspic, and chill it until it is set. Sprinkle half of the sliced asparagus and half of the chopped hard-boiled egg in an even layer over the chilled aspic. Cover with more vegetable aspic, and chill again until set. Continue layering the chicken and herbs and the asparagus and egg in the tin to make three more layers, pouring aspic over each layer and leaving it to chill and set for about 15 minutes between each new layer. Pour the remaining vegetable aspic over the final layer and chill the terrine until it is very firm — at least 4 hours, or overnight.

To make the lemon yogurt sauce, mix the lemon rind and juice with the chopped tarragon and parsley and the sugar. Stir in the yogurt and chill the sauce thoroughly before serving — about 1 hour.

To unmould the terrine, dip the loaf tin in hot water for 5 seconds, then invert it on to a flat serving plate. Serve the terrine garnished with the lettuce leaves and accompanied by the sauce.

EDITOR'S NOTE: *If you are making the vegetable aspic especially for this recipe, the reserved chicken-cooking liquid can be incorporated into the aspic before it is clarified.*

Jellied Asparagus and Chicken Terrine

Serves 12 as a first course
Working time: about 1 hour
Total time: about 7 hours (includes chilling)

Calories **72**
Protein **10g**
Cholesterol **20mg**
Total fat **3g**
Saturated fat **1g**
Sodium **40mg**

2	boneless chicken breasts (about 175 g/6 oz each), skinned	2
1 tsp	grated lemon rind	1 tsp
1	small garlic clove, finely chopped	1
4 tbsp	dry white wine	4 tbsp
2	sprigs fresh tarragon, plus 1 tbsp chopped fresh tarragon	2
12	thin asparagus spears (about 350 g/ 12 oz), trimmed and peeled	12
1.25 litres	vegetable aspic (recipe, page 13), melted	2 pints
1 tbsp	cut chives	1 tbsp
2 tbsp	chopped parsley	2 tbsp
1	hard-boiled egg, finely chopped	1
	red lollo or other lettuce leaves, for garnish	
Lemon yogurt sauce		
1	lemon, grated rind plus 1 tbsp juice only	1
1 tsp	chopped fresh tarragon	1 tsp
2 tsp	chopped parsley	2 tsp

Chicken and Asparagus Moulds

Serves 4 as a first course
Working time: about 30 minutes
Total time: about 2 hours

Calories **145**
Protein **23g**
Cholesterol **45mg**
Total fat **5g**
Saturated fat **2g**
Sodium **150mg**

2	skinned and boned chicken breasts (about 125 g/4 oz each)	2
1	large sprig fresh tarragon, plus ½ tsp chopped fresh tarragon	1
1	strip lemon rind	1
¼ tsp	salt	¼ tsp
	freshly ground black pepper	
8	slender asparagus spears (about 125 g/4 oz)	8
2 tbsp	dry white wine	2 tbsp
3 tsp	powdered gelatine	3 tsp
100 g	low-fat fromage frais	3½ oz
2 tsp	fresh lemon juice	2 tsp
1	tomato, cut into wedges, for garnish	1

Place the chicken breasts in a saucepan together with the tarragon sprig, lemon rind, half of the salt, some pepper and 15 cl (¼ pint) of water. Cover the pan, gently bring the water to the boil and simmer the chicken for 20 minutes.

Meanwhile, cook the asparagus in a saucepan of simmering water until it is just tender — about 6 minutes. Drain the asparagus spears, refresh them under cold running water and drain them again. Cut off a 5 cm (2 inch) tip from each spear and set the tips aside. Roughly chop the stalks.

Remove the chicken breasts from the pan and drain them on paper towels. Strain the stock through a muslin-lined sieve and make it up to 15 cl (¼ pint) with cold water if necessary. Stir the wine into the stock.

To make an aspic, dissolve ½ teaspoon of the gelatine in 4 tablespoons of the wine stock *(page 13)*. Pour 1 tablespoon of the aspic into each of four 15 cl (¼ pint) moulds. Leave the aspic to partially set in the refrigerator — about 5 minutes. Arrange two of the asparagus tips on the partially set jelly in each mould, then return the moulds to the refrigerator until the aspic is set firmly — about 10 minutes.

Meanwhile, roughly chop the chicken and process it to a smooth paste in a food processor. Dissolve the remaining gelatine in the rest of the stock and add it to the chicken, together with the *fromage frais* and lemon juice. Process briefly to blend the ingredients. Turn the chicken mousseline into a bowl, add the chopped asparagus stalks, chopped tarragon, the remaining salt and some pepper, and mix well. Spoon the mousseline over the set jelly in the moulds. Chill the moulds in the refrigerator until the mousseline has set — about 1 hour.

To serve the moulds, dip them briefly in hot water and unmould them on to individual plates. Garnish the moulds with the tomato wedges.

Poached Chicken and Pistachio Sausage

IN THIS LOW-FAT ADAPTATION OF CLASSIC FRENCH *BOUDIN BLANC* — "WHITE PUDDING" — A SPICED MINCED CHICKEN MIXTURE IS POACHED AND SERVED IN THINLY-SLICED ROUNDS.

Serves 6 as a main course
Working time: about 2 hours and 45 minutes
Total time: 30 hours (includes chilling)

Calories **220**
Protein **25g**
Cholesterol **55mg**
Total fat **8g**
Saturated fat **2g**
Sodium **275mg**

1	onion, chopped	1
1	blade of mace	1
5 tbsp	skimmed milk	5 tbsp
60 g	crème fraîche	2 oz
60 g	fresh white breadcrumbs	2 oz
250 g	skinned chicken breast, minced or finely chopped	8 oz
250 g	lean veal, minced or finely chopped	8 oz
1	egg, shell washed and reserved	1
3	egg whites	3
¼ tsp	grated nutmeg	¼ tsp
¼ tsp	ground allspice	¼ tsp
¼ tsp	ground cinnamon	¼ tsp
½ tsp	salt	½ tsp
¼ tsp	white pepper	¼ tsp
30 g	shelled pistachio nuts, skinned	1 oz
1 litre	unsalted brown stock (recipe, page 11)	1 ¾ pints
10 cl	dry Madeira	3½ fl oz
4 tsp	powdered gelatine	4 tsp
1 tsp	red wine vinegar	1 tsp

Place the onion, mace and milk in a saucepan. Slowly bring the milk to boiling point, remove the pan from the heat and leave the milk to infuse for 15 to 30 minutes. Strain the milk through a fine-meshed sieve into a small saucepan, pressing down hard on the onion to extract its juice. Stir the *crème fraîche* into the flavoured milk, then stir in the breadcrumbs. Cook the mixture over low heat, stirring continuously, until it thickens and comes away cleanly from the sides of the pan — 2 to 3 minutes. Set it aside to cool.

Process the chicken and veal in a food processor until they form a smooth paste. Blend in the bread mixture, then the whole egg. With the processor running, gradually add two of the egg whites. Blend in the nutmeg, allspice, cinnamon, salt and pepper. Transfer the mixture to a bowl, fold in the pistachio nuts and chill the mixture for at least 2 hours.

Lay a 30 by 30 cm (12 by 12 inch) piece of plastic film on the work surface. Form the chicken and veal mixture into a 25 cm (10 inch) long oblong on the plastic film and use the film to roll the mixture into a neat sausage. Rinse a square of muslin, wring it out, lay it on the work surface and brush it lightly with oil. Carefully unroll the sausage on to one edge of the muslin square, removing the plastic film, then roll up the sausage firmly in the muslin. Tie one end of the roll with string, ensure the filling is packed down firmly, then tie the other end tightly. Chill the sausage for 24 hours, to allow the flavours to develop.

To cook the sausage, bring the stock to the boil in a saucepan, then pour it into a 30 by 10 by 10 cm (12 by 4 by 4 inch) loaf tin. Add the Madeira, and stand the loaf tin in a deep roasting pan on the hob. Pour boiling water into the roasting pan until it comes half way up the side of the loaf tin. Heat the water until the stock in the loaf tin is just simmering. Using string, tie the two ends of the muslin sausage to the handle of a long wooden spoon. Lower the sausage into the stock, resting the spoon on the rim of the loaf tin; the sausage must not touch the bottom of the tin. Add enough boiling water to the stock to cover the sausage by about 2.5 cm (1 inch). Poach the sausage at a bare simmer for 30 minutes, topping up the boiling water in the roasting pan if necessary.

Remove the sausage from the tin and drain it. Cut off the tied ends of the muslin, unwrap the sausage and place it on a wire rack set over a tray. Baste the sausage generously with its cooking liquid, then wrap it in foil and leave it to cool — about 30 minutes.

Meanwhile, strain the stock and reduce it over high heat to 30 cl (½ pint). Using the reduced stock, gelatine, the remaining egg white, the egg shell and vinegar, make a vegetable aspic *(page 12)*. When the stock has cooled, chill it until it sets to a firm jelly — about 1 hour. Chop the aspic into small cubes.

Serve the sausage at room temperature, cut into thin slices and garnished with the chilled aspic cubes.

SUGGESTED ACCOMPANIMENT: *wholemeal bread.*

EDITOR'S NOTE: *To skin pistachio nuts, drop them into boiling water and simmer them for 1 minute. Drain them, enfold them in a towel and rub them briskly.*

Chicken and Spinach Timbales

Serves 10 as a first course
Working time: about 1 hour and 30 minutes
Total time: about 3 hours

Calories **195**
Protein **28g**
Cholesterol **45mg**
Total fat **7g**
Saturated fat **2g**
Sodium **175mg**

5 tsp	safflower oil	5 tsp
2	carrots, finely chopped	2
1	onion, finely chopped	1
3	sticks celery, finely chopped	3
2	garlic cloves, finely chopped	2
3 tbsp	plain flour	3 tbsp
2 tbsp	curry powder	2 tbsp
12.5 cl	dry white wine	4 fl oz
1.75 kg.	chicken, skinned and jointed, all fat removed	3½ lb
1	bouquet garni	1
60 cl	unsalted chicken stock (recipe, page 10)	1 pint
750 g	spinach, washed and stemmed	1½ lb
⅛ tsp	salt	⅛ tsp
	freshly ground black pepper	
4	egg whites	4
10	fresh vine leaves, for garnish (optional)	10
	red grapes, for garnish (optional)	

Heat 3 teaspoons of the oil in a fireproof casserole. Add the carrots, onion, celery and garlic, and cook them over medium heat, stirring frequently, until lightly browned — about 5 minutes. Stir in the flour and curry powder and cook for a further 3 minutes. Pour in the wine, stirring continuously, and arrange the chicken portions on top of the vegetables. Add the bouquet garni and pour in the stock to cover the chicken. Heat the stock slowly until it is just boiling, then reduce the heat, cover the casserole and simmer the chicken until it is cooked through — about 40 minutes.

Using a slotted spoon, remove the chicken from the casserole; discard the bouquet garni. Strain the cooking liquid through a muslin-lined sieve and return it to the pan; reserve the vegetables. Skim any fat from the surface of the liquid and, if necessary, boil the liquid to reduce it to 50 cl (16 fl oz). Meanwhile, remove the chicken meat from the bones, discarding any fat and gristle, and cut the meat into chunks.

Preheat the oven to 190°C (375°F or Mark 5). Lightly grease ten 12 cl (4 fl oz) ramekins with the remaining oil. Cut out 10 circles of baking parchment and use them to line the base of each ramekin.

Select 175 g (6 oz) of the largest spinach leaves. Dip them, a few at at time, into simmering water just until they become pliable, then drain them and lay them on paper towels to dry. Line the prepared ramekins with the leaves, overlapping them and allowing the edges to hang over the rims of the dishes. Blanch the remaining spinach leaves for 1 minute, drain them well in a fine sieve and squeeze them dry by hand.

Purée the squeezed spinach leaves in a food processor. Add the chicken meat and pulse the processor to chop it finely. Transfer the mixture to a large bowl. Add the reserved vegetables and the reduced cooking liquid, mix well and season with the salt and some pepper. Beat the egg whites until they form stiff peaks. Using a metal spoon, gently fold them into the chicken mixture and divide it among the ramekins. Fold the edges of the spinach leaves over the filling, then cover each timbale with foil. Stand the ramekins in a roasting pan or dish and pour in boiling water to come half way up their sides. Bake the timbales until they are firm to the touch — about 35 minutes.

Invert the cooked timbales on to individual serving plates. Lift off the ramekins and remove the lining paper. If you like, garnish the timbales with vine leaves and grapes; serve them immediately.

Chicken and Ham Mousses

Serves 4 as a first course
Working time: about 50 minutes
Total time: about 1 hour and 45 minutes

Calories **230**
Protein **27g**
Cholesterol **60mg**
Total fat **11g**
Saturated fat **5g**
Sodium **520mg**

15 g	unsalted butter	½ oz
1	small onion, finely chopped	1
250 g	boneless chicken breast, skinned and diced	8 oz
125 g	lean cooked ham, roughly diced	4 oz
125 g	low-fat fromage frais	4 oz
⅛ tsp	ground mace	⅛ tsp
	freshly ground black pepper	
2	egg whites	2
	watercress sprigs, for garnish	
	Green sauce	
75 g	low-fat fromage frais	2½ oz
8 cl	plain low-fat yogurt	3 fl oz
60 g	watercress, washed and finely chopped, thick stems removed	2 oz
2 tsp	chopped parsley	2 tsp

Melt the butter in a non-stick frying pan and fry the onion over low heat until it begins to soften — about 3 minutes. Add the chicken and cook it gently, stirring frequently, until it is opaque, firm and cooked through — 8 to 10 minutes. Remove the pan from the heat, leave the chicken and onion to cool for a few minutes, then place them in a food processor. Process until the chicken is finely chopped, add the ham and process again until it, too, is finely chopped. Turn the mixture into a bowl, add the *fromage frais*, mace and some pepper, and mix very thoroughly.

Preheat the oven to 180°C (350°F or Mark 4). Lightly grease four 15 cl (¼ pint) ovenproof moulds or ramekin dishes with a little oil.

Whisk the egg whites until they are stiff. Beat about 2 tablespoons of the stiffened whites into the chicken and ham mixture, then use a metal spoon to fold in the remaining egg whites quickly and evenly. Divide the mixture among the prepared moulds, giving each one a sharp tap on a flat surface to release air bubbles.

Stand the moulds in a roasting pan and add enough boiling water to come two thirds of the way up their sides. Cook the mousses in the oven until they are firm to the touch — 30 to 35 minutes.

While the mousses are cooking, make the sauce. Place the *fromage frais*, yogurt, chopped watercress and parsley in a food processor or blender and process until smooth — about 1 minute.

Allow the cooked mousses to cool slightly, then carefully turn out each one on to a small plate. Spoon a little of the green sauce over and around the mousses. Serve while the mousses are still warm, garnished with watercress sprigs.

EDITOR'S NOTE: *The mousses can be served as either a first course or the main course for a light lunch.*

Jellied Lemon Chicken

Serves 12 as a main course
Working time: about 45 minutes
Total time: about 15 hours (includes chilling)

Calories **140**
Protein **26g**
Cholesterol **70mg**
Total fat **4g**
Saturated fat **2g**
Sodium **170mg**

3 kg	chicken, giblets reserved except for the liver	6 ½ lb
3	lemons, one quartered, the grated rind only of two	3
1	onion, roughly chopped	1
2	carrots, roughly chopped	2
2	sticks celery, roughly chopped	2
60 g	parsley, finely chopped, plus one parsley sprig	2 oz
1 tsp	salt	1 tsp
8	black peppercorns	8
	freshly ground black pepper	
4 tsp	capers	4 tsp

Rinse the chicken and giblets well under cold running water and pat them dry with paper towels. Put the lemon quarters inside the chicken. Place the chicken and giblets in a large pan and pour in 60 cl (1 pint) of cold water. Add the onion, carrots, celery, parsley sprig, ½ teaspoon of the salt and the peppercorns. Bring the liquid to the boil over medium heat, then reduce the heat to low. Partially cover the saucepan and simmer gently until the chicken is cooked and the juices run clear when a thigh is pierced with a skewer — 1 ½ to 2 hours. Remove the chicken from the pan, partially cover it with foil and set it aside.

Strain the stock through a muslin-lined sieve into a heatproof bowl; discard the solids. Let the stock cool for about 1 hour, then chill it for 3 to 4 hours, until the fat rises to the surface and solidifies and the stock becomes jellied. Remove and discard the fat. Stand the bowl in hot water until the stock becomes liquid again.

Meanwhile, remove the flesh from the chicken, discarding the skin and bones, and cut it into 2.5 cm (1 inch) cubes. Place one third of the cubes in a large, round serving bowl and add a little of the remaining salt and some pepper. Sprinkle on one third each of the capers, chopped parsley and grated lemon rind. Repeat twice more, ending with a layer of capers, parsley and lemon rind. Carefully pour the stock into the bowl to cover the chicken completely. Cover the bowl and chill the chicken overnight before serving.

2 *Raw marinated sea bass, rice and shellfish feature in a Japanese-inspired terrine wrapped in dried nori seaweed (recipe, page 66).*

Lightness and Flavour from Fish

It is not surprising that fish plays a leading role in the new style of cookery. Low in calories and saturated fat, fish of all kinds is generously endowed with protein and other vital nutrients. Moreover, where terrines and pâtés are concerned, fish is infinitely versatile. Its delicate flesh is easily flaked or pounded down for creamy, quickly prepared pâtés, or puréed to form the basis of a silk-smooth mousseline. Slender fillets of white fish or pink-fleshed trout or salmon can be wrapped round a filling or used as a colourful lining for a terrine. Chunks of lightly cooked white fish and morsels of shellfish, held in suspension in a wine or lemon aspic, provide a refreshing first course for a summer lunch, while a whole fish such as sea bass — boned, stuffed, poached and presented as a galantine — makes a spectacular centrepiece for a formal buffet.

Some of the recipes on the following pages call for white-fleshed fish such as haddock, whiting or lemon sole; others require oily species such as mackerel or salmon. In all cases, substitutions can be made, so long as you keep to fish of the same basic type. A dish of delicately flavoured elements, such as the three-fish pie with prawns on page 78, would not be improved by the inclusion of an assertive, oily fleshed species such as mackerel. In turn, the robust flavourings in the curried prawn pâté on page 77 would overpower the subtlety of sea bass or sole.

Indispensable to every successful fish terrine, pâté or galantine is a first-class fishmonger. As well as supplying seafood of impeccable freshness, a good fish merchant will provide a fund of information, and enough practical help to cut your working time virtually in half. If the day's catch does not include the species called for in a recipe, the fishmonger will suggest the best alternatives. He will also free the cook from such necessary but time-consuming chores as gutting, filleting or boning a fish. If you intend to serve a raw fish preparation, such as the Terrine Mikado on page 66, a trusted source is essential. It is a cardinal rule that dishes containing uncooked fish should only be made with seafood that is absolutely fresh, and they should be eaten on the same day.

Because freshness is such a vital factor, even those pâtés and terrines based on cooked fish or shellfish are better served on the day that they are made. Those that are to be served well chilled should be prepared a few hours before they are needed, and kept in the refrigerator, closely covered with plastic film. Freezing is not advisable for fish terrines: it could mar both their flavour and their texture.

Mullet and Pasta Timbale Wrapped in Spinach

Serves 6 as a main course
Working time: about 1 hour
Total time: about 2 hours

Calories **360**
Protein **28g**
Cholesterol **110mg**
Total fat **9g**
Saturated fat **3g**
Sodium **250mg**

200 g	fresh fettuccine or noodles	7 oz
750 g	red or grey mullet, cleaned and scaled	1½ lb
15 cl	skimmed milk	¼ pint
1	onion, grated or finely chopped	1
1	stick celery, cut into four pieces	1
4	black peppercorns	4
250 g	large spinach leaves, stems removed, washed	8 oz
2 tbsp	chopped flat-leaf parsley	2 tbsp
2 tbsp	chopped fresh coriander	2 tbsp
½	lemon, grated rind and juice	½
	freshly ground black pepper	
2 tbsp	cornflour	2 tbsp
15 cl	unsalted fish stock (recipe, page 11)	¼ pint
2	eggs, beaten	2
30 g	halloumi cheese, finely grated	1 oz
Tomato sauce		
1 tbsp	virgin olive oil	1 tbsp
1	onion, finely chopped	1
1	garlic clove, finely chopped	1
1 kg	ripe beef tomatoes, skinned, seeded and roughly chopped	2 lb
15 cl	dry white wine	¼ pint
1 tbsp	white wine vinegar	1 tbsp
1 tsp	sugar	1 tsp
2 tbsp	chopped fresh basil	2 tbsp
¼ tsp	salt	¼ tsp
	freshly ground black pepper	

Bring 3 litres (5 pints) of lightly salted water to the boil in a large saucepan. Add the pasta, bring the water back to the boil and cook the pasta until it is *al*

dente — about 2 minutes. Drain the pasta, rinse it under cold running water and set it aside.

Place the mullet in a large saucepan, add the milk, onion, celery pieces and black· peppercorns, and poach the fish over low heat until it is just tender and will flake — about 8 minutes.

Meanwhile, blanch the spinach leaves for 1 minute in a large pan of rapidly boiling water. Drain the spinach, refresh it under cold running water and drain it again. Spread out the leaves on paper towels to dry.

Using a slotted spoon, remove the cooked fish from the pan, and set it aside in a bowl. Strain the fish-cooking liquid into another bowl; discard the vegetables and peppercorns. Remove the skin and bones from the fish, and flake the flesh with a fork. Mix the parsley, coriander, lemon rind and juice and some black pepper into the flaked fish.

Preheat the oven to 180°C (350°F or Mark 4). Mix the cornflour into the bowl of fish-cooking liquid to form a paste, then stir in the fish stock. Pour the liquid into a saucepan, slowly bring it to the boil and cook it, stirring continuously until the sauce thickens. Remove the pan from the heat and mix in the beaten eggs. Put the pasta in a bowl and add the sauce. Sprinkle on the halloumi cheese and mix thoroughly.

Line a 1.2 litre (2 pint) ovenproof bowl with most of the blanched spinach leaves, overlapping them to prevent any liquid from seeping through, and allowing their ends to overhang the sides of the bowl. Spoon half of the pasta mixture into the bowl, pressing it down lightly. Spoon the fish mixture over the pasta and cover the fish with the remaining pasta, again pressing down lightly. Cover the pasta layer with the reserved spinach leaves, and fold the overhanging leaves over them. Place a small ovenproof plate, upside down, on the top to hold the leaves in place.

Place the bowl in a deep roasting pan and pour boiling water into the pan to come two thirds of the way up the side of the bowl. Bake the timbale until a skewer inserted into the centre feels hot to the touch when removed — 40 to 50 minutes.

Meanwhile, make the tomato sauce. Heat the oil in a saucepan over medium heat, then gently fry the onion and garlic until the onion is transparent — about 4 minutes. Add the tomatoes and cook for a further 3 minutes, stirring, then add the wine, vinegar, sugar, basil, salt and some pepper. Bring the liquid to the boil and simmer it for 10 minutes. Allow the mixture to cool slightly, then purée it in a food processor or blender.

Remove the roasting pan from the oven and allow the timbale to cool for 5 minutes. If necessary, gently reheat the tomato sauce. Remove the plate from the timbale. Turn out the timbale on to a serving dish and serve it hot, accompanied by the tomato sauce.

SUGGESTED ACCOMPANIMENT: *mixed green salad.*

EDITOR'S NOTE: *Halloumi cheese is a Greek goat cheese with a salty tang. If it is unavailable, substitute 2 tablespoons of grated Parmesan cheese.*

Smoked Salmon Parcels with a Chive and Pink Trout Filling

Serves 8 as a first course
Working time: about 45 minutes
Total time: about 4 hours (includes chilling)

Calories **120**
Protein **19g**
Cholesterol **40mg**
Total fat **5g**
Saturated fat **1g**
Sodium **370mg**

400 g	pink trout fillets	14 oz
¼	onion, chopped	¼
2	lemon slices, plus extra lemon slices, for garnish (optional)	2
1	bay leaf	1
6	black peppercorns	6
175 g	low-fat fromage frais	6 oz
⅛ tsp	salt	⅛ tsp
	freshly ground black pepper	
⅛ tsp	ground coriander	⅛ tsp
2 tsp	powdered gelatine	2 tsp
1 tbsp	fresh lemon juice	1 tbsp
1 tbsp	cut chives, plus 16 long chives	1 tbsp
1	egg white	1
125 g	smoked salmon, trimmed into eight 16 by 5 cm (6½ by 2 inch) rectangles	4 oz
	curly endive, for garnish (optional)	

Lay the trout fillets in a frying pan. Add the onion, lemon slices, bay leaf and peppercorns, then pour in 30 cl (½ pint) of water to barely cover the fish. Bring the water just to the boil, reduce the heat and cover the pan. Simmer the trout gently until it is cooked — 7 to 10 minutes. Leave the fish to cool in the cooking liquid. Meanwhile, line a 20 by 10 by 5 cm (8 by 4 by 2 inch) loaf tin with non-stick parchment paper *(page 34)*.

Lift the cooled trout fillets from the pan and discard the cooking liquid. Flake the fish finely, discarding the skin and any bones. Place the flaked trout in a bowl and beat in the *fromage frais*, the salt, a little pepper and the ground coriander. Dissolve the gelatine in the lemon juice and 2 tablespoons of water, following the method on page 13. Stir the dissolved gelatine into the trout mixture and add the cut chives. Immediately whisk the egg white until it is very stiff. Beat 2 tablespoons of the whisked egg white into the fish mixture, then use a metal spoon to fold in the remaining egg white, making sure that it is evenly distributed. Turn the trout mousse into the prepared tin and chill it until it is firmly set — at least 3 hours.

Just before serving the mousse, turn it out of the tin and remove the paper. Cut the mousse into eight even-sized blocks whose lengths are the width of the smoked salmon rectangles. Wrap each portion of mousse in a piece of smoked salmon, leaving the ends of the mousse portion exposed. Pass two chives round the long and short dimensions of the parcel respectively, and lightly knot the ends of the chives together. Serve the smoked salmon parcels on individual plates, garnished, if you wish, with slices of lemon and a little curly endive.

Pink and Green Fish Terrine

Serves 16 as a first course
Working time: about 45 minutes
Total time: about 4 hours (includes chilling)

Calories **50**
Protein **7g**
Cholesterol **30mg**
Total fat **2g**
Saturated fat **1g**
Sodium **85mg**

500 g	pink trout fillets, skinned	1 lb
1 ½ tsp	chopped wild fennel	1 ½ tsp
1 ½ tsp	chopped fresh dill	1 ½ tsp
4	egg whites	4
½ tsp	salt	½ tsp
	white pepper	
15 g	unsalted butter	½ oz
90 g	parsley, stalks removed	3 oz
500 g	whiting or haddock fillets, skinned	1 lb
1 tbsp	chopped fresh tarragon, or 1 tsp dried tarragon	1 tbsp
1 tbsp	dry sherry or vermouth	1 tbsp

Line a 20 by 6 by 7.5 cm (8 by 2½ by 3 inch) terrine or loaf tin with non-stick parchment paper.

Roughly chop the trout fillets, then purée them in a food processor. Add the fennel, dill, two of the egg whites, ¼ teaspoon of the salt and some white pepper, and blend again to form a smooth paste. Transfer the pink paste to the prepared terrine, smoothing it down with the back of a spoon, then make a deep groove lengthwise down the centre. Chill the paste while you prepare the green layer.

Preheat the oven to 190°C (375°F or Mark 5). Melt the butter in a small saucepan, add the parsley and cook it over low heat until it is soft — about 10 minutes. Allow the parsley to cool, then place it in the food processor. Roughly chop the white fish and add it to the parsley. Process the parsley and fish until they are well blended. Add the tarragon, the remaining egg whites, the sherry, the remaining salt and some white pepper. Process the mixture to a smooth purée. Transfer the purée to the terrine and smooth it into an even layer with the back of a spoon.

Cover the terrine loosely with non-stick parchment paper and stand it in a large roasting pan or dish. Pour boiling water into the roasting pan to come two thirds of the way up the side of the terrine. Bake the terrine until the mixture is set and firm to the touch — about 35 minutes. Leave the terrine to cool, then chill it for at least 2 hours. Turn out the terrine on to a platter, and serve it cut into slices.

SUGGESTED ACCOMPANIMENTS: *curly endive and radish salad; Melba toast.*

Haddock Terrine with Dill

Serves 16 as a first course
Working time: about 45 minutes
Total time: about 5 hours (includes chilling)

Calories **70**			
Protein **11g**	90 g	fine fresh white breadcrumbs	3 oz
Cholesterol **30mg**	25 cl	skimmed milk	8 fl oz
Total fat **2g**	275 g	boned and skinned smoked Finnan haddock, cut into pieces	9 oz
Saturated fat **trace**	300 g	boned and skinned fresh haddock, cut into pieces	10 oz
Sodium **295mg**	1	egg	1
	3	egg whites	3
	1 tbsp	dry white vermouth	1 tbsp
	½ tsp	finely grated lemon rind	½ tsp
	1½ tbsp	fresh lemon juice	1½ tbsp
	2½ tbsp	chopped parsley	2½ tbsp
	3 tbsp	chopped fresh dill	3 tbsp
	30 cl	vegetable aspic (recipe, page 13), melted	½ pint
	3	quail's eggs, hard-boiled (optional)	3

Preheat the oven to 180°C (350°F or Mark 4). Put 60 g (2 oz) of the breadcrumbs in a bowl, pour the milk over them, and leave them for 5 minutes until they have absorbed the milk. Place the smoked Finnan haddock and 275 g (6 oz) of the fresh haddock in a food processor. Add the egg, two of the egg whites, the vermouth, lemon rind and lemon juice, and the milk-soaked breadcrumbs, then process the ingredients to a smooth purée. Set the purée aside.

Clean the food processor. Place the remaining fresh haddock, egg white and breadcrumbs, the parsley and 2 tablespoons of the dill in the processor, and process until the ingredients form a smooth, thick purée.

Line a 15 by 10 by 7.5 cm (6 by 4 by 3 inch) terrine or loaf tin with non-stick parchment paper *(page 34)*. Spoon half of the smoked haddock purée into the terrine, making sure that the corners of the dish are neatly filled. Lightly smooth the top of the mixture with the back of the spoon. Carefully place the herbed fresh haddock mixture, a tablespoon at a time, down the centre of the smoked haddock purée, along the length of the terrine. (The herbed mixture will sink slightly into the smoked haddock purée.) Carefully spread the remaining smoked haddock purée on top, disturbing the herbed purée as little as possible.

Cover the terrine with a lid or foil and stand it in a large roasting pan or dish. Pour in enough boiling water to come two thirds of the way up the side of the terrine. Bake the terrine in the oven until a skewer inserted in the centre is hot to the touch when withdrawn — 1 to 1¼ hours. Pour off any excess cooking liquid. Leave the terrine to cool — about 1 hour — then chill it in the refrigerator for 2 hours.

Pour a thin layer of aspic over the surface of the terrine and chill it until it has almost set — about 10 minutes. Sprinkle the remaining chopped dill over the aspic, pressing it in lightly, then chill the terrine again until the aspic is completely set — a further 10 minutes. If you are using quail's eggs, cut them into thin, vertical slices and arrange the best slices on top of the terrine. Pour over the remaining aspic and chill the terrine until it is set — 10 to 15 minutes.

Pink Trout Mousse

Serves 12 as a first course
Working time: about 30 minutes
Total time: about 4 hours (includes chilling)

Calories **75**	2	shallots, finely chopped	2
Protein **12g**	30 cl	unsalted fish stock (recipe, page 11)	½ pint
Cholesterol **25mg**	½	lime, juice only	½
Total fat **2g**	2 tbsp	dry vermouth	2 tbsp
Saturated fat **trace**	500 g	trout fillets	1 lb
Sodium **120mg**	1 tbsp	tomato paste	1 tbsp
	90 g	thick Greek yogurt	3 oz
	½ tsp	salt	½ tsp
		white pepper	
	1 tbsp	powdered gelatine	1 tbsp
	3	egg whites	3
	¼	cucumber, sliced, for garnish	¼

Place the shallots in a large, shallow pan with the fish stock, lime juice and vermouth. Bring the liquid to the boil, reduce the heat and simmer gently for 3 minutes, until the shallots have softened. Lay the trout fillets in the stock, skin side down. Cover the pan and simmer gently for 3 minutes, then remove the pan from the heat and leave the fish to cool in the stock.

Remove the fish from the pan with a slotted spoon. Roughly flake the fish, discarding the skin and any bones. Strain the stock. Place the fish in a food processor or blender, together with the strained stock, and blend the ingredients until smooth. Turn out the mixture into a bowl and beat in the tomato paste, yogurt, salt and some pepper.

Dissolve the gelatine in 3 tablespoons of cold water, following the instructions on page 13. Slowly pour the dissolved gelatine over the fish mixture, beating it well all the time. Chill the fish mixture until it is just beginning to set — 15 to 20 minutes.

Whisk the egg whites until they are stiff but not dry. Using a large metal spoon, stir one third of the egg whites into the fish mixture to lighten it, then gently fold in the remaining egg whites; avoid overmixing. Turn the mousse into a dampened serving dish and chill it until it is set — about 3 hours.

Serve the mousse garnished with the cucumber.

SUGGESTED ACCOMPANIMENT: *granary toast.*

Salmon Coulibiaca

THIS IS A VARIATION OF A CLASSIC RUSSIAN FISH PIE.
TRADITIONALLY, THE PIE IS LADEN WITH BUTTER AND
EGGS; HERE, MOISTNESS IS PROVIDED BY
A LOW-FAT COD MOUSSELINE.

Serves 20 as a main course
Working time: about 1 hour and 40 minutes
Total time: about 8 hours (includes rising and cooling)

Calories **270**	500 g	cod fillet, skinned and any bones removed	1 lb
Protein **16g**	2	egg whites	2
Cholesterol **75mg**	1¼ tsp	salt	1¼ tsp
Total fat **10g**	250 g	thick Greek yogurt	8 oz
Saturated fat **3g**		white pepper	
Sodium **200mg**	1 tbsp	virgin olive oil	1 tbsp
	1	onion, finely chopped	1
	250 g	Italian round-grain rice	8 oz
	¾ litre	unsalted chicken stock (recipe, page 10)	1½ pints
	2 tbsp	chopped fresh marjoram	2 tbsp
	2 tbsp	chopped fresh oregano	2 tbsp
	1 kg	middle-cut piece of fresh salmon, skinned and boned, cut into 1 cm (½ inch) slices	2 lb
	6 tbsp	chopped fresh dill	6 tbsp
		freshly ground black pepper	
	½	lemon, juice only	½
	1	egg, beaten	1
	Brioche dough		
	20 g	fresh yeast, or 15 g (½ oz) dried yeast	¾ oz
	500 g	strong plain flour	1 lb
	¼ tsp	salt	¼ tsp
	2	eggs, beaten	2
	2	egg whites	2
	60 g	polyunsaturated margarine	2 oz

First prepare the brioche dough. Dissolve the fresh yeast in 4 tablespoons of tepid water, or reconstitute the dried yeast according to the manufacturer's instructions. Sift the flour and salt into a mixing bowl and make a well in the centre. Add the two beaten eggs, the egg whites, margarine and yeast liquid. Mix the ingredients together well to form a firm dough. Knead

the dough on a lightly floured surface for 10 minutes, until it is smooth and elastic. Place the dough in a clean, lightly floured bowl. Cover the bowl with plastic film and refrigerate it for at least 4 hours, allowing the dough to rise slowly until it doubles in size.

Meanwhile, prepare the filling. Put the cod, egg whites and ¼ teaspoon of the salt into a food processor, and process them to a smooth paste. Press the fish mixture through a nylon sieve into a clean bowl, to remove all coarse fibre. Cover the bowl and refrigerate it for 1 hour.

Gradually beat the yogurt into the chilled cod. Season it well with white pepper, then cover the bowl again and return it to the refrigerator until required.

To prepare the rice, first heat the oil in a large saucepan over medium heat, then add the onion and cook it for 6 to 8 minutes, until it is softened but not browned. Add the rice and stir in the unsalted chicken stock, the fresh marjoram and oregano, and ¼ teaspoon of the salt. Bring the stock to the boil over high heat. Reduce the heat to low, cover the saucepan with a tightly fitting lid, and simmer for 20 to 25 minutes, until the rice is cooked and the stock has been absorbed. Set the rice aside to cool.

Turn the risen brioche dough on to a lightly floured surface and knead it for 1 to 2 minutes, until smooth. Roll out the dough to a large oblong measuring about 50 by 45 cm (20 by 18 inches). Lift the dough carefully on to a large, clean tea towel.

Spoon half of the rice down the centre of the dough in a neat strip measuring about 35 by 15 cm (14 by 6 inches). Cover the rice with half of the salmon slices. Sprinkle the salmon with half of the dill, then season it with half of the remaining salt, some black pepper and half of the lemon juice. Spread the cod mousseline on top of the salmon, covering it completely. Place the remaining salmon on top of the mousseline, sprinkle it with the remaining dill and season with the remaining salt, some more black pepper and the remaining lemon juice. Very carefully spoon the remaining rice over the salmon to cover it neatly and evenly.

Cut off a 10 cm (4 inch) square from each corner of the pastry and set the squares aside. Lift the two short ends of the pastry up and over the filling, then brush them with a little of the beaten egg. Lift one of the long sides of the pastry up and over the filling and brush it with a little more of the beaten egg. Bring the remaining side of the pastry up and over the first side to en- ▶

close the filling completely. Gently press the pastry joins together to seal them.

Grease a large baking sheet. With the aid of the tea towel, very carefully turn the coulibiaca on to the baking sheet, with the joins underneath. Make three evenly spaced holes in the top of the coulibiaca. Re-knead and re-roll the brioche trimmings quite thinly, and cut out some oval petal shapes. Brush the coulibiaca with a little of the beaten egg and decorate the top with the pastry petals. Brush the petals with the remaining beaten egg.

Tear a length of aluminium foil about 120 cm (48 inches) long. Fold the foil into three or four, lengthwise, so that its width is about the same as the coulibiaca's depth — about 10 cm (4 inches). Grease the foil well on one side, then wrap it, greased side inwards, right round the circumference of the coulibiaca. Secure the ends together firmly with paper clips. (The foil will stop the coulibiaca from spreading as it rises.) Set the wrapped coulibiaca aside in a warm place for 30 minutes.

Preheat the oven to 200°C (400°F or Mark 6). Bake the coulibiaca for 20 minutes; reduce the oven temperature to 190°C (375°F of Mark 5), and continue cooking for another 30 minutes. Remove the foil and cook, uncovered, for 15 to 20 minutes, until the pastry is golden-brown, and a skewer inserted in the centre of the coulibiaca feels hot to the touch when removed.

Allow the coulibiaca to cool to room temperature on the baking sheet — about 1 hour — then transfer it to a serving dish or board. Serve the coulibiaca at room temperature, or chilled.

SUGGESTED ACCOMPANIMENT: *green salad*.

EDITOR'S NOTE: *If the coulibiaca is to be served chilled, it may be made the day before and then stored overnight in the refrigerator.*

Jellied Bouillabaisse

THIS JELLIED TERRINE TAKES ITS INSPIRATION FROM BOUILLABAISSE, A SAFFRON-SCENTED SOUP MADE WITH AN ASSORTMENT OF MEDITERRANEAN FISH.

Serves 10 as a first course
Working time: about 1 hour
Total time: about 8 hours

Calories **45**
Protein **8g**
Cholesterol **20mg**
Total fat **trace**
Saturated fat **trace**
Sodium **30mg**

350 g	sea bass fillets (or other non-oily firm-textured white fish such as Dover sole, cod, grouper or hake), skinned	12 oz
1.5 litres	unsalted fish stock (recipe, page 11)	2½ pints
2	small fennel bulbs, stalks and feathery leaves reserved, bulbs finely chopped	2
¼ tsp	saffron threads	¼ tsp
4	leeks, trimmed, washed thoroughly to remove all grit, chopped	4
½	onion, chopped	½
2	sticks celery, chopped	2
1	garlic clove, finely chopped	1
3 tbsp	powdered gelatine	3 tbsp
3	eggs, whites and washed shells only	3
1	sweet green pepper, skinned (page 90), seeded and chopped	1
1	sweet red pepper, skinned (page 90), seeded and chopped	1
350 g	firm ripe tomatoes, skinned, seeded and finely chopped, drained on paper towels	12 oz

Place the fish fillets in a wide, shallow saucepan and pour in enough fish stock to cover them. Heat the stock gently until it is just simmering, then poach the fish for 7 to 10 minutes, until it is just firm. Using a slotted spoon, remove the fish from the pan. Cut the fillets into 6 mm (¼ inch) cubes and set them aside on paper towels to drain.

Add the chopped fennel bulbs to the fish-cooking liquid and simmer until they are tender — about 15 minutes. Reserving the cooking liquid, drain the fennel and place it on paper towels to dry.

Put the saffron threads, leeks, onion, celery and garlic in a heavy-bottomed saucepan. Trim off the feathery leaves from the fennel stalks, chop them and set them aside. Slice the stalks and add them to the pan. Pour in the remaining stock and the reserved fish-cooking liquid. Bring the liquid slowly to the boil, then simmer it for 20 minutes. Strain the stock through a nylon sieve into a large bowl; discard the vegetables. Add the gelatine, egg whites and shells to the stock and clarify it following the instructions on page 12. There should be about 1.5 litres (2½ pints) of aspic: pour off any excess, or add a little water to make up the quantity, if necessary. Set the aspic aside until it is cool and has just begun to set — about 40 minutes.

Ladle a little of the aspic into a 30 by 10 by 7.5 cm (12 by 4 by 3 inch) loaf tin to cover the bottom to a depth of about 6 mm (¼ inch), and place it in the refrigerator until the aspic is set — about 10 minutes.

Arrange about a third of the cubed fish and some of the chopped green and red peppers in the bottom of the tin. Cover the fish and peppers with aspic and chill until it is set. Sprinkle about half of the chopped tomatoes and half of the cooked, chopped fennel evenly over the layer of fish and peppers, cover them with aspic and chill until set. Continue layering the ingredients in this way, chilling the aspic between each layer and finishing with a layer of fish and peppers. Sprinkle the chopped fennel leaves over the top layer and cover them with the remaining aspic. Chill the terrine in the refrigerator until it is completely set — at least 4 hours, or overnight.

To unmould the bouillabaisse, dip the base and sides of the terrine in hot water for 5 seconds, then invert it on to a platter. Serve the terrine cut into slices.

Terrine Niçoise

Serves 10 as a first course
Working time: about 1 hour
Total time: about 3 hours

Calories **155**
Protein **14g**
Cholesterol **60mg**
Total fat **7g**
Saturated fat **2g**
Sodium **280mg**

½	lemon	½
3	large artichokes	3
175 g	very small new potatoes	6 oz
90 g	French beans, topped and tailed	3 oz
8 to 10	large lettuce leaves	8 to 10
1	sweet red pepper, skinned (page 90) and seeded	1
1	sweet yellow pepper, skinned (page 90) and seeded	1
2	eggs	2
2	egg whites	2
1 tsp	salt	1 tsp
40 cl	plain low-fat yogurt	14 fl oz
350 g	fresh tuna, trimmed into five long strips, each about 2 cm (¾ inch) thick	12 oz
	white pepper	
	Anchovy vinaigrette	
2 tbsp	virgin olive oil	2 tbsp
2 tbsp	fresh lemon juice	2 tbsp
1 tbsp	fresh apple or orange juice	1 tbsp
¼ tsp	Dijon mustard	¼ tsp
	freshly ground black pepper	
½	garlic clove, finely chopped (optional)	½
2 or 3	thyme sprigs, leaves separated	2 or 3
2 or 3	dill sprigs, finely cut	2 or 3
1 tsp	finely cut chives	1 tsp
1 tsp	finely chopped parsley	1 tsp
2	black olives, finely diced	2
3	anchovy fillets, larger bones picked out, finely diced	3

Bring a large, non-reactive pan of water to the boil. Squeeze the juice of the half lemon into the water and add the lemon half itself. Cook the artichokes in the acidulated water for 15 minutes, then drain them upside down. When they are cool enough to handle, remove the leaves and the hairy choke. Neaten the artichoke bottoms with a knife, and remove a slice from two opposite sides of each one, so that they will lie closely side by side when arranged in the terrine.

Cook the potatoes in boiling water for 10 to 12 minutes, until just tender but slightly under-done (test them with a skewer). Drain the potatoes, refresh them under cold water, then peel them or leave the skins on, as preferred. Cut a slice from both ends of each potato. Blanch the French beans in boiling water for about 40 seconds; refresh them under cold water, drain them and set them aside.

Remove the centre rib from each lettuce leaf. Dip the leaves in boiling water for a few seconds, away from the heat, until soft. Refresh them in cold water, drain them and spread them out to dry on paper towels. Cut the sweet peppers into 1 cm (⅜ inch) wide strips.

Whisk the eggs and egg whites lightly with ¾ teaspoon of the salt, until they are blended but not frothy. Add the yogurt to the eggs and mix well.

Preheat the oven to 180°C (350°F or Mark 4). Line a 1.5 litre (2 pint) terrine or loaf tin with the lettuce leaves, leaving about 6 cm (2½ inches) overhanging at the top. Season the tuna and the artichoke bottoms with the remaining salt and some white pepper. Spread a thin layer of the yogurt mixture in the terrine, then lay the artichokes along the centre with a strip of tuna on each side. Spread enough yogurt mixture over the artichokes and tuna to cover them, lay the yellow pepper strips on top with a tuna strip down the centre, and cover with more yogurt mixture. Continue layering, using first the French beans, then the red pepper strips, and separating each layer with some of the yogurt mixture. Finally, place two lines of potatoes on either side and two tuna strips along the centre, and cover with the remaining yogurt mixture.

Fold the lettuce leaves over the top, making sure that the terrine is completely enclosed (patch any gaps with extra leaves). Cover the terrine with foil, piercing a few holes in the foil to let out steam during cooking. Stand the terrine in a roasting pan and pour in boiling water to come two thirds up the side of the terrine. Bake it for 1 hour; remove the foil and bake for about 10 minutes more, until a skewer inserted into the centre feels hot to the touch when removed.

Meanwhile, make the anchovy vinaigrette. Blend together the oil, fruit juices, mustard, some black pepper and the garlic, if you are using it. Gently stir in the herbs, olives and diced anchovy fillets. Set the dressing aside for 20 to 30 minutes at room temperature, to let the flavours blend.

Rest the terrine in the tin in a warm place, covered loosely with foil, for 15 minutes. Invert it on to a slightly inclined board and leave to drain for 5 minutes. Serve warm, cut into slices, with the vinaigrette.

Sole and Watercress Terrine with Smoked Eel

Serves 6 as a main course
Working time: about 1 hour
Total time: about 9 hours (includes chilling)

Calories **120**
Protein **17g**
Cholesterol **125mg**
Total fat **5g**
Saturated fat **2g**
Sodium **250mg**

500 g	skinned lemon sole fillets	1 lb
30 g	watercress	1 oz
15 g	flat-leaf parsley	½ oz
15 g	fresh chervil, plus sprigs for garnish	½ oz
15 g	fresh dill or fennel tops	½ oz
350 g	skinned whiting fillets	12 oz
2	egg whites	2
4 tbsp	crème fraîche	4 tbsp
4 tbsp	thick Greek yogurt	4 tbsp
¼ tsp	quatre épices	¼ tsp
¼ tsp	white pepper	¼ tsp
½ tsp	salt	½ tsp
45 g	smoked eel fillet, cut into long, thin strips	1½ oz

Lightly oil an 18 by 7.5 by 7.5 cm (7 by 3 by 3 inch) terrine or loaf tin. Flatten and stretch the sole fillets between two sheets of plastic film by beating them gently, then rolling them with a rolling pin. Make three light, diagonal cuts in the skinned side of each fillet to prevent shrinking and curling. Line the terrine with the fillets; place them skinned side upwards across the terrine, overlapping them a little if possible. Press the fillets into the base of the terrine, allowing the ends to overhang its sides. Set the terrine aside.

Blanch the watercress and parsley in rapidly boiling water for 15 seconds; refresh them immediately under cold water and squeeze them dry in a paper towel. Finely chop the watercress, parsley, chervil and dill or fennel tops together, either in a food processor or using a large, sharp knife. Set the herbs aside.

Preheat the oven to 180°C (350°F or Mark 4). Cut the whiting into chunks and process it finely in a food processor, scraping down the bowl from time to time. Add one egg white, process briefly and scrape down the bowl, then add the second egg white and process the mixture to a smooth purée. If the mixture feels warm at this stage, chill it for 30 minutes before processing it with the crème fraîche and yogurt. Finally, add the chopped herbs, quatre épices, pepper and salt, and process briefly to amalgamate the ingredients.

Spoon half of the mousseline into the terrine and use the back of the spoon to form a narrow channel in the centre, running the length of the terrine. Arrange the eel strips down the length of the channel. Spoon the remaining mousseline over the eel and smooth down the surface with the back of the spoon. Fold the overhanging ends of sole over the mousseline.

Cover the terrine with a piece of foil and stand it in a large roasting pan or dish. Pour boiling water into the pan to come two thirds of the way up the side of the terrine. Bake the terrine for about 40 minutes, until the upper surface is firm to the touch. Remove the terrine from the roasting pan and set it aside to cool.

When the terrine is cool, place a wire rack or similar flat drainer over it, then invert the terrine and rack together on to a tray. Leave the terrine to drain for about 20 minutes, then chill it for at least 6 hours. Serve the terrine sliced, garnished with chervil or fennel tops.

SUGGESTED ACCOMPANIMENT: moist, dark rye bread.

Terrine Mikado

THIS RECIPE COMBINES INTO A EUROPEAN-STYLE TERRINE THE
ELEMENTS OF TWO QUINTESSENTIALLY JAPANESE HORS-
D'OEUVRE: SUSHI — SMALL MORSELS OF RICE AND SEAFOOD
WRAPPED IN SEAWEED; AND SASHIMI — RAW FISH SERVED
WITH SOY SAUCE AND WASABI (JAPANESE HORSERADISH).

Serves 10 as a first course
Working time: about 40 minutes
Total time: about 2 hours and 15 minutes
(includes marinating)

Calories **140**
Protein **11g**
Cholesterol **40mg**
Total fat **2g**
Saturated fat **trace**
Sodium **75mg**

600 g	sea bass fillet, skinned	1¼ lb
10 cl	rice vinegar	3½ fl oz
2 tsp	grated or finely chopped fresh ginger root	2 tsp
¼ tsp	wasabi powder	¼ tsp
250 g	sushi rice	8 oz
2 tbsp	dried wakame seaweed, soaked for 10 minutes in 20 cl (7 fl oz) of cold water (optional)	2 tbsp
¾ tsp	sugar	¾ tsp
¼ tsp	salt	¼ tsp
4	sheets nori seaweed	4
4 tsp	red salmon caviare (Keta), for garnish (optional)	4 tsp
	mixed seaweed, for garnish (optional)	

Cut the sea bass fillet diagonally into thin slices and lay the slices on a platter large enough to hold them in a single layer without overlapping. Blend 3 tablespoons of the vinegar with the ginger and wasabi powder, and pour the mixture over the fish. Cover the fish with plastic film and put it in the refrigerator to marinate for 1½ to 3 hours, turning it once during this time. The marinade's acidity will turn the fish opaque.

Rinse the rice in cold water and drain it in a sieve. Pour the rice into a pan with 30 cl (½ pint) of water, and bring the water to the boil. Cover the pan and simmer the rice over very low heat for 10 minutes. Remove the pan from the heat but let the rice steam through for 15 to 20 minutes more before you remove the lid.

Meanwhile, drain the wakame, if you are using it, in a square of muslin; bring the corners of the muslin together into a parcel and squeeze the wakame dry. Shred it finely with your fingers and set it aside.

Scoop out the rice into a large — preferably shallow — bowl. In a small jug, mix the sugar and salt with 2½ tablespoons of the rice vinegar, stirring until they are dissolved, then pour the mixture evenly over the rice. Add the shredded wakame to the rice and toss the rice gently to mix it in well, wielding a bamboo rice paddle or wooden spoon with a cutting and turning motion. With the other hand, fan the rice using a fan or a piece of cardboard, to cool it quickly so that the grains become glossy. Cover the rice with a damp cloth or with plastic film, and set it aside.

Remove the fish from the refrigerator. Drain it on layers of paper towels; wipe off the grated ginger, if you wish. Line a 22 by 12 by 6 cm (9 by 5 by 2½ inch) loaf tin with plastic film, leaving enough overhanging to meet and wrap over at the top. Mix the remaining rice vinegar with 5 tablespoons of water and moisten your fingers when you are working with the rice, to prevent the rice from sticking to them. Wet a brush in the vinegared water, and use it to lightly moisten the inside of the lined tin. Toast the nori sheets by waving them 12 cm (5 inches) above a flame or electric ring for a few seconds, until they are fragrant.

To assemble the terrine, line the bottom and the long sides of the prepared tin with two of the nori sheets, overlapping them by about 1 cm (½ inch) along the bottom. Bend the nori sheets over the tin at the top to determine how much to trim away: they should cover the top of the tin, and overlap by about 2 cm (¾ inch). Trim off any excess with kitchen scissors. Tear the nori trimmings and remaining sheets into strips. Arrange the tin so that a short side is facing you. Moisten your finger in the vinegared water and layer the fish, rice and nori pieces in the tin to create a random pattern, making sure that the final layer is level.

When all the rice and fish are used up, fold the overhanging nori over the terrine and wrap the plastic film over the nori. Weight the terrine with a 500 g (1 lb) weight, following instructions on page 19; leave it to firm in the refrigerator for at least 15, but not more than 30, minutes. If the terrine is left in the tin for longer than 30 minutes, the nori will absorb too much moisture and will tear easily when the terrine is turned out.

To serve the terrine, turn it out and remove the plastic film; cut the terrine into slices. Place a slice of the terrine in the centre of each individual plate and garnish with a little of the caviare and the mixed seaweed, if you are using them.

EDITOR'S NOTE: *Other fine-flavoured, firm white fish such as bream or red mullet can be used instead of sea bass; cooked, shelled mussels could be added for colour and texture contrast. Sushi rice, wasabi powder and the seaweeds can be purchased from Oriental grocers and some health food shops. If sushi rice is unobtainable, another glutinous rice such as pudding rice may be substituted.*

If you wish to prepare the terrine in advance, turn it out and slice it, then cover the slices with plastic film and leave them in the refrigerator for 5 to 10 minutes before serving.

Terrine of Salmon and Sole

Serves 6 as a main course
Working time: about 50 minutes
Total time: about 2 hours and 30 minutes (includes cooling)

Calories **170**
Protein **21g**
Cholesterol **55mg**
Total fat **9g**
Saturated fat **3g**
Sodium **290mg**

8	cabbage leaves, tough stems trimmed	8
250 g	salmon tail fillet, skinned	8 oz
90 g	monkfish fillet	3 oz
½ tsp	salt	½ tsp
	white pepper	
250 g	lemon sole fillets, skinned	8 oz
4	egg whites	4
2	slices stale white bread, crusts removed	2
2 tbsp	double cream	2 tbsp
12.5 cl	milk	4 fl oz

Blanch the cabbage leaves in boiling water for 2 minutes. Drain them, refresh them under cold running water, then drain them again on paper towels. Line an 18 by 7.5 by 7.5 cm (7 by 3 by 3 inch) loaf tin with all but two of the blanched cabbage leaves, arranging them so that they overhang the rim by at least 5 cm (2 inches). Set the tin aside.

Cut a strip from the salmon fillet the same length as the tin and 1 cm (½ inch) wide. Trim the monkfish fillet to the same size as the salmon strip; reserve the trimmings. Season both strips of fish with a little of the salt and some pepper. Wrap each strip in one of the remaining cabbage leaves and set them aside.

Cut the sole into several pieces. Place the pieces, with the monkfish trimmings, in a food processor, and process to a smooth purée. Add two of the egg whites and continue to process until evenly mixed. Moisten the slices of bread in cold water, then squeeze them

dry; keep the slices separate. Add one moistened bread slice to the sole purée together with 1 tablespoon of the cream and 4 tablespoons of the milk. Season the purée with half of the remaining salt and some pepper, and process it for a further 30 seconds. Transfer the sole purée to a small bowl and place it in the refrigerator.

Cut the remaining salmon fillet into several pieces and process them to a smooth purée in the food processor — about 30 seconds. Add the remaining egg whites and continue to process until they are well mixed with the salmon. Add the remaining moistened bread, cream, milk and salt, and some pepper, and process for a further 30 seconds.

Preheat the oven to 180°C (350°F or Mark 4). To assemble the terrine, spread 3 tablespoons of the salmon mixture against one side and along the bottom of the cabbage-lined tin. Lay the cabbage-wrapped strip of monkfish down the length of the salmon purée, and cover it with the remaining salmon purée, spreading it evenly with a small palette knife so that it fills exactly half of the mould diagonally. Gently spread about 5 tablespoons of the sole purée into the remaining space, lay the cabbage-wrapped strip of salmon on the mixture and cover it with the remaining sole purée, smoothing the surface gently with the back of the spoon. Fold the overhanging cabbage leaves over the top of the terrine to cover it. Cover the tin with foil.

Stand the tin in a large roasting pan or dish. Pour boiling water into the roasting pan to come two thirds of the way up the sides of the tin. Bake the terrine for about 35 minutes, until it is springy yet firm to the touch. Allow the terrine to cool completely — about 1 hour — before turning it out and slicing it.

SUGGESTED ACCOMPANIMENT: *rice and vegetable salad.*

Fresh and Smoked Mackerel Pâté

Serves 10 as a first course
Working time: about 20 minutes
Total time: about 1 hour and 30 minutes (includes chilling)

Calories **145**
Protein **14g**
Cholesterol **40mg**
Total fat **10g**
Saturated fat **3g**
Sodium **265mg**

350 g	fresh mackerel, filleted and skinned	12 oz
250 g	smoked mackerel fillets, skin and any bones removed	8 oz
250 g	low-fat fromage frais	8 oz
1	lemon, grated rind and juice of half, the other half cut into wedges	1
1 tbsp	chopped fresh dill or fennel tops, plus whole sprigs for garnish	1 tbsp
	freshly ground black pepper	

Pour water into a saucepan to fill it to a depth of 2.5 cm (1 inch). Set a vegetable steamer in the pan and bring the water to the boil. Put the fresh mackerel in the steamer, cover the pan tightly and steam the fish until it is cooked — about 10 minutes.

Place the cooked fresh mackerel and the smoked mackerel in a food processor or blender, together with all but 1½ tablespoons of the *fromage frais*, the lemon rind and juice, and the chopped dill or fennel, and process the ingredients to a smooth paste. Season the pâté with some pepper. Transfer the pâté to a bowl, cover it and chill it for at least 1 hour.

Remove the pâté from the refrigerator just before serving, stir it and divide it among 10 individual ramekins. Garnish each portion with a little of the reserved *fromage frais* and the dill or fennel sprigs, and serve immediately with the wedges of lemon.

SUGGESTED ACCOMPANIMENT: *wholemeal bread*.

Speckled Cod Timbales with Yellow Pepper Sauce

Serves 6 as a first course
Working time: about 45 minutes
Total time: about 1 hour

Calories **90**			
Protein **13g**	1 tsp	cornflour	1 tsp
Cholesterol **10mg**	20 cl	skimmed milk	7 fl oz
Total fat **1g**	500 g	cod fillet, skinned and cut into pieces	1 lb
Saturated fat **trace**	1 tbsp	prepared horseradish	1 tbsp
Sodium **295mg**	¾ tsp	salt	¾ tsp
		freshly ground black pepper	
	1	large sweet yellow pepper	1
	2	egg whites	2
	½ tsp	white wine vinegar	½ tsp
	1 tbsp	black lumpfish roe, for garnish (optional)	1 tbsp
		flat-leaf parsley, for garnish (optional)	

Preheat the oven to 190°C (375°F or Mark 5).

Blend the cornflour with a little of the milk in a small, heavy-bottomed saucepan. Stir in remaining milk and bring it to the boil over medium heat. Cook the sauce for 2 minutes, stirring continuously, until it has thickened. Leave it to cool slightly — about 10 minutes.

Pour the thickened sauce into a food processor or blender, add the pieces of cod, and purée them until the mixture is completely smooth. Turn the purée into a bowl and beat in the horseradish, ½ teaspoon of the salt and some freshly ground black pepper. Roughly grate a quarter of the sweet yellow pepper and add it to the bowl. Whisk the egg whites until they are stiff. Using a metal spoon, mix 2 tablespoons of the egg whites into the cod mixture, then fold in the remainder.

Lightly grease six 7.5 cm (3 inch) ramekins and spoon in the cod mixture, smoothing the surface with the back of the spoon. Stand the ramekins in a baking dish. Pour in boiling water to a depth of 1 cm (½ inch). Cover the ramekins with lightly greased foil, and bake the timbales for 20 to 25 minutes, until they have risen and feel just firm. Leave them to cool for 10 minutes.

Meanwhile, skin the remainder of the yellow pepper, following the instructions on page 90. Seed and derib the skinned pepper, then roughly chop it and purée it in a food processor or blender with 4 tablespoons of water. Using a spoon, push the pepper purée through a sieve into a small, heavy-bottomed saucepan. Stir in the wine vinegar and the remaining salt, and heat the sauce gently over low heat for 2 minutes.

Loosen the edges of the timbales with a knife and turn them out on to paper towels to drain for 1 minute. Using a spatula, transfer them to warmed serving plates. Garnish each timbale with lumpfish roe and parsley, if you are using them; spoon a little sauce round the base of each one and serve.

Seafood Mosaic

Serves 12 as a first course
Working time: about 1 hour and 30 minutes
Total time: about 7 hours (includes chilling)

Calories **155**
Protein **25g**
Cholesterol **120mg**
Total fat **3g**
Saturated fat **1g**
Sodium **295mg**

4	large eggs, whites and shells only, shells washed and crushed	4
125 g	tomatoes, finely chopped	4 oz
125 g	lean chicken, minced	4 oz
2	leeks, white parts only, cleaned thoroughly and finely chopped	2
90 g	mushrooms, finely chopped	3 oz
2	sticks celery, finely chopped	2
1 tsp	finely chopped fresh ginger root	1 tsp
1.5 litres	unsalted fish stock (recipe, page 11)	2½ pints
2 tbsp	fresh lemon juice	2 tbsp
75 g	powdered gelatine	2½ oz
1 tsp	salt	1 tsp
140 g	peeled cooked prawns	4½ oz
250 g	turbot or haddock fillet	8 oz
175 g	salmon or pink trout fillet	6 oz
8	oysters (optional)	8
15 to 20	small mussels	15 to 20
6	squid, with pouches measuring about 12 cm (5 inches), cleaned (opposite)	6
2	lemons, grated rind only	2
5 tbsp	finely chopped mixed fresh herbs, such as parsley with tarragon and chervil	5 tbsp
15 to 18	green peppercorns, finely crushed	15 to 18
5	shallots, finely chopped	5
Court-bouillon		
25 cl	dry white wine	8 fl oz
90 g	carrots, sliced	3 oz
1	leek, white part only, cleaned thoroughly and sliced	1
60 g	onion, chopped	2 oz
1½	sticks celery, sliced	1½
1	small garlic clove, unpeeled	1
4	parsley sprigs	4
3	thyme sprigs	3
½	bay leaf	½
4	peppercorns	4
4	coriander seeds	4

First prepare the court-bouillon. Put the wine in a non-reactive pan with 1 litre (1 ¾ pints) of water. Bring the liquid to the boil, then add the rest of the ingredients and leave them to simmer gently for 15 minutes. Allow the contents of the pan to cool and infuse for 1 hour at room temperature, or for no more than 24 hours in the refrigerator. Strain the court-bouillon and set it aside.

To make the aspic, first put the tomatoes, chicken, leeks, mushrooms, celery and ginger in a saucepan with 60 cl (1 pint) of the fish stock. Bring to the boil, simmer for about 15 minutes, then strain the liquid and discard the solids. Add the lemon juice, gelatine and the strained liquid to the remaining stock and, using the egg whites and crushed shells, clarify the combined liquid as described on page 12.

Add ¾ teaspoon of the salt to the clarified stock and set it aside in a cool place, stirring every now and then to prevent it from setting too firmly (it must be kept in a syrupy state until you are ready to use it).

Cut the prawns in half crosswise. Slice the narrower ends into little rounds, and set them aside; leave the other halves intact. Cut the turbot and salmon, along the grain, into 2 cm (¾ inch) wide strips. If using oysters, open them carefully; collect the juice and strain it into the court-bouillon. Detach the oysters from their shells. Scrub and debeard the mussels.

Bring the court-bouillon to the boil, then reduce the heat to a simmer. Put in the squid pouches. As soon as they start to shrink and float to the surface, remove them with a slotted spoon and refresh them in cold water. Leave them to drain in a colander, open ends downwards. Meanwhile, poach the tentacles in the court-bouillon, removing them as soon as they curl. Refresh them in cold water and drain. Stand the pouches with their open ends up in a bowl just large enough to hold them all without squashing them. Cover with plastic film and chill in the refrigerator.

Keeping the court-bouillon at a low simmer, slip the turbot and salmon strips into the pan. Cook them for 1½ minutes, then remove them using a slotted spoon. Plunge the fish briefly into cold water to prevent further cooking. Remove the fish from the water, drain, then season with the remaining salt and set aside.

Repeat this procedure with the oysters, if you are using them, poaching them for 30 seconds only, or until firm to the touch. Bring the court-bouillon to the boil again and drop in the cleaned mussels. As soon as they open, remove them with the slotted spoon, then refresh them as above and drain. Detach the mussels from their shells. Cover the poached seafood and put it in the refrigerator until required.

Chop the squid tentacles into small dice and mix them with the sliced prawns. Pour about 8 cl (3 fl oz) of the unset aspic into a small bowl and put it in the refrigerator until it thickens slightly — about 30 minutes — then stir in the diced squid and prawns. (The jelly should be set just enough to keep the solids in suspension, but no more.) Using a small spoon, fill the squid pouches with this jelly; cover the bowl and put the squid in the refrigerator until the jelly has set.

Blanch the grated lemon rind in boiling water for 10 seconds. Drain it in a fine strainer, refresh it under cold running water and dry it on paper towels. Mix the lemon rind into the remaining unset jelly, together with the chopped herbs, green peppercorns and shallots. Pour a thin layer of jelly into the bottom of a 25 by 7.5 by 7.5 cm (10 by 3 by 3 inch) terrine, then put it into the refrigerator to set — about 15 minutes. When the jelly inside the squid pouches has set, trim about 2 cm (¾ inch) from the pointed ends of the body sacs.

Arrange a layer of seafood in the terrine in a random fashion, using some of each variety and packing the gaps with the halved prawns and the mussels. Spoon a generous layer of jelly over the seafood and return the terrine to the refrigerator to set. Continue layering and chilling in the same way, making sure that the arrangement varies between layers. Leave the terrine in the refrigerator for 3 to 4 hours to set completely.

To unmould the terrine, dip the base and sides in hot water for 5 seconds, turn the terrine out on to a platter and cut it into 2 cm (¾ inch) slices.

Preparing a Squid for Cooking

1 *SEPARATING THE POUCH AND TENTACLES. Working over a bowl of water or a sink, hold the squid's pouch in one hand and its tentacles in the other. Gently pull the tentacles until the viscera separate from the inside of the pouch. Place the tentacles, with the head and viscera still attached, in the bowl.*

2 *REMOVING THE PEN. Feel inside the pouch with your fingers to locate the pen, or quill — a cartilaginous structure running nearly the length of the pouch. Pull out the pen and discard it. Reach inside the pouch again and scrape out any remaining gelatinous material with your fingers; wash the pouch thoroughly.*

3 *SKINNING THE POUCH. Carefully pull off the edible triangular fins on either side of the pouch and skin them. Starting at the open end of the pouch, use your fingers to pull the mottled purplish skin away from the pale flesh. Continue peeling off the skin from the pouch; discard the skin. Rinse the pouch and wings, then set them aside in a bowl of fresh cold water.*

4 *CUTTING OFF THE TENTACLES. Lay the viscera, head and tentacles on a cutting board. Sever the tentacles from the head below the eyes; the tentacles should remain joined together by a narrow band of flesh. Discard the head and viscera. If any of the bony beak remains in the tentacle section, squeeze it out.*

Terrine of White Fish, Salmon and Squid

Serves 12 as a first course
Working time: about 1 hour
Total time: about 3 hours and 30 minutes (includes cooling)

Calories **135**
Protein **14g**
Cholesterol **95mg**
Total fat **6g**
Saturated fat **3g**
Sodium **130mg**

2	large leeks, measuring at least 30 cm (12 inches) when trimmed, three cleaned outer layers from each leek only	2
175 g	French beans, topped and tailed	6 oz
350 g	whiting fillets, skinned and cut into pieces	12 oz
4	egg whites	4
2	slices stale white bread, crusts removed	2
4 tbsp	double cream	4 tbsp
12.5 cl	milk	4 fl oz
½ tsp	salt	½ tsp
	white pepper	
350 g	salmon fillet, skinned, cut into pieces	12 oz
1 tbsp	chopped fresh dill	1 tbsp
4	squid, pouches only, cleaned and skinned (page 71)	4

Blanch the outer layers of the leeks in boiling water for 4 minutes, until they are soft. Remove the layers with a slotted spoon, reserving the cooking water. Refresh the layers under cold running water, drain them and set them aside on paper towels to dry. Blanch the French beans in the leek liquid for 3 minutes, drain them, refresh them under cold running water, drain them again and set them aside.

Line a 25 by 7.5 by 7.5 cm (10 by 3 by 3 inch) terrine or non-reactive loaf tin with the leek layers. Open them out flat and place them, overlapping, across the terrine so that they overhang the sides; they will be folded over the filling to enclose it. Set the lined terrine aside.

Place the whiting in a food processor and process it until it is smooth. Lightly beat two of the egg whites and add them to the whiting, one third at a time, while the processor is running. Moisten the two slices of bread and squeeze them dry. Add one of the moistened slices to the whiting, together with 2 tablespoons of the double cream, 4 tablespoons of the milk, ¼ teaspoon of salt and some white pepper, and process for 30 seconds. Transfer the white fish mixture to a small bowl and place it in the refrigerator.

Place the salmon in the food processor and process it until it is smooth. Lightly beat the remaining egg whites and add them to the salmon in three additions, as above. Add the remaining moistened bread slice, double cream, milk and salt, some more pepper and the chopped dill, and process for 30 seconds.

Preheat the oven to 180°C (350°F or Mark 4). Place one quarter of the salmon mixture in a piping bag fitted with a 10 mm (½ inch) plain nozzle and fill each of the squid pouches with the mixture. Using the back of a spoon, spread the remainder of the salmon mixture evenly over the bottom and sides of the leek-lined terrine. Spoon half of the white fish mixture into the bottom of the terrine. With the spoon, create a channel along the centre, slightly wider than the stuffed squid pouches. Line the channel with a single layer of beans, then place the stuffed squid pouches in the bean-lined hollow. Carefully cover the pouches with the remaining beans, to create a ring of beans round the pouches along the length of the terrine. Cover the beans and fill the terrine with the remaining white fish mixture. Fold the overhanging leeks over the top of the terrine, completely enclosing the filling.

Cover the terrine with foil, stand it in a roasting pan and pour in enough boiling water to come two thirds of the way up the side of the terrine. Bake for 40 minutes. Cool for about 2 hours before turning out.

EDITOR'S NOTE: *The unused squid pieces can be incorporated in a seafood salad or a fish soup or stew.*

Layered Seafood in Wine Jelly

Serves 6 as a first course
Working time: about 45 minutes
Total time: about 4 hours and 30 minutes (includes chilling)

Calories **110**
Protein **18g**
Cholesterol **110mg**
Total fat **2g**
Saturated fat **1g**
Sodium **100mg**

250 g	whole rainbow trout, cleaned, filleted and skinned, bones and head reserved	8 oz
300 g	whole lemon sole, cleaned, filleted and skinned, bones and head reserved	10 oz
2	long sticks celery, one roughly chopped, one finely sliced	2
1	carrot, roughly chopped	1
½	leek, trimmed, washed thoroughly and roughly chopped	½
1	bay leaf	1
1	parsley sprig	1
1	small onion, sliced	1
⅛ tsp	salt	⅛ tsp
3	white peppercorns	3
15 cl	dry white wine	¼ pint
2 tsp	powdered gelatine	2 tsp
1 tsp	fresh lemon juice	1 tsp
1 tbsp	chopped fresh dill, plus a few whole dill sprigs	1 tbsp
60 g	peeled cooked prawns	2 oz
2 tsp	red lumpfish roe	2 tsp

Place the fish bones and heads in a saucepan and add the chopped celery, the carrot, leek, bay leaf, parsley, onion and salt. Pour ¼ litre (8 fl oz) of water into the pan, and bring it to the boil; cover the pan and simmer for 15 minutes. Add the peppercorns and wine to the stock and bring it back to a simmer.

Place a sheet of non-stick parchment paper in the bottom of a steamer. Arrange the trout and sole fillets in layers in the steamer, with non-stick parchment paper between the layers. Set the steamer over the pan of stock, and continue to simmer the stock for about 10 minutes, until the fish is just firm.

Remove the fish fillets from the steamer and leave them to cool. Line a sieve with a double thickness of muslin or coffee filter paper and strain the stock, discarding the fish trimmings; the stock will take between 30 minutes and 1 hour to filter. If necessary, make the strained stock up to 30 cl (½ pint) with cold water.

Meanwhile, place the sliced celery in a small saucepan, add water to cover and bring it to the boil. Reduce the heat and simmer for 3 minutes, until the celery is just tender. Drain the celery and set it aside.

Dissolve the gelatine in 3 tablespoons of the fish stock, following the method on page 13. Stir the gelatine mixture into the remaining stock, and add the lemon juice. Spoon enough jelly into a 20 by 10 by 6 cm (8 by 4 by 2½ inch) loaf tin to cover its base with a thin layer. Arrange some dill sprigs in the jelly and leave it to set in the refrigerator — about 15 minutes.

Arrange the trout fillets and half of the cooked celery slices over the set jelly, and sprinkle them with half of the chopped dill. Spoon in enough jelly just to cover the fish and chill again until set — a further 15 minutes. Arrange the prawns and lumpfish roe in a layer over the set jelly. Add enough jelly to cover and chill again until set — about 15 minutes.

Lastly, arrange the sole fillets and remaining celery slices over the prawns, sprinkle on the remaining chopped dill and gently pour over the remaining jelly. Chill in the refrigerator for at least 2 hours.

To unmould, dip the sides and base of the tin in hot water for 5 seconds. Invert it on to a serving plate and lift off the tin. If you like, garnish with more dill sprigs.

EDITOR'S NOTE: *Jellied terrines of this type can be difficult to slice without breaking up the main ingredients. For the best results, use a wet, serrated knife to cut the terrine and hold a fish slice or palette knife against the piece being cut as you slice; use a gentle sawing motion.*

Sea Bass
Galantine Orientale

IF THE FISH CONTAINS ROE, THIS CAN BE INCLUDED
IN THE STUFFING, BUT IT MUST FIRST BE FRIED IN
A TEASPOON OF SESAME OIL OVER MEDIUM HEAT
FOR ABOUT 2 MINUTES.

Serves 12 as a first course
Working time: about 2 hours
Total time: about 7 hours (includes marinating and chilling)

Calories **150**
Protein **14g**
Cholesterol **80mg**
Total fat **5g**
Saturated fat **1g**
Sodium **160mg**

1.25 kg	sea bass, boned and gutted through the back, head and tail left intact, bones and trimmings reserved	2½ lb
1 tbsp	low-sodium soy sauce or shoyu	1 tbsp
1 tbsp	light sesame oil	1 tbsp
3 tbsp	rice vinegar	3 tbsp
5 cm	piece fresh ginger root, peeled	2 inch
1	small carrot, sliced	1
1	leek, white part only, slit and cleaned thoroughly to remove all grit	1
1	small shallot, sliced	1
1	garlic clove	1
1	parsley sprig	1
1	fresh tarragon sprig	1
4	black peppercorns	4
45 cl	dry white wine	¾ pint
1 tsp	powdered gelatine	1 tsp
2 tsp	white sesame seeds, toasted	2 tsp
2 tsp	black sesame seeds	2 tsp
1	black olive, stoned and halved	1
	whole cooked prawns, for garnish (optional)	
Prawn and shiitake stuffing		
60 g	round-grain rice	2 oz
1 tbsp	light sesame oil	1 tbsp
75 g	fresh shiitake mushrooms, very finely sliced	2½ oz
350 g	raw giant prawns, shells removed and reserved, prawns deveined	12 oz
2	garlic cloves	2
2.5 cm	piece fresh ginger root, peeled	1 inch
¼ tsp	salt	¼ tsp
1 tsp	arrowroot	1 tsp
1	egg white	1
150 g	cooked giant prawns, shells removed and reserved, prawns deveined and finely diced	5 oz

Rinse the fish thoroughly and pat it dry on paper towels. Pour the soy sauce, light sesame oil and 1 tablespoon of the rice vinegar into a bowl. Using a garlic press, squeeze the juice from the ginger into the bowl. Whisk these together to make a marinade. Sit the fish, belly side down, on a dish, pour the marinade inside it, and leave it to marinate for about 1 hour.

Meanwhile, prepare the stuffing. Put the rice and 17.5 cl (6 fl oz) of water in a small saucepan and bring to the boil over medium-high heat. Reduce the heat, cover the saucepan and simmer the rice until the liquid has been absorbed and the rice is tender — about 20

minutes. Set the rice aside to cool. Heat the oil in a small frying pan and gently cook the mushrooms, covered, for about 10 minutes. Remove the lid and drain off any liquid. Set the mushrooms aside to cool.

Using a food processor or a mortar and pestle, reduce the raw prawns and the cooled rice to a paste. With a garlic press, squeeze the juices of the garlic and ginger into the prawn paste. Blend the ingredients thoroughly, then beat in the salt, arrowroot and egg white to form a fluffy mass.

Fold the diced cooked prawns into the raw prawn mixture, together with the shiitake mushrooms. Add the cooked sea bass roe, if you are using any, and stir the stuffing thoroughly.

Pour off any unabsorbed marinade from the sea bass, and pack the stuffing into the fish. Wrap the fish in a 30 cm (12 inch) square of muslin and secure it with thread. Sit the fish on its belly on the rack of a fish kettle. Pour 2.5 cm (1 inch) of boiling water into the kettle, keeping the water level below the belly of the fish.

Cover the kettle and steam the fish over medium heat for 25 to 35 minutes, or until the flesh in the middle of the back is opaque. Remove the bass from the kettle and leave it to rest, again on its belly, for 5 minutes, then invert it on to its back to drain and cool. When the fish is cool enough to handle, turn it back on to its belly, unwrap it and carefully remove the skin, leaving the head intact. Leave the fish in the refrigerator to chill thoroughly for about 1 hour.

While the fish is chilling, make the stock. Put all reserved bones and trimmings, the carrot, leek, shallot, garlic clove, parsley, tarragon, peppercorns, wine and the remaining rice vinegar in a large saucepan. Add 30 cl (½ pint) of water and simmer the liquid for 20 minutes. Strain the stock through muslin, then return it to the pan and simmer until it is reduced to about 6 tablespoons. Dissolve the gelatine in the reduced stock *(page 13)* and set it aside until it cools and begins to set — about 20 minutes.

Place the chilled fish on a serving platter. As soon as the aspic has just begun to set, brush some of it all over the fish. Place the fish in the refrigerator for 5 minutes, then garnish it with rows of white and black sesame seeds. Spoon over the remaining aspic. Set the olive halves in the fish's eye sockets. Chill the bass for at least 2 hours before serving it, garnished with whole cooked prawns, if you wish.

EDITOR'S NOTE: *To bone and gut a bass through the back, slit it from head to tail on either side of the dorsal fin, and work the blade of a small, flexible knife round the rib cage of the fish. Cut the backbone at the head and tail ends with kitchen scissors, leaving both the head and tail in position. Pull out and discard the backbone, gut, entrails and gills, then rinse the fish. Alternatively, you can ask your fishmonger to bone the fish for you.*

If you do not have a fish kettle or steamer pan of suitable size, wrap the fish in a double layer of oiled cooking foil instead of muslin. Sit the fish on a rack in a roasting pan, pour in 2.5 cm (1 inch) of boiling water, and steam it for 25 minutes. Leave the fish to cool in the foil.

Sea Bass Stuffed with Spinach and Mushrooms

Serves 6 as a main course
Working time: about 45 minutes
Total time: about 5 hours
(includes chilling)

Calories **140**
Protein **21g**
Cholesterol **65mg**
Total fat **4g**
Saturated fat **2g**
Sodium **435mg**

200 g	spinach, washed and stemmed	7 oz
4	raw Dublin Bay prawns, peeled	4
15 g	unsalted butter	½ oz
1	shallot, finely chopped	1
60 g	button mushrooms, chopped	2 oz
½ tsp	chopped fresh thyme	½ tsp
2	egg whites	2
1 tsp	salt	1 tsp
	white pepper	
90 g	whiting fillet, skinned, cut into pieces	3 oz
1 tbsp	double cream	1 tbsp
750 g	sea bass, boned and gutted through the back, head and tail left intact	1½ lb
2 tbsp	white wine vinegar	2 tbsp
1	small carrot, finely sliced	1
1	small onion, sliced	1
2	parsley stalks	2
1	thyme sprig	1
½	bay leaf	½

Blanch the spinach in a large pan of boiling water for 1 minute. Drain the spinach, refresh it under cold running water and drain it again. Set five of the leaves aside on paper towels to dry; squeeze the remaining spinach dry, then chop it finely. Arrange the reserved leaves flat on a work surface side by side, overlapping their edges. Place the prawns, end to end, in a line across the spinach leaves, and tightly roll them round the prawns into a cigar shape. Set the roll aside.

Melt the butter in a small, heavy-bottomed saucepan, add the shallot, cover the pan and soften the shallot over medium heat for 2 minutes. Add the chopped mushrooms and thyme, and cook, uncovered, for 5 minutes to evaporate the moisture. Remove the pan from the heat, stir in the chopped spinach and one egg white, and season with ¼ teaspoon of the salt and some white pepper. Allow the mixture to cool.

Place the whiting in a food processor and process it until smooth. Add the remaining egg white a little at a time while the processor is running. Add the cream, ¼ teaspoon of the remaining salt and some pepper, and process until smooth. Allow the mixture to cool.

Moisten a 30 cm (12 inch) square of muslin and stretch it out on the work surface. Rinse the sea bass well and pat it dry with paper towels. Sit it upright on its belly and spoon the spinach mixture into the cavity, smoothing it with the back of the spoon. Spoon the whiting mixture over the spinach mixture and form a channel along the centre. Place the spinach-prawn roll in the channel. Push the sides of the fish together to enclose the stuffing, wrap the fish tightly in the muslin and secure the muslin with thread.

Put the white wine vinegar, carrot, onion, parsley stalks, thyme, bay leaf and the remaining salt in a small fish kettle with 1.75 litre (3 pints) of water. Bring the liquid to the boil and simmer it for 3 to 4 minutes. Lower the sea bass into the bouillon, set it on the rack and simmer it gently for 15 minutes. Remove the fish kettle from the heat and allow the fish to cool in its cooking liquid — about 1 hour. Unwrap the sea bass carefully and chill it for about 3 hours before serving.

SUGGESTED ACCOMPANIMENTS: *wild rice and mushrooms; parslied carrots.*

EDITOR'S NOTE: *To bone and gut a bass through the back, slit it from head to tail on either side of the dorsal fin, and work the blade of a small, flexible knife round the rib cage. Cut the backbone at the head and tail ends with kitchen scissors, leaving both head and tail in position. Pull out and discard the backbone, gut, entrails and gills, then rinse the fish. Alternatively, ask your fishmonger to bone the fish for you.*

If you do not have a fish kettle, wrap the fish and the carrot, onion, parsley, thyme, bay leaf and salt (omit the vinegar) tightly in a double layer of oiled cooking foil, instead of muslin. Sit the fish on a rack in a roasting pan, pour in 2.5 cm (1 inch) of boiling water and steam the fish for 20 minutes. Leave the fish to cool in the foil.

Curried Prawn Pâté

MAKE THIS PÂTÉ THE DAY BEFORE SERVING TO ALLOW
THE FLAVOURS TO DEVELOP

Serves 8 as a first course
Working time: about 45 minutes
Total time: about 12 hours (includes chilling)

Calories **125**
Protein **17g**
Cholesterol **100mg**
Total fat **4g**
Saturated fat **1g**
Sodium **265**

175 g	unpeeled cooked prawns	6 oz
1 tbsp	virgin olive oil	1 tbsp
1	onion, finely chopped	1
1	garlic clove, finely chopped	1
1 tbsp	paprika	1 tbsp
½ tsp	cayenne pepper	½ tsp
½ tsp	ground turmeric	½ tsp
4½ tsp	coriander seeds, ground	4½ tsp
1 tsp	peppercorns, ground	1 tsp
½ tsp	fenugreek seeds, ground	½ tsp
½ tsp	fennel seeds, ground	½ tsp
1 tsp	finely chopped fresh ginger root	1 tsp
1 tbsp	tomato paste	1 tbsp
1 tsp	sugar	1 tsp
1 tbsp	creamed coconut	1 tbsp
750 g	haddock fillets, skinned and cut into 2.5 cm (1 inch) chunks	1½ lb
1	lemon, juice only	1
30 g	fresh breadcrumbs	1 oz
1	egg	1
	freshly ground black pepper	
	fresh coriander leaves, for garnish (optional)	

Peel the prawns. Place the shells and any roe in a small saucepan; cover the prawns and refrigerate them until required. Pour ¼ litre (8 fl oz) of water over the prawn shells, then heat gently until the liquid is just boiling. Cover the saucepan, reduce the heat and simmer the shells for 15 minutes. Strain the shell stock and discard the shells. Pour the strained stock back into the saucepan and boil it, uncovered, until it is reduced to 4 tablespoons.

Preheat the oven to 180°C (350°F or Mark 4). Line an 18 by 9 by 6 cm (7 by 3½ by 2½ inch) loaf tin with greaseproof paper *(page 34)* and set it aside.

Heat the oil in a heavy-bottomed saucepan. Add the onion and garlic and cook them gently until they are just soft — about 3 minutes. Stir in the paprika, cayenne pepper, turmeric, coriander seeds, peppercorns, fenugreek, fennel and ginger. Cook for a further minute, then stir in the tomato paste, sugar, coconut and reduced stock. Gently mix in the haddock. Cover the pan and simmer the fish for about 10 minutes, until it is cooked but still firm. Remove the pan from the heat and leave the haddock to cool slightly.

Place the cooled fish with all the cooking juices and spices in a food processor or blender and add the lemon juice, fresh breadcrumbs and egg. Process the ingredients to a smooth purée, then transfer the purée to a bowl. Reserve a few whole peeled prawns for garnish; roughly chop the remainder and mix them into the haddock purée. Season the purée with some freshly ground black pepper.

▶

Spoon the pâté into the prepared loaf tin, smoothing the surface with the back of the spoon. Cover the tin loosely with foil, stand it in a large roasting pan or dish, and pour boiling water into the roasting pan to come two thirds of the way up the side of the tin. Bake the pâté until it is firm to the touch — about 1¼ hours. Weight the pâté with a 500 g (1 lb) weight *(page 19)* and leave it to cool — about 2 hours — then chill it overnight in the refrigerator.

To serve the pâté, turn it out on to a board or serving platter and garnish it with the reserved whole prawns and, if desired, some fresh coriander leaves.

SUGGESTED ACCOMPANIMENT: *poppadoms.*

Three-Fish Pie with Prawns

MAKE THIS PIE THE DAY BEFORE YOU WISH
TO SERVE IT.

Serves 20 as a first course
Working time: about 1 hour and 15 minutes
Total time: about 12 hours (includes chilling)

Calories **235**
Protein **21g**
Cholesterol **75mg**
Total fat **9g**
Saturated fat **2g**
Sodium **250mg**

500 g	whole lemon sole or plaice	1 lb
1 kg	haddock fillets, skinned	2 lb
500 g	middle-cut piece of fresh salmon, or 750 g (1½ lb) pink trout	1 lb
6	large raw prawns	6
1	lemon	1
1	onion, sliced	1
1	small bunch parsley	1
1	fresh thyme sprig	1
1	fresh rosemary sprig	1
1 tsp	salt	1 tsp
30 cl	dry white wine	½ pint
	white pepper	
1	egg, beaten	1
3 tsp	powdered gelatine	3 tsp
Hot-water crust pastry		
350 g	plain flour	12 oz
¼ tsp	salt	¼ tsp
1	egg yolk	1
125 g	polyunsaturated margarine	4 oz

Using a very sharp filleting knife, remove the four fillets from the sole, then carefully remove and discard the skin. Set the fillets aside. Put the bones and head into a large saucepan. Cut the haddock flesh into long strips, about 4 cm (1½ inch) wide, and set them aside. Cut the salmon flesh away from the bones, discarding the skin and any small bones; add the larger bones to the saucepan. Cut the salmon into long strips, about 4 cm (1½ inch) wide, and set them aside.

Remove the shells from the prawns and add the shells to the saucepan. Make a long slit along the back of each prawn and remove the black intestinal tract. Rinse the prawns well under cold water, then set them aside with the other fish. Cover all of the fish and refrigerate it while you make the stock and pastry.

Pour 1.75 litres (3 pints) of cold water into the saucepan to cover the fish trimmings. Cut half of the lemon into slices and add these to the pan with the onion, parsley, thyme, rosemary, half of the salt and the white wine. Set the pan over medium heat and bring the liquid almost to the boil (do not allow it to boil as this would make the stock cloudy). Reduce the heat to low and simmer the stock gently for 20 minutes, skimming off the scum as it rises to the surface.

Meanwhile, preheat the oven to 220°C (425°F or Mark 7). Thoroughly grease a 30 by 7.5 by 7.5 cm (12 by 3 by 3 inch) oblong hinged pie mould.

To make the pastry, sift the flour and salt into a mixing bowl and make a well in the centre; drop the egg yolk into the well. Put the margarine in a pan with 12.5 cl (4 fl oz) of cold water. Heat gently until the margarine melts, then bring to the boil. Immediately, pour the hot liquid into the flour, stirring with a round-bladed knife to form a soft dough. Knead the dough on a lightly floured surface until smooth.

Cut off one third of the pastry, wrap it in plastic film and set it aside. Roll the remainder out to an oblong measuring about 45 by 22 cm (18 by 9 inches). Line the pie mould with the pastry, pressing it firmly into position across the base and up the sides; leave a little excess overhanging the edge of the mould.

Fill the lined mould with the fish: place half of the haddock strips in the bottom, then add the prawns, sole fillets, salmon strips and finally the remaining haddock strips. Season each layer with a little of the remaining salt, some white pepper, and some juice squeezed from the remaining lemon half.

Roll out the remaining pastry to an oblong large enough to cover the top of the pie. Brush the overhanging pastry with a little cold water, then place the pastry lid in position; press the edges of the pie firmly together to seal them. Using kitchen scissors, trim the edges of the pie to neaten them. Re-knead and re-roll the trimmings to an oblong measuring about 10 by 15 cm (4 by 6 inches). Cut eight strips from the pastry, each one 5 mm (½ inch) wide. Brush the top of the pie with some of the beaten egg. Decorate the top with the pastry strips, arranged in a lattice pattern. Trim the ends of the strips, then brush the pie again with egg. Reserve the remaining egg. Make three evenly spaced holes in the top of the pie.

Place the pie on a baking sheet and bake it for 20 minutes, then reduce the oven temperature to 190°C (375°F or Mark 5) and continue cooking for 40 minutes. Remove the pie from the oven and carefully remove the sides of the mould. Brush the sides of the pie with the remaining beaten egg and return it to the oven for about 10 minutes, until it is golden-brown all over.

Remove the pie from the oven and allow it to cool for 1 hour, then refrigerate it until cold — 3 to 4 hours.

Strain the fish stock through a nylon sieve lined with a double thickness of muslin. Return the stock to the saucepan. Bring it to the boil over medium heat and allow it to simmer gently until it is reduced to 30 cl (½ pint) — about 20 minutes. Meanwhile, put 3 tablespoons of cold water into a small bowl, sprinkle over the gelatine, and set it aside to soften. When the stock is reduced, add the softened gelatine to the hot stock and stir until it is completely dissolved. Allow the stock to become quite cold, but not set.

Using a small funnel, carefully pour the fish stock into the pie through the holes in the top. Refrigerate the pie overnight before serving it.

EDITOR'S NOTE: *If preferred, ready-filleted sole or plaice, haddock and salmon may be used in the recipe, with 60 cl (1 pint) of unsalted fish stock (page 11) reduced to 30 cl (½ pint), as described above.*

Layered Crab Terrine with Mushrooms

Serves 8 as a first course
Working time: about 45 minutes
Total time: about 5 hours and 30 minutes (includes chilling)

Calories **120**
Protein **15g**
Cholesterol **55mg**
Total fat **5g**
Saturated fat **1g**
Sodium **340mg**

1	large crab, dressed, brown and white meat kept separate (about 500 g/1 lb crab meat)	1
60 cl	unsalted vegetable stock (recipe, page 10)	1 pint
10 g	unsalted butter	⅓ oz
2 tsp	Dijon mustard	2 tsp
175 g	open mushrooms, wiped clean, finely chopped	6 oz
1 tsp	fresh lemon juice	1 tsp
6 tbsp	dry sherry	6 tbsp
½ tsp	salt	½ tsp
3½ tsp	powdered gelatine	3½ tsp
60 g	celery heart, finely sliced	2 oz
2 tbsp	crème fraîche or thick Greek yogurt	2 tbsp
1 tbsp	tomato paste	1 tbsp
½ tsp	ground coriander	½ tsp
	freshly ground black pepper	

Break up any large pieces of white crab meat and add sufficient of the smaller pieces of white meat to the brown to give equal quantities of each type of meat. Chill the crab meat until required.

In a wide, shallow saucepan, bring the vegetable stock to the boil over high heat. Reduce the heat to low and boil the stock gently until it is reduced to one third of its volume — about 15 minutes.

Meanwhile, melt the butter in a non-stick frying pan over medium heat and stir in the mustard. Add the mushrooms, lemon juice, 1 tablespoon of the sherry and ¼ teaspoon of the salt, and stir lightly. Cover the pan and cook the mushrooms until they give up their juice — 1 to 2 minutes. Remove the lid from the pan and continue to cook over medium heat, stirring continuously, until the mushroom mixture is soft and all excess moisture has evaporated — about 10 minutes. Set the mixture aside to cool.

If the reduced stock is cloudy, pass it through a sieve lined with a double layer of muslin. Dissolve 2 teaspoons of the gelatine in 3 tablespoons of the reduced stock, following the method on page 13. Add the dissolved gelatine to the remaining stock, together with 3 tablespoons of the remaining sherry and the remaining salt. Set the jelly aside to cool.

Rinse a 22 by 12 by 6 cm (9 by 5 by 2½ inch) loaf tin with cold water. Pour just enough of the cooled jelly into the tin to coat the bottom thinly. Chill the tin until the jelly has set — 10 to 15 minutes. Stir the white crab meat and the sliced celery into the remaining jelly. Spoon this mixture into the tin to form an even layer. Return the tin to the refrigerator until the white crab meat layer is set — about 30 minutes.

Process the brown crab meat in a food processor or blender until smooth. Add the mushroom mixture and blend again. Blend in the *crème fraîche*, the tomato paste, ground coriander and some pepper. Dissolve the remaining gelatine in the remaining sherry, again following the method on page 13, then pour this into the brown meat mixture with the processor motor running, to produce a mousse.

Spoon the brown meat mousse into the mould, smoothing the surface with the back of the spoon. Chill the terrine until it is set — about 3 hours.

To unmould the terrine, dip its base and sides in hot water for 5 seconds, then invert it on to a flat plate or board. Serve the terrine cut into slices.

Devilled Crab

Serves 4 as a first course
Working (and total) time: about 20 minutes

Calories **125**
Protein **17g**
Cholesterol **85mg**
Total fat **5g**
Saturated fat **1g**
Sodium **390mg**

1	crab, dressed, brown and white meat kept separate (about 300 g/10 oz crab meat)	1
3 tbsp	plain low-fat yogurt	3 tbsp
25 g	fine fresh wholemeal breadcrumbs	¾ oz
½	lemon, finely grated rind and juice only	½
1 tsp	Dijon mustard	1 tsp
2 tsp	Worcester sauce	2 tsp
½ tsp	paprika	½ tsp
⅛ tsp	salt	⅛ tsp
½	hard-boiled egg, yolk and white separated, white finely chopped	½

Mash the white crab meat with the back of a fork to break it into separate strands, then set it aside. Place the brown crab meat in a food processor. Add the yogurt, breadcrumbs, lemon rind and juice, mustard, Worcester sauce, paprika and salt, and process to a smooth purée. Transfer the purée to a bowl, and stir in the white crab meat. Turn the crab into a serving dish.

Press the egg yolk through a sieve. Sprinkle the egg yolk and egg white over the devilled crab and serve it at room temperature.

SUGGESTED ACCOMPANIMENT: *Melba toast.*

Scallop Timbales with Grated Orange Rind

Serves 6 as a first course
Working time: about 40 minutes
Total time: about 3 hours (includes marinating)

Calories **90**
Protein **12g**
Cholesterol **30mg**
Total fat **3g**
Saturated fat **2g**
Sodium **290mg**

350 g	shelled scallops, bright white connective tissue removed	12 oz
½ tsp	coriander seeds	½ tsp
1 tbsp	vodka	1 tbsp
1	orange, juice and ¼ tsp grated rind only	1
60 g	crème fraîche	2 oz
60 g	thick Greek yogurt	2 oz
¼ tsp	salt	¼ tsp
¼ tsp	white pepper	¼ tsp
1	egg white	1

Separate the corals from the scallops and set the corals aside. Slice two of the scallop cushions horizontally into three round sections, and place them in a small dish. Put the remaining scallop cushions in the refrigerator to chill.

In a small, heavy-bottomed frying pan, toast the coriander seeds over medium heat, shaking the pan continuously until the seeds become aromatic — about 30 seconds. Remove the frying pan from the heat and immediately stir the toasted coriander seeds into the vodka. Allow the vodka to infuse for 10 minutes. Strain the flavoured vodka and mix it with 1 tablespoon of the orange juice. Spoon this marinade over the six scallop rounds, coating them evenly. Cover the dish and put it in the refrigerator for at least 2 hours for the scallop rounds to marinate.

Meanwhile, poach the corals gently in the remaining orange juice over low heat for 1 to 2 minutes, until they are firm. Drain the corals and dice them finely, then set them aside in the refrigerator. Purée the chilled whole scallop cushions in a food processor. Add the *crème fraîche* and yogurt, and blend well. Transfer the purée to a bowl, cover it and chill it for 30 minutes. Stir in the salt, the white pepper and the grated orange rind, then chill the scallop mousseline again, covered, until the sliced scallops are ready.

Preheat the oven to 180°C (350°F or Mark 4).

Remove the scallop slices from their marinade and drain them on paper towels; reserve the marinade to dress an accompanying salad, if you wish. Whisk the egg white until it forms soft peaks, then gently fold it into the chilled mousseline, together with the diced corals. Spoon half of the mousseline into six very lightly greased 7 cl (2½ fl oz) timbale moulds. Place a scallop slice on top of the mousseline in each mould, then spoon in the remaining mousseline. Tap the moulds on the work surface to even out the mousseline. Stand the timbales in a large roasting pan and pour boiling water into the pan to come two thirds of the way up the sides of the timbales. Cover them with a piece of non-stick parchment paper or foil, and bake them in the oven until they are firm to the touch in the centre — about 35 minutes.

Leave the timbales to rest for about 5 minutes. Gently loosen the edges with a knife and invert the timbales on to a double thickness of paper towels, to absorb any excess liquid. Serve the timbales warm.

SUGGESTED ACCOMPANIMENT: *mixed green salad.*

EDITOR'S NOTE: *The timbales may also be served chilled: unmould them just before serving.*

Spinach and Crab Terrine

Serves 8 as a first course
Working time: about 40 minutes
Total time: about 3 hours (includes chilling)

Calories **150**
Protein **16g**
Cholesterol **50mg**
Total fat **7g**
Saturated fat **1g**
Sodium **300mg**

250 g	spinach, washed and stemmed	8 oz
30 g	polyunsaturated margarine	1 oz
30 g	plain flour	1 oz
30 cl	semi-skimmed milk	½ pint
¼ tsp	salt	¼ tsp
	white pepper	
1	large crab, dressed, brown and white meat kept separate (about 500 g/1 lb crab meat)	1
2 tbsp	fresh lemon juice	2 tbsp
3 tsp	powdered gelatine	3 tsp
	lemon wedges, for garnish	
	cucumber slices, for garnish	
	lettuce leaves, for garnish	

Blanch the spinach in a large pan of boiling water for 1 minute, then drain it and refresh it under cold running water. Drain the spinach in a colander, pressing it with the back of a spoon to remove all the water. Chop the spinach in a blender or food processor.

Melt the margarine in a saucepan. Add the flour and cook it over low heat for 1 minute, stirring continuously. Gradually pour in the milk, still stirring continuously, and cook over medium heat until the sauce boils. Reduce the heat and simmer the sauce for 2 minutes. Stir in the salt and some pepper, then divide the sauce equally between two bowls. Add the white crab meat, the spinach and 1 tablespoon of the lemon juice to one bowl of sauce, and mix thoroughly. Add the brown crab meat and the remaining lemon juice to the second bowl, and mix well.

Dissolve the gelatine in 4 tablespoons of water, following the instructions on page 13. Divide the gelatine between the white crab and the brown crab mixtures, and mix it in thoroughly.

Spoon half of the white crab meat and spinach mixture into a greased 18 by 7.5 by 6 cm (7 by 3 by 2½ inch) loaf tin, levelling it with the back of the spoon. Chill the tin in the refrigerator until the mixture is just setting — about 15 minutes. Spoon the brown crab meat mixture into the tin and level the surface, then gently spoon the remaining white crab meat and spinach mixture over the brown crab meat. Chill the terrine until it is firm — about 2 hours.

To unmould the terrine, dip the base and sides of the tin in hot water for 5 seconds, then invert it on to a flat serving plate. Serve the terrine garnished with the lemon wedges, cucumber slices and lettuce leaves.

3 Blanched vegetable morsels and poached quail's eggs, set in a golden vegetable aspic, make a picture-perfect first course (recipe, page 92).

Vegetables in Novel Guises

Few dishes express the new style of cooking as well as the vegetable pâtés and terrines on the following pages. Light, fresh, colourful and healthy, they are based on ingredients that are not only rich in valuable nutrients, but low in calories and virtually devoid of fat.

Delicate timbales of fresh green peas and mange-tout *(page 90)*, an aromatic terrine of wild and cultivated mushrooms set in a creamy mushroom mousse *(page 100)*, or individual red pepper ramekins *(page 99)*, would make an elegant and intriguing prelude to a sophisticated dinner party menu; a vibrantly spiced black-eyed pea pâté *(page 108)*, or puréed carrots spiked with balsamic vinegar, fresh herbs and cumin *(page 89)*, provide a simple, quickly prepared picnic treat or snack. Some vegetable terrines and pâtés are substantial enough to form a main course for a lunch or supper; many could serve either as a separate vegetable course or as an accompaniment to a main dish of poultry or meat.

The few recipes in this chapter that incorporate meat or poultry do so in only modest quantities. A little bacon, for instance, lends its distinctive flavour to the mushroom and chestnut pâté on page 93 and the stuffed cabbage terrine on page 96, which is further enriched by a wrapping of caul. The mushroom and parsley mousselines on page 91 are based on pounded chicken breast, although similar mousselines could be made with whiting or other lean white fish.

Since vegetables take centre stage, their quality is all important. Use only vegetables in the peak of condition, and take advantage of those at their seasonal best. The moulded spinach and pasta terrine on page 103, for instance, is an ideal dish for the hot days of high summer, when the finest fresh basil and sun-ripened tomatoes are available. In winter, when a wide selection of genuinely first-rate produce is harder to come by, pâtés based on pulses, or the potatoes layered with Gruyère and onions *(page 102)*, are inspired, and inviting, ways to begin a meal.

To take full advantage of their fresh colour and flavour, vegetable terrines and pâtés are best prepared on the day they are to be served. Those intended to be eaten cold should be wrapped closely in plastic film and kept in the refrigerator until shortly before serving time. Large pâtés are best given about 30 minutes at a cool room temperature to take the chill off them; smaller items will rise to an ideal serving temperature in about half that time.

Spicy Cauliflower Pâté

Serves 10 as a first course
Working time: about 30 minutes
Total time: about 1 hour and 15 minutes

Calories **70**
Protein **1g**
Cholesterol **0mg**
Total fat **5g**
Saturated fat **1g**
Sodium **200mg**

60 g	polyunsaturated margarine	2 oz
1	onion, finely chopped	1
2 tsp	tomato paste	2 tsp
2	large tomatoes, skinned, seeded and chopped	2
1	garlic clove, finely chopped	1
¼ tsp	ground cumin	¼ tsp
¼ tsp	ground turmeric	¼ tsp
¼ tsp	paprika, plus a little extra for garnish	¼ tsp
¼ tsp	garam masala	¼ tsp
⅛ tsp	chili powder	⅛ tsp
½ tsp	salt	½ tsp
1	large cauliflower (about 750g/1 ½ lb), broken into small florets	1
2 tsp	chopped fresh ginger root	2 tsp
	freshly ground black pepper	

Melt the margarine in a large, heavy-bottomed saucepan over medium heat, then add the onion and sauté it for about 1 minute. Add the tomato paste, chopped tomatoes, garlic, cumin, turmeric, paprika, garam masala, chili powder and salt. Cook the mixture, stirring it frequently, until the tomatoes have broken down — about 5 minutes. Add the cauliflower florets and mix them in thoroughly. Cover the pan and cook the florets gently until they soften and begin to break up — 15 to 20 minutes; stir them regularly during this time to ensure that they do not stick to the bottom of the pan, and add a tablespoon of water, if necessary. Add the chopped ginger root to the pan for the last few minutes of cooking.

Allow the mixture to cool slightly, then blend it in a food processor or blender until it is smooth. Season the purée with freshly ground black pepper. Turn it into a serving bowl, smooth the top and leave it to cool, then chill it in the refrigerator for about 15 minutes.

Just before serving, place a few strips of non-stick parchment paper over the pâté in a decorative pattern. Sift a little paprika over the exposed surfaces as a garnish, then remove the paper strips and serve.

SUGGESTED ACCOMPANIMENT: *warm naan or pitta bread.*

EDITOR'S NOTE: *The pâté may be kept in the refrigerator for a few hours, if necessary, though it should be eaten on the day that it is made. Remove it from the refrigerator half an hour before serving as it is best eaten at about room temperature.*

Cauliflower Terrine with a Spinach-Herb Sauce

Serves 8 as a first course
Working time: about 30 minutes
Total time: about 4 hours (includes cooling)

Calories **115**
Protein **10g**
Cholesterol **70mg**
Total fat **7g**
Saturated fat **6g**
Sodium **200mg**

2	lemon slices	2
350 g	small cauliflower florets	12 oz
2	eggs	2
1	egg white	1
35 cl	skimmed milk	12 fl oz
	freshly ground black pepper	
½ tsp	dry mustard	½ tsp
¼ tsp	grated nutmeg	¼ tsp
90 g	matured Cheddar cheese, finely grated	3 oz
	assorted fresh salad leaves, for garnish	
Spinach-herb sauce		
60 g	spinach, washed and stemmed	2 oz
60 g	watercress, washed and stemmed	2 oz
2 tsp	chopped parsley	2 tsp
1 tsp	chopped fresh tarragon	1 tsp
1 tbsp	finely cut chives	1 tbsp
1 tbsp	fresh lemon juice	1 tbsp
12.5 cl	low-fat fromage frais	4 fl oz
12.5 cl	plain low-fat yogurt	4 fl oz
¼ tsp	salt	¼ tsp
	freshly ground black pepper	
	cayenne pepper	

Lightly grease a 21 by 11 by 6 cm (8½ by 4½ by 2½ inch) non-stick loaf tin. Preheat the oven to 180°C (350°F or Mark 4).

Put the lemon slices in a saucepan of water, bring the water to the boil and add the cauliflower florets. Cover the saucepan, reduce the heat and simmer the florets for 3 minutes. Drain them well, discard the lemon slices and spread the florets out on paper towels to drain and cool completely.

Meanwhile, whisk the whole eggs, egg white, milk, a little black pepper, the mustard and the grated nutmeg together in a bowl. Layer the cauliflower florets in the prepared tin alternately with the grated Cheddar cheese, then pour the egg and milk mixture over them. Cover the tin lightly with foil and place it in a baking dish. Pour boiling water into the dish to come two thirds of the way up the side of the tin, and bake the terrine for about 50 minutes, or until it is set. Remove the tin from the baking dish and allow the terrine to cool completely.

Shortly before serving the terrine, prepare the sauce. Blanch the spinach and watercress together for 1 minute in a saucepan of boiling water. Drain them thoroughly; squeeze them out in paper towels to remove excess liquid. Using a sharp knife, chop the spinach and watercress very finely. Place them in a mixing bowl and add the parsley, tarragon, chives, lemon juice, *fromage frais*, yogurt, salt, some black pepper and some cayenne. Mix the ingredients together well. Transfer the sauce to a serving bowl.

Turn out the terrine on to a flat serving platter. Serve it sliced, garnished with the fresh salad leaves and accompanied by the sauce.

Broccoli and Blue Cheese Pâté

Serves 10 as a first course
Working time: about 30 minutes
Total time: about 1 hour

Calories **150**
Protein **6g**
Cholesterol **10mg**
Total fat **8g**
Saturated fat **5g**
Sodium **240mg**

350 g	broccoli	12 oz
60 g	polyunsaturated margarine	2 oz
1	leek, cleaned thoroughly to remove all grit, finely sliced	1
¼ tsp	grated nutmeg	¼ tsp
¼ tsp	salt	¼ tsp
	freshly ground black pepper	
60 g	blue cheese	2 oz
500 g	low-fat soft cheese	1 lb
60 g	low-fat fromage frais	2 oz
6 cl	vegetable aspic (recipe, page 13)	2 fl oz

Using a pair of kitchen scissors, trim six florets from the broccoli and blanch them for 30 seconds in a small pan of boiling water. Drain the florets and refresh them under cold running water. Set them aside for garnish Roughly chop the remaining broccoli.

Melt the margarine in a heavy-bottomed saucepan and add the chopped broccoli, the leek, nutmeg, salt, some black pepper and 1 tablespoon of water. Cover the pan and cook the vegetables until they soften — 5 to 8 minutes; stir them occasionally as they cook to prevent them from burning.

While the vegetables are cooking, mash the blue cheese in a bowl. Gradually incorporate the soft cheese until the two cheeses are well mixed. Set the bowl aside at room temperature.

Purée the cooked vegetables in a food processor until smooth, then transfer the purée to a large bowl and allow it to cool until it is tepid. Using a large fork, beat the cheese mixture into the vegetable purée. Transfer the pâté to a 1.25 litre (2 pint) oval mould and smooth the surface. Chill the pâté in the refrigerator for at least 30 minutes.

Meanwhile, combine the *fromage frais* and vegetable aspic in a bowl, and chill the mixture in the refrigerator until it is well thickened but not quite set — about 30 minutes. Remove the pâté from the refrigerator and pour the aspic mixture over the surface in a thin layer. Chill the pâté for a further 5 to 10 minutes, to set the aspic topping.

Cut the reserved broccoli florets in half lengthwise, so that they will lie flat. Arrange the broccoli florets on top of the pâté in the form of a tree. Serve the pâté on the day it is prepared.

SUGGESTED ACCOMPANIMENT: *granary rolls or Melba toast.*

Carrot and Herb Ramekins

Serves 4 as a first course
Working time: about 30 minutes
Total time: about 1 hour

Calories **120**
Protein **2g**
Cholesterol **0mg**
Total fat **9g**
Saturated fat **2g**
Sodium **410mg**

30 g	parsley	1 oz
30 g	chives	1 oz
45 g	polyunsaturated margarine	1 ½ oz
500 g	carrots, thinly sliced	1 lb
1	garlic clove, finely chopped	1
2 tsp	balsamic or sherry vinegar	2 tsp
½ tsp	grated lemon rind	½ tsp
1 tbsp	fresh lemon juice	1 tbsp
½ tsp	ground cumin	½ tsp
½ tsp	salt	½ tsp
	freshly ground black pepper	

Set aside four small parsley sprigs and a few chives for garnish. Chop the remainder.

Melt the margarine in a heavy-bottomed saucepan over medium heat. Add the carrots and cook them, covered, until they soften — about 10 minutes — stirring them occasionally to prevent them from burning. When they are almost cooked, add the garlic, vinegar, lemon rind and juice, and the cumin. Stir the contents of the pan well and continue cooking for a further 2 minutes. Add the chopped parsley and chives to the pan, stirring them in thoroughly.

Transfer the mixture to a food processor or blender and add the salt and some freshly ground black pepper. Process the ingredients to a purée. Spoon the purée into four individual ramekins and chill them in the refrigerator until the pâté has set — at least 30 minutes. Decorate the pâté with the reserved parsley sprigs and chives before serving.

SUGGESTED ACCOMPANIMENT: *wholemeal toast fingers.*

mould. Add the tomato juice to the remaining mixture in the pan and simmer it for 3 minutes. Transfer the mixture to a food processor and purée it to form a smooth sauce. Add ¼ teaspoon of the salt, some black pepper and the vinegar, then set the sauce aside.

Put the mint in a pan of water and bring the water to the boil. Add the peas and cook them, covered, until tender — about 10 minutes for fresh peas and 6 minutes for frozen. Drain the peas and refresh them under cold running water. Transfer them to the food processor and blend them to a smooth purée.

Dissolve the gelatine in 3 tablespoons of water *(page 13)*. Add the gelatine solution and 2 tablespoons of the *fromage frais* to the pea purée. Blend the mixture well, and season it with the remaining ¼ teaspoon of salt and some black pepper.

Whisk the egg white until it is stiff, then fold it into the pea purée. Spoon the mixture into the moulds and chill them for 30 minutes, or until the timbales are set.

Turn out the timbales on to individual plates and serve them with a little of the tomato sauce spooned round them. To feather the sauce, mix together the remaining *fromage frais* and the lemon juice. Divide 1 teaspoon of this mixture into a line of eight or nine small mounds positioned in the tomato sauce near the edge of each plate. Use the tip of a skewer to link each line of mounds in a decorative, scrolled pattern.

EDITOR'S NOTE: *Although feathering a sauce is not difficult, it is a good idea to practise before attempting it for guests.*

Pea and Tomato Timbales

Serves 6 as a first course
Working time: about 30 minutes
Total time: about 1 hour

Calories **65**
Protein **4g**
Cholesterol **0mg**
Total fat **4g**
Saturated fat **1g**
Sodium **140mg**

200 g	mange-tout, strings removed	7 oz
1 tbsp	safflower oil	1 tbsp
1	small onion, finely chopped	1
1 ½ tsp	chopped fresh oregano, or ½ tsp dried oregano	1 ½ tsp
250 g	tomatoes, skinned, seeded and chopped	8 oz
5 tbsp	tomato juice	5 tbsp
½ tsp	salt	½ tsp
	freshly ground black pepper	
1 tsp	red wine vinegar	1 tsp
1	mint sprig	1
350 g	fresh peas, shelled, or 125 g (4 oz) frozen peas	12 oz
1 tbsp	powdered gelatine	1 tbsp
4 tbsp	low-fat fromage frais	4 tbsp
1	egg white	1
¼ tsp	fresh lemon juice	¼ tsp

Lightly oil six 15 cl (¼ pint) dariole moulds.

Bring a saucepan of water to the boil, add the mange-tout, cover the pan and cook them for 3 minutes. Drain the mange-tout, refresh them under cold running water and pat them dry on paper towels. Line the sides of the prepared moulds with overlapping mange-tout, ensuring that they all face the same way and that their tips just touch the base of the moulds. Set the moulds aside.

Heat the oil in a small, heavy-bottomed pan and add the onion and oregano. Cover the pan and cook the onion over gentle heat for 3 to 4 minutes, until it is soft but not coloured. Add the tomatoes and stir the mixture briefly. Remove the pan from the heat.

Put a teaspoon of the tomato mixture into each

Skinning a Sweet Pepper

LOOSENING AND REMOVING THE SKIN. Place the pepper about 5 cm (2 inches) below a preheated grill. Turn the pepper as its sides become slightly scorched, until the skin has blistered all round. Transfer the pepper to a bowl and cover it with plastic film, or put the pepper in a paper bag and fold it shut; the trapped steam will make the pepper limp and loosen its skin. With a paring knife, peel off the pepper's skin in sections, from top to bottom. The pepper may then be seeded and deribbed.

Vegetables in a Chicken Mousseline

Serves 12 as a first course
Working time: about 2 hours
Total time: about 12 hours (includes chilling)

Calories **150** Protein **19g** Cholesterol **10mg** Total fat **6g** Saturated fat **3g** Sodium **200mg**		
30 g	unsalted butter	1 oz
1	large onion, finely chopped	1
250 g	chestnut mushrooms, wiped clean, roughly chopped	8 oz
250 g	long carrots, cut lengthwise into 5 mm (¼ inch) wide strips	8 oz
175 g	baby sweetcorn, trimmed if necessary	6 oz
3	long asparagus spears, trimmed and peeled	3
175 g	thin French beans, topped and tailed	6 oz
750 g	skinless boned chicken breasts	1½ lb
3	egg whites	3
¾ tsp	salt	¾ tsp
	white pepper	
375 g	thick Greek yogurt	12 oz
3 tbsp	chopped parsley	3 tbsp
1	large sweet red pepper, skinned (left), seeded and cut into 5 mm (¼ inch) wide strips	1

Melt the butter in a large, heavy frying pan over medium heat. Add the onion and cook it gently until it is soft but not brown — about 5 minutes. Add the mushrooms to the pan and cook them for 12 to 15 minutes, until they are soft and all the excess moisture has evaporated. Remove the pan from the heat and allow the mushroom mixture to cool while you prepare the remaining vegetables.

Steam the carrot strips and the baby sweetcorn for 15 to 20 minutes, until they are just tender. Transfer them from the steamer to paper towels to drain and cool. Steam the asparagus spears for 4 to 5 minutes, until they are just tender, then drain them on paper towels. Meanwhile, cook the French beans in boiling water for 3 to 4 minutes until they, too, are just tender. Pour them into a colander and refresh them under cold running water. Drain them well on paper towels.

Preheat the oven to 190°C (375°F or Mark 5). Line a 25 by 11 by 7.5 cm (10 by 4½ by 3 inch) loaf tin with non-stick parchment paper *(page 34)*.

Halve three of the baby sweetcorn lengthwise. Arrange the asparagus spears, the halved baby sweetcorn and some of the carrot strips diagonally across the bottom of the loaf tin; alternate carrot strips and beans lengthwise in the spaces that remain. Do not leave any gaps.

Remove all sinews from the chicken breasts and cut the flesh into large cubes. Place the cubes in a food processor with the egg whites, the salt and some white pepper. Process for about 1 minute, until a smooth paste is formed. Add the Greek yogurt and process for another minute, until the mixture is very smooth. Divide the chicken mousseline into two equal portions; mix the mushroom mixture into one half and the chopped parsley into the other.

Carefully spoon half of the parsley mousseline into the prepared loaf tin and spread it evenly. Cover it with a layer of alternating lines, arranged lengthwise, of red pepper strips and French beans. Spoon half of the mushroom mousseline on top of the pepper strips and beans, spreading it evenly. Arrange alternating lines of carrot strips and baby sweetcorn lengthwise on top of the mousseline. Spoon the remaining parsley mousseline into the tin and spread it evenly. Cover it with the remaining beans. Finally, spoon in the remaining mushroom mousseline and level the top.

Cover the terrine with a sheet of greased non-stick parchment paper. Stand it in a large, deep roasting pan or dish and pour in sufficient boiling water to come two thirds of the way up the side of the loaf tin. Cook the terrine for 30 to 40 minutes, until the surface is firm and a skewer inserted into the centre feels hot to the touch when removed.

Remove the terrine from the water bath and allow it to cool for about 1 hour. Refrigerate it overnight, until it is completely cold and firm.

Turn out the terrine on to a flat serving plate and remove the parchment paper. Use a sharp knife to slice the terrine for serving.

Spring Vegetables and Quail's Eggs in an Aspic Valentine

Serves 4 as a first course
Working time: about 45 minutes
Total time: about 3 hours (includes chilling)

Calories **55**
Protein **4g**
Cholesterol **55mg**
Total fat **2g**
Saturated fat **1g**
Sodium **315mg**

½ tsp	cider vinegar	½ tsp
4	quail's eggs	4
8	slender asparagus spears, trimmed to a length of 7.5 cm (3 inches)	8
8	baby sweetcorn	8
4	baby carrots, halved lengthwise	4
4	small broccoli florets	4
1 ½ tsp	powdered gelatine	1 ½ tsp
35 cl	vegetable aspic (recipe, page 13)	12 fl oz
6 tbsp	rosé or white wine	6 tbsp
4 to 6	small button mushrooms, halved, tossed in ½ tbsp fresh lemon juice	4 to 6
4	small chervil sprigs, plus chervil sprigs for garnish	4

Bring a shallow saucepan of water to the boil, add the vinegar and reduce the heat to a low simmer. Carefully break the quail's eggs into the water and poach them gently for about 3 minutes, or until the whites are just firm and the yolks are still creamy. Using a slotted spoon, transfer the poached eggs to a bowl of cold water to arrest the cooking. Neaten the edges of the whites with a pair of scissors. Leave the eggs in the water until you are ready to assemble the valentines.

Blanch the asparagus tips, sweetcorn and carrots in a saucepan of boiling, salted water for 2 minutes. Blanch the broccoli florets for 1 minute. Refresh the vegetables under cold running water and leave them to drain on paper towels.

Lightly wet the insides of four 12.5 cl (4 fl oz) heart-shaped moulds. Dissolve the gelatine in 1 tablespoon of water *(page 13)*. Mix the gelatine solution into the vegetable aspic, then stir in the wine. Pour a 5 mm (¼ inch) layer of wine aspic into the bottom of each mould. Chill the moulds in the refrigerator for 15 minutes, to set the aspic.

Using a slotted spoon, transfer the poached eggs to paper towels to drain. Pat the button mushroom halves dry on paper towels. Arrange the vegetables, eggs and small chervil sprigs decoratively in the prepared moulds, bearing in mind that the base of the mould will be the top of the valentine when it is turned out. Half fill the moulds with aspic, taking care not to disturb the position of the eggs and vegetables. Chill the moulds in the refrigerator for 15 minutes, then fill the moulds with the rest of the aspic and chill them for 2 hours, or until they are firmly set.

To serve, turn the valentines out on to individual plates and garnish them with sprigs of chervil.

Mushroom and Chestnut Pâté with Madeira

Serves 10 as a first course
Working time: about 30 minutes
Total time: about 11 hours (includes soaking and chilling)

Calories **130**
Protein **4g**
Cholesterol **5mg**
Total fat **5g**
Saturated fat **1g**
Sodium **100mg**

250 g	dried chestnuts, soaked overnight and drained	8 oz
30 g	dried mushrooms (optional)	1 oz
4 tbsp	Madeira	4 tbsp
1 tbsp	safflower oil	1 tbsp
750 g	button mushrooms, sliced	1 ½ lb
1 tbsp	sherry vinegar	1 tbsp
1 tsp	fresh thyme leaves	1 tsp
4 ½ tsp	low-sodium soy sauce or shoyu	4 ½ tsp
	freshly ground black pepper	
2	rashers streaky bacon (about 45 g/ 1 ½ oz), rind removed	2
1 tbsp	chopped parsley	1 tbsp

Place the chestnuts in a saucepan and cover them with fresh water. Bring the water to the boil, cover the saucepan and simmer the chestnuts for 30 to 45 minutes, until they are soft.

Meanwhile, soak the dried mushrooms, if you are using them, in 1 tablespoon of the Madeira and 4 tablespoons of tepid water for 20 minutes.

Drain the chestnuts and purée them in a food processor; leave the purée in the machine. Squeeze out as much moisture as possible from the dried mushrooms; strain the soaking liquid through a double layer of muslin or a coffee filter paper, and set it aside. Rinse the mushrooms thoroughly in a bowl of fresh water, squeezing them gently under the water to expel any grit. Pat the mushrooms dry on paper towels.

Heat the oil in a large, heavy frying pan. Add the fresh button mushrooms and cook them over medium heat until they are soft — about 5 minutes. Add the sherry vinegar, together with the dried mushrooms and their strained soaking liquid. Stir the mixture and cook it over medium heat for 1 minute. Pour in the remaining Madeira, increase the heat and cook the mixture fast for 3 minutes to burn off the alcohol.

Add the mushroom mixture and the thyme leaves to the chestnut purée in the food processor. Process until a smooth paste is formed. Add the soy sauce and some freshly ground black pepper, and process again briefly. Transfer the pâté to a serving bowl and chill it in the refrigerator for 2 hours.

Preheat the grill to hot, and cook the bacon until it is crisp, turning it once. Leave the bacon to cool, then crumble it over the top of the pâté. Sprinkle on the chopped parsley, and serve.

SUGGESTED ACCOMPANIMENTS: *celery sticks; crusty French bread or oatcakes.*

Courgette, Spinach and Carrot Terrine

Serves 8 as a main course
Working time: about 45 minutes
Total time: about 13 hours (includes chilling)

Calories **145**
Protein **7g**
Cholesterol **0mg**
Total fat **4g**
Saturated fat **1g**
Sodium **220mg**

2	large carrots, cut into 1 cm (½ inch) dice	2
2 tbsp	virgin olive oil	2 tbsp
1 kg	courgettes, grated	2½ lb
250 g	spring onions, chopped	8 oz
3	garlic cloves, finely chopped	3
750 g	fresh spinach, stems removed	1½ lb
4 tbsp	chopped fresh dill	4 tbsp
½ tsp	cayenne pepper	½ tsp
2 tsp	low-sodium soy sauce or shoyu	2 tsp
125 g	dry breadcrumbs	4 oz
4	egg whites, lightly whisked	4

Place the carrots in a saucepan and pour in cold water to cover them. Bring the water to the boil, reduce the heat and simmer the carrots until they are tender — about 5 minutes. Drain the carrots and refresh them under cold running water. Drain them again and set them aside on paper towels.

Heat the oil in a large, heavy frying pan. Add the courgettes and spring onions to the pan, and stir. Cover the pan and cook the vegetables over medium-low heat until they are tender — about 15 minutes; stir them occasionally during this time. Add the garlic, increase the heat slightly and continue cooking the vegetables, uncovered, until most of the moisture has evaporated — 8 to 10 minutes. Leave the mixture to cool a little, then transfer half of it to a food processor. Set the other half aside until required.

Preheat the oven to 170°C (325°F or Mark 3). Line a 22 by 12 by 6 cm (9 by 5 by 2½ inch) terrine with non-stick parchment paper (page 34).

Blanch the spinach for 1 minute in a large pan of boiling water. Drain the spinach and squeeze out as much moisture as possible. Chop the spinach coarsely and add it to the courgette mixture in the food processor. Add the dill, cayenne pepper and soy sauce, and process the mixture briefly. Add the breadcrumbs and process again, just enough to mix the ingredients. Transfer the purée to a bowl and stir in the reserved courgette mixture. Mix the egg whites in well.

Spread one third of the spinach mixture in the base of the prepared terrine. Arrange half of the carrots on top of the spinach mixture. Spread another third of the spinach mixture in the terrine and top it with the remaining carrots. Finally, add the remaining spinach mixture and level the top. Lightly press a piece of non-stick parchment paper on to the surface of the mixture, and cover the terrine with aluminium foil.

Stand the terrine in a large roasting pan and pour in sufficient boiling water to come two thirds of the way up the side of the loaf tin. Bake the terrine until the mixture is set and firm to the touch — about 1½ hours. Uncover the mould, turn off the heat and allow the terrine to cool in the oven. When the terrine is cold, cover it with plastic film and chill it overnight.

To unmould the terrine, turn it out on to a flat serving platter and peel off the parchment paper. Serve the terrine cut into slices.

SUGGESTED ACCOMPANIMENTS: *crusty bread; bean salad.*

Watercress and Broccoli Timbales

Serves 4 as a first course
Working time: about 40 minutes
Total time: about 4 hours (includes chilling)

Calories **65**
Protein **6g**
Cholesterol **60mg**
Total fat **4g**
Saturated fat **2g**
Sodium **75mg**

15 cl	vegetable aspic (recipe, page 13)	¼ pint
1	egg, hard-boiled	1
250 g	broccoli, trimmed	8 oz
2	small spring onions, trimmed and sliced	2
1	bunch watercress, coarse stems removed	1
6 tbsp	plain low-fat yogurt	6 tbsp
2 tbsp	single cream	2 tbsp
⅛ tsp	salt	⅛ tsp
	freshly ground black pepper	
2 tsp	powdered gelatine	2 tsp
1 tsp	fresh lemon juice	1 sp

Rinse out four 15 cl (¼ pint) dariole moulds with water; select moulds that measure about 6 cm (2½ inches) in diameter at the rim. Spoon a thin layer of vegetable aspic into the bottom of each damp mould, and chill the moulds for about 15 minutes, to set the aspic. Cut four thin slices, crosswise, from the widest part of the hard-boiled egg. Place one slice of egg in the bottom of each mould. Divide the remaining aspic among the moulds, spooning it over the egg slices. Chill the moulds for another 15 minutes.

Meanwhile, cook the broccoli in a pan of boiling water until it is just tender — 3 to 4 minutes. Drain the broccoli, refresh it under cold running water and drain it again very thoroughly. Put the broccoli in a food processor with the spring onions and three quarters of the watercress, and process until smooth. Add the yogurt, cream, salt and some freshly ground black pepper, and process again. Transfer the purée to a mixing bowl. Finely chop the remaining hard-boiled egg and stir it into the broccoli and watercress purée.

Dissolve the gelatine in 2 tablespoons of water and the lemon juice (page 13), and stir the dissolved gelatine thoroughly into the broccoli mixture. Spoon the mixture into the moulds and chill them for 3 to 4 hours, until the timbales are firmly set.

To serve, dip the base and sides of each mould in hot water for 2 or 3 seconds, and invert the timbales on to individual serving plates. Garnish the timbales with the remaining watercress.

Cabbage Stuffed with Chestnuts, Chard and Bacon

Serves 6 as a main course
Working time: about 45 minutes
Total time: about 3 hours

Calories **165**
Protein **10g**
Cholesterol **75mg**
Total fat **8g**
Saturated fat **2g**
Sodium **235mg**

8	fresh chestnuts	8
1 kg	firm cabbage	2 lb
1 tbsp	virgin olive oil	1 tbsp
2	small shallots, chopped	2
250 g	Swiss chard, stems removed, chopped	8 oz
100 g	spinach, stems removed, chopped	3½ oz
8	large sorrel leaves, stems removed, shredded	8
90 g	parsley, chopped	3 oz
1 tbsp	chopped fresh tarragon, or 1 tsp dried tarragon	1 tbsp
1	sprig summer savory	1
1	garlic clove, crushed	1
150 g	pork caul, soaked for 15 minutes in warm water mixed with 1 tsp of malt vinegar	5 oz
60 g	back bacon, rind removed, chopped	2 oz
60 g	fresh breadcrumbs	2 oz
½ tsp	quatre épices	½ tsp
	freshly ground black pepper	
2	small eggs, lightly beaten	2

First, peel and cook the chestnuts. Cut a cross in the hull of each chestnut and drop them into boiling water. Parboil the nuts for about 10 minutes, to loosen their hulls. Using a slotted spoon, lift the chestnuts, a few at a time, from the boiling water. Peel off the hulls and inner skins while the nuts are still warm. Discard the cooking water, return the peeled nuts to the pan, pour in fresh water to cover them and simmer for a further 30 minutes, to cook them through. Drain the chestnuts and break them up roughly.

Meanwhile, remove six outer leaves from the cabbage and blanch them for 1 to 2 minutes in boiling water, to make them supple. Drain the leaves thoroughly and lay them out on paper towels. Quarter the remaining cabbage; discard the hard stem and chop the leaves roughly. Put the chopped cabbage in a large, heavy-bottomed saucepan with 2 tablespoons of water. Cook the cabbage, tightly covered, over low heat until it is beginning to soften — about 20 minutes. While the cabbage is cooking, heat the oil in a heavy frying pan and sweat the shallots gently in the oil until they are transparent — about 5 minutes.

Add the chard and spinach to the cabbage and cook for a further 5 minutes, to soften them. Remove the pan from the heat and stir in the sorrel, parsley, tarragon, summer savory, shallots, garlic and chestnuts. Transfer the mixture to a large bowl and set it aside.

Preheat the oven to 170°C (325°F or Mark 3). Remove the caul from its soaking water and pat it dry on paper towels. Stretch it out as thinly as possible and drape it over a round terrine or soufflé dish measuring about 18 cm (7 inches) in diameter. Press the caul gently into the terrine to line the base and sides, and leave the edges of it overhanging the rim of the dish. Arrange the reserved cabbage leaves inside the terrine, overlapping them to line the dish completely; again, allow the edges of the leaves to overhang the rim of the dish.

Process the bacon briefly in a food processor. Using

a wooden spoon, mix the bacon into the cabbage mixture, together with the breadcrumbs, *quatre épices* and some freshly ground black pepper. Thoroughly mix in the beaten eggs. Turn the filling into the prepared terrine, packing it down tightly and mounding it slightly in the centre. Fold the overhanging cabbage leaves over the filling, pressing them down well, then drape and fold the edges of the caul over the top, tucking them down inside the edges of the terrine.

Place the terrine in a large, deep roasting pan and pour in sufficient boiling water to come two thirds of the way up the side of the terrine. Bake the terrine for 1½ hours, or until a skewer inserted into the middle meets with little resistance, then increase the oven temperature to 220°C (425°F or Mark 7) and continue to bake the terrine until it is lightly browned on top — about 30 minutes more.

Carefully pour off and discard all the fat at the top of the terrine. Invert the terrine first on to a flat plate, then back on to a chopping board so that it is the right way up. Serve the terrine sliced or cut into wedges.

EDITOR'S NOTE: *If sorrel leaves are unavailable, increase the quantity of spinach to 125 g (4 oz).*

Red Pepper, Spinach and Mushroom Loaf

Serves 6 as a main course
Working time: about 1 hour and 30 minutes
Total time: about 7 hours and 30 minutes (includes chilling)

Calories **115**
Protein **8g**
Cholesterol **0mg**
Total fat **4g**
Saturated fat **1g**
Sodium **220mg**

1 kg	sweet red peppers, skinned (page 90) and seeded	2 lb
1 tbsp	virgin olive oil	1 tbsp
4	egg whites	4
60 g	dry breadcrumbs	2 oz
750 g	button mushrooms, sliced	1½ lb
1 tsp	chopped fresh basil	1 tsp
1 tsp	chopped fresh marjoram, or ¼ tsp dried marjoram	1 tsp
1 tsp	chopped fresh oregano, or ¼ tsp dried oregano	1 tsp
¼ tsp	salt	¼ tsp
350 g	fresh spinach leaves, stems removed	12 oz

Dice one large red pepper, and set the dice aside. Roughly chop the remaining peppers. Heat ½ tablespoon of the olive oil in a heavy-bottomed saucepan over low heat. Add the roughly chopped peppers and cook them, stirring occasionally, until they are tender — about 10 minutes. Cool the peppers slightly, then purée them in a food processor. Add two of the egg whites and 2 tablespoons of the dry breadcrumbs, and process again until the ingredients are thoroughly combined. Transfer the mixture to a bowl and set it aside while you make the mushroom purée.

Heat the remaining olive oil in a clean saucepan. Add the button mushrooms and cook them over medium heat, stirring occasionally, until they are tender — about 5 minutes. Increase the heat and continue to cook until all the moisture has evaporated — about 10 minutes. Stir the mushrooms occasionally, to prevent them from sticking to the pan. Allow them to cool a little, then purée them in the food processor. Add the remaining egg whites and breadcrumbs and process again, then add the basil, marjoram, oregano and salt, and process briefly to mix these into the purée. Set the mixture aside.

Blanch the spinach leaves for 1 minute in a large pan of boiling water. Drain the spinach, refresh it under cold running water and drain it again. Open out the leaves and lay them on paper towels to allow the remaining moisture to be absorbed.

Preheat the oven to 220°C (425°F or Mark 7). Line an 18 by 7.5 by 7.5 cm (7 by 3 by 3 inch) loaf tin with non-stick parchment paper *(page 34)*. Sprinkle half of the reserved diced pepper over the bottom of the tin. Spoon in half of the pepper purée and spread it evenly, then lay a third of the spinach leaves over the top. Spread the mushroom mixture over the spinach. Lay another third of the spinach over the mushroom mixture, then scatter on the remaining diced pepper. Pour in the rest of the pepper purée, smooth it level, and lay the last of the spinach leaves over the top. Cover the terrine with non-stick parchment paper.

Bake the terrine for 50 minutes to 1 hour, or until a knife inserted into the centre comes out clean. Leave the terrine to cool in the tin, then chill it in the refrigerator for several hours, or overnight.

Turn out the terrine on to a flat serving dish and peel off the lining paper. Serve the terrine cut into slices.

SUGGESTED ACCOMPANIMENT: *crisp young lettuce leaves dressed with a light vinaigrette.*

Asparagus and Red Pepper Mousse

Serves 12 as a first course
Working time: about 1 hour and 10 minutes
Total time: about 8 hours (includes chilling)

Calories **65**
Protein **6g**
Cholesterol **5mg**
Total fat **3g**
Saturated fat **2g**
Sodium **105mg**

1 kg	long asparagus spears, trimmed and peeled	2 lb
30 g	unsalted butter	1 oz
30 g	plain flour	1 oz
30 cl	unsalted chicken stock (recipe, page 10)	½ pint
45 g	thick Greek yogurt	1½ oz
¾ tsp	salt	¾ tsp
	white pepper	
1	sweet red pepper, skinned (page 90) and seeded	1
100 g	low-fat fromage frais	3½ oz
2 tbsp	cut chives	2 tbsp
8 tsp	powdered gelatine	8 tsp
1	egg white	1

Place the asparagus spears in a steamer, and steam them for 15 to 20 minutes, or until they are tender. Select eight of the best spears and set them aside. Purée the remaining asparagus in a food processor or blender. Trim the reserved asparagus spears so that they will fit exactly, lengthwise, in the bottom of a 22 by 12 by 6 cm (9 by 5 by 2½ inch) non-reactive loaf tin. Arrange the spears side by side in the bottom of the tin, alternating the orientation.

Melt the butter in a small, heavy-bottomed saucepan over medium heat. Stir in the flour, then stir in the chicken stock. Bring the sauce to the boil, stirring con-tinuously. Reduce the heat to low and allow the sauce to simmer for 5 to 6 minutes, or until no taste of raw flour remains. Remove the pan from the heat and stir in the asparagus purée and the yogurt. Season the mixture with ½ teaspoon of the salt and some white pepper. Allow the mixture to cool for about 1 hour, stirring frequently to prevent a skin from forming.

While the asparagus mixture cools, purée the red pepper in a food processor. Put the purée in a small bowl and season it with ⅛ teaspoon of the salt and some white pepper. Put the *fromage frais* in another small bowl and stir in the chives, the remaining salt, and a little white pepper.

Dissolve the gelatine in 6 tablespoons of water (*page 13*). Stir 1 teaspoon of the gelatine solution into the pepper purée, and 1 teaspoon into the *fromage frais*. Stir the remainder into the asparagus mixture. Whisk the egg white until it will hold soft peaks and fold it gently into the asparagus mixture; refrigerate the mixture until it begins to thicken — 20 to 30 minutes. Keep the pepper purée and *fromage frais* at room temperature, to prevent them from setting.

Pour one third of the asparagus mixture into the prepared tin. Spoon half of the pepper purée and the *fromage frais* over the asparagus mixture, in random dollops. Pour in another third of the asparagus mix-ture, add the remaining pepper purée and *fromage frais* as before, and then pour in the remaining asparagus mixture. Level the top and chill the terrine for 4 to 5 hours, or until it has set firmly.

To unmould the terrine, dip the base and sides of the tin in hot water for 2 or 3 seconds and invert it on to a serving plate. Serve the terrine cut into slices.

SUGGESTED ACCOMPANIMENT: *toast fingers.*

Red Pepper Ramekins

Serves 8 as a first course
Working time: about 1 hour
Total time: about 5 hours and 30 minutes
(includes chilling)

Calories **50**
Protein **5g**
Cholesterol **0mg**
Total fat **1g**
Saturated fat **trace**
Sodium **25mg**

1 kg	sweet red peppers, seeded, deribbed and sliced	2 lb
90 g	shallots, sliced	3 oz
125 g	young leeks, trimmed, cleaned thoroughly to remove all grit, and chopped	4 oz
¼ litre	unsalted vegetable stock (recipe, page 10)	8 fl oz
1	bouquet garni	1
2 tbsp	powdered gelatine	2 tbsp
15 cl	plain low-fat yogurt	¼ pint
17.5 cl	tomato juice	6 fl oz
10	drops Tabasco sauce	10
½ tsp	fresh lime juice	½ tsp
	sprigs of basil, for garnish	
	frisée or other salad leaves, for garnish	
Pepper salad		
1	sweet red pepper, skinned (page 90) seeded and cut into thin strips	1
1	sweet yellow pepper, skinned (page 90), seeded and cut into thin strips	1
½ tsp	fresh lime juice	½ tsp
	freshly ground black pepper	

Place the red peppers, shallots and leeks in a saucepan. Pour in the stock and add the bouquet garni. Bring the stock to the boil over low heat, then cover the pan and cook the vegetables until they are very soft — 30 to 40 minutes. Drain the vegetables and reserve the cooking liquid; discard the bouquet garni. Purée the vegetables in a food processor and strain the purée to remove any coarse fibres.

Pour 12.5 cl (4 fl oz) of the reserved cooking liquid into a small bowl and set it aside to cool. Combine the remaining cooking liquid with the vegetable purée in a large measuring jug; stir in the yogurt and enough tomato juice to make the purée up to 90 cl (1½ pints). Dissolve the gelatine in the cooled reserved cooking liquid (page 13). Stir the gelatine solution into the vegetable purée, and add the Tabasco sauce and the lime juice. Whisk vigorously, to ensure that the yogurt is thoroughly incorporated. Divide the mixture among eight 12.5 cl (4 fl oz) moulds. Chill the moulds in the refrigerator for at least 4 hours, or overnight, until the mixture is completely set.

For the pepper salad, toss the red and yellow pepper strips with the lime juice. Season the salad with some freshly ground black pepper.

Dip the bases and sides of the moulds in hot water for 2 or 3 seconds and turn the ramekins out on to individual serving plates. Spoon a small portion of the pepper salad on to each plate, and garnish with sprigs of basil and a few salad leaves.

Layered Mushroom Terrine

Serves 10 as a first course
Working time: about 2 hours
Total time: about 6 hours (includes chilling)

Calories **75**
Protein **4g**
Cholesterol **25mg**
Total fat **3g**
Saturated fat **1g**
Sodium **150mg**

15 g	dried ceps	½ oz
7 g	dried horn of plenty mushrooms	¼ oz
30 g	dried morels	1 oz
40 cl	unsalted brown stock (recipe, page 11)	15 fl oz
125 g	flat mushrooms, finely chopped	4 oz
125 g	grey oyster mushrooms, finely chopped	4 oz
2	garlic cloves	2
2 tbsp	chopped parsley	2 tbsp
4 tbsp	Madeira	4 tbsp
¾ tsp	salt	¾ tsp
	freshly ground black pepper	
15 g	unsalted butter	½ oz
1 tsp	Dijon mustard	1 tsp
1 tsp	fresh lemon juice	1 tsp
200 g	button mushrooms, finely chopped	7 oz
100 g	golden oyster mushrooms, finely chopped	3½ oz
	white pepper	
30 g	fresh breadcrumbs	1 oz
1	small egg	1
100 g	low-fat fromage frais	3½ oz
1 tsp	cornflour, sifted	1 tsp
1	egg white	1
1½ tsp	powdered gelatine	1½ tsp

Place the dried ceps, dried horn of plenty mushrooms and dried morels in three separate bowls. Add 8 cl (3 fl oz) of stock to both the ceps and the horn of plenty mushrooms, and add 17.5 cl (6 fl oz) to the morels. Leave the mushrooms to soak for about 30 minutes. At the end of this time, remove the mushrooms from their soaking liquids and squeeze them out, reserving the soaking liquids. Strain the soaking liquids through a coffee filter paper and set them aside. Keeping them separate, rinse the mushrooms in a bowl of water and squeeze them gently to rid them of all their grit.

Place the ceps in a small, heavy-bottomed saucepan with the flat mushrooms, grey oyster mushrooms, garlic, parsley, the remaining stock, 2 tablespoons of the Madeira, ¼ teaspoon of the salt and some freshly ground black pepper. Cover the pan and simmer the ingredients gently for about 20 minutes, until the mushrooms are soft. Remove the lid, increase the heat and continue cooking until all the moisture has evaporated. Remove the garlic cloves if you wish,

or crush them into the mixture. Turn the cep mixture into a bowl and leave it to cool.

Pat the horn of plenty mushrooms dry on paper towels and chop them finely. Set them aside.

Melt the butter in a small, heavy frying pan and stir in the Dijon mustard and the fresh lemon juice. Add the button mushrooms, golden oyster mushrooms, ¼ teaspoon of the salt and some white pepper. Cover the pan and cook the mushrooms until they are tender — 15 to 20 minutes. Remove the lid, increase the heat and continue to cook, stirring constantly, until all the moisture has evaporated. Transfer the mixture to a bowl and leave it to cool.

Preheat the oven to 180°C (350°F or Mark 4). Line an 18 by 18 by 5 cm (7 by 7 by 2 inch) baking tin with a double thickness of non-stick parchment paper (page 34). Stir the breadcrumbs and egg into the cooled cep mixture and press the mixture into the bottom of the tin. Purée the second mushroom mixture in a food processor until smooth. Beat in the fromage frais, cornflour and egg white, then fold in the horn of plenty mushrooms. Spoon this mixture into the tin and level the surface. Cover the terrine with a piece of lightly oiled foil, and place the tin in a roasting pan. Pour in boiling water to come two thirds of the way up the side of the tin, and bake the terrine for 40 to 50 minutes, or until the centre is firm to the touch. Remove the terrine from the water bath and allow it to cool.

Meanwhile, steam the morel mushrooms in a steamer set over a saucepan of boiling water for 5 minutes. Dissolve the gelatine in 2 tablespoons of the reserved mushroom-soaking liquid (page 13) and stir the gelatine solution into 15 cl (¼ pint) of the remaining soaking liquid. Stir in the remaining 2 tablespoons of Madeira and ¼ teaspoon of salt. Set the liquid jelly aside in the refrigerator until it is on the point of setting — about 20 to 30 minutes.

Arrange the steamed morels on the surface of the terrine and press them down lightly. Spoon the partially set jelly over the morels and chill the terrine for at least 2 hours, or until the jelly is set firmly.

To unmould the terrine, run a sharp knife gently round all four sides of the baking tin to loosen the jelly, then use the lining paper to lift the terrine out of the tin. Fold down the paper and use a large palette knife to slide the terrine off its paper base and on to a large serving plate. Neaten the edges, if necessary. Serve the terrine cut into slices.

SUGGESTED ACCOMPANIMENTS: *crusty bread; lettuce leaves.*

Potatoes Layered with Gruyère and Onions

Serves 6 as a main course
Working time: about 35 minutes
Total time: about 2 hours

Calories **250**			
Protein **9g**	1 kg	large potatoes, scrubbed	2½ lb
Cholesterol **25mg**	1 tbsp	virgin olive oil	1 tbsp
Total fat **9g**	125 g	spring onions, trimmed and thinly sliced	4 oz
Saturated fat **4g**	1	garlic clove, crushed	1
Sodium **210mg**	1	large sweet red pepper, seeded, deribbed and thinly sliced	1
	½ tsp	salt	½ tsp
		freshly ground black pepper	
	125 g	Gruyère cheese, coarsely grated	4 oz
	6 tbsp	unsalted chicken stock (recipe, page 10)	6 tbsp
	1 tbsp	chopped parsley	1 tbsp

Put the potatoes into a large saucepan and cover them with cold water. Put on the lid and bring the water to the boil, then reduce the heat and simmer the potatoes for 25 to 30 minutes, until they are almost, but not quite, tender.

Meanwhile, heat the oil in a heavy frying pan over medium heat. Add the spring onions and garlic, and cook them gently until soft but not browned — 2 to 3 minutes. Using a slotted spoon, remove the onions and garlic from the pan and set them aside. Add the sweet red pepper slices to the oil remaining in the frying pan. Cover the pan and sweat the pepper slices over low heat for 15 to 20 minutes, until they are soft. Remove the pan from the heat.

Preheat the oven to 220°C (425°F or Mark 7). Grease a 25 by 11 by 7.5 cm (10 by 4½ by 3 inch) loaf tin. Line the base with non-stick parchment paper (page 34).

Drain the potatoes and, holding each one in turn in a clean tea towel, carefully peel off the skins while the potatoes are still hot. Allow the peeled potatoes to cool for 15 to 20 minutes, then cut them into slices a little less than 5 mm (¼ inch) thick.

Arrange the best and largest potato slices in two neatly overlapping rows in the bottom of the loaf tin. Season them with a little of the salt and some black pepper. Cover the potato slices with half of the onions and garlic, and scatter on a quarter of the grated cheese. Sprinkle 1½ tablespoons of the chicken stock over the top. Add another layer of potato slices, season them with a little more of the salt and some black pepper, and cover them with the red pepper slices. Sprinkle on another quarter of the cheese and 1½ tablespoons of the stock. Arrange another layer of potato slices in the tin, season them as before, and add the remaining onions and garlic, another quarter of the cheese and 1½ tablespoons of the stock. Finally, layer the remaining potato slices in the tin, add the remaining salt and a little more black pepper, and sprinkle on the remaining cheese and stock.

Bake the vegetables for 30 to 40 minutes, until the topmost potatoes are golden-brown and all the potatoes are cooked through. Remove the tin from the oven and allow it to stand for 5 minutes. Loosen the sides with a palette knife, then turn the vegetables out on to a flat serving platter. Peel off the lining paper, scatter the chopped parsley over the dish and serve it hot, cut into slices.

Spinach and Pasta Terrine

Serves 16 as a first course
Working time: about 40 minutes
Total time: about 3 hours (includes chilling)

Calories **135**
Protein **7g**
Cholesterol **0mg**
Total fat **5g**
Saturated fat **1g**
Sodium **200mg**

1.5 kg	fresh spinach, 20 leaves set aside, the remainder chopped	3 lb
250 g	dried tortiglioni, penne or other large tubular pasta shapes	8 oz
4 tbsp	plus 1 tsp virgin olive oil	4 tbsp
1 kg	tomatoes, skinned and seeded	2 lb
2 tsp	tomato paste	2 tsp
1 ½ tsp	salt	1 ½ tsp
	freshly ground black pepper	
2 tbsp	powdered gelatine	2 tbsp
2 tsp	ready-made pesto	2 tsp
4 tsp	chopped fresh basil	4 tsp
2 tbsp	white wine vinegar	2 tbsp

Remove the stalks from the whole spinach leaves. Blanch the leaves in a saucepan of boiling water for 30 seconds, then drain them and plunge them into iced water. Drain them again thoroughly and pat them dry on paper towels. Line a 28 by 7.5 by 7.5 cm (11 by 3 by 3 inch) terrine with plastic film, pulling the film as tight as possible and pressing it into the corners. Arrange the blanched spinach leaves in the terrine, allowing them to overhang its sides.

Add the pasta to 3 litres (5 pints) of boiling water with 1 ½ teaspoons of salt. Start testing the pasta after 10 minutes and continue to cook it until it is *al dente*. Drain the pasta and toss it in the teaspoon of olive oil. Set the pasta aside.

In a food processor or blender, purée the tomatoes with the tomato paste, ½ teaspoon of the salt and some black pepper. Pass the purée through a nylon sieve into a bowl. Dissolve the gelatine in 6 tablespoons of water *(page 13)*, and whisk the gelatine solution into the tomato purée. Set the mixture aside.

Blanch the chopped spinach in a large pan of boiling water for 1 minute. Drain it well, then squeeze it very thoroughly in a clean tea towel or a piece of muslin to remove all excess liquid. Put the spinach in a bowl and mix in the pesto, the chopped basil, ½ teaspoon of the salt and some black pepper.

Place half of the pasta in the terrine and pour half of the tomato mixture over it. Add the spinach mixture and gently smooth the surface to cover the pasta and tomatoes, then add the remaining pasta and the rest of the tomato mixture. Cover the terrine with the overhanging spinach leaves, and chill it for 2 to 3 hours.

Just before unmoulding the terrine, make a vinaigrette. In a small bowl, stir the remaining ½ teaspoon of salt and the vinegar together until the salt dissolves. Whisk in the 4 tablespoons of olive oil, beating until the oil and vinegar are thoroughly blended. Add some black pepper and set the vinaigrette aside.

To serve, unmould the terrine on to a large platter or board, remove the plastic film and slice the terrine using a sharp knife. Pass the vinaigrette separately.

Potted Chili Beans

Serves 8 as a main course
Working time: about 35 minutes
Total time: about 5 hours (includes soaking)

Calories **200**
Protein **15g**
Cholesterol **0mg**
Total fat **1g**
Saturated fat **trace**
Sodium **370mg**

250 g	dried red kidney beans, picked over	8 oz
125 g	dried haricot beans, picked over	4 oz
125 g	dried peas, picked over	4 oz
2	bay leaves	2
2	large onions, chopped	2
3	carrots, finely diced	3
2	sticks celery, finely diced	2
6	garlic cloves, finely chopped	6
3	fresh green chili peppers, seeded and chopped (caution, page 9)	3
4 tsp	chopped fresh oregano, or 1 tsp dried oregano	4 tsp
2	lemons, grated rind and juice	2
2 tsp	caster sugar	2 tsp
1 tbsp	paprika	1 tbsp
1½ tsp	salt	1½ tsp
	freshly ground black pepper	
5 tbsp	chopped fresh coriander	5 tbsp
	fresh coriander sprigs, for garnish	

Rinse the kidney beans, haricot beans and peas under cold running water and put them into a large saucepan with enough cold water to cover them by about 7.5 cm (3 inches). Discard any pulses that float to the surface. Cover the saucepan, leaving the lid ajar, and slowly bring the water to the boil. Boil the pulses for 2 minutes, then turn off the heat and leave them to soak, covered, for at least an hour. (Alternatively, soak the pulses overnight in cold water.)

Rinse the pulses and place them in a clean saucepan with enough cold water to cover them by about 7.5 cm (3 inches). Bring the water to the boil. Boil the pulses rapidly for 10 minutes, then drain and rinse them and discard the water. Wash out the pan, replace the pulses and add the bay leaves and 1.25 litres (2 pints) of water. Bring the water to the boil, cover the pan and reduce the heat. Simmer the beans and peas gently for 1 hour.

Add the onions, carrots, celery, garlic, chilies and oregano to the pan, and stir them in to the beans and peas. Continue to cook the mixture, uncovered, for a further 20 to 30 minutes, stirring frequently, until the vegetables and beans are completely tender and all the cooking liquid has been absorbed.

Remove the pan from the heat and discard the bay leaves. Stir in the lemon rind and juice, the sugar, paprika, salt and some black pepper. Use a food processor to reduce the beans and vegetables to a coarse purée. Do this in batches, transferring the processed pâté to a mixing bowl. Stir in the chopped coriander and leave the pâté to cool completely.

Divide the pâté among eight individual bowls, and garnish each portion with a sprig of coriander.

SUGGESTED ACCOMPANIMENTS: *salad of sliced tomatoes and onion rings; corn muffins.*

Place the red lentils and carrots in a heavy-bottomed, non-reactive saucepan and pour in sufficient water to cover them. Grate the rind from one half of the orange and set it aside. Squeeze the juice from both halves of the fruit and add it to the pan with the lentils and carrots. Bring the liquid to the boil, then cover the pan and reduce the heat. Simmer gently until the carrots are tender and the lentils are very soft — about 30 minutes. Stir the contents of the pan from time to time, to prevent them from burning, and add a little more water if necessary; all the liquid should have been absorbed by the end of the cooking time.

Meanwhile, place the green lentils and the ceps in a second heavy-bottomed saucepan. Pour in 30 cl (½ pint) of water, add the soy sauce and bay leaf halves, and bring the liquid to the boil. Cover the pan and reduce the heat. Simmer the lentils gently until they are completely tender — about 50 minutes. Uncover the saucepan towards the end of the cooking time to allow the moisture to evaporate, but do not allow the lentils to catch on the bottom of the pan. Place the lentils in a sieve over a bowl to cool and drain.

Lightly oil a 25 by 10 by 7.5 cm (10 by 4 by 3 inch) terrine and line it with non-stick parchment paper (*page 34*). Lightly oil the lining paper. Preheat the oven to 180°C (350°F or Mark 4).

Purée the red lentils and carrots by pressing them through a sieve into a mixing bowl; a food processor may be used to do this, but take care not to over-process, or the purée will be too runny. Add the reserved orange rind, the vinegar, cumin, ¼ teaspoon of the salt and some white pepper. Lightly beat one of the eggs, then add it to the mixture with 60 g (2 oz) of the *fromage frais* and stir well. Spoon half of this mixture into the prepared terrine and smooth the surface level with the back of the spoon.

Lightly beat the remaining egg. Discard the bay leaf halves from the cooked green lentils. Stir in the parsley, thyme, mint, the remaining *fromage frais*, the beaten egg and the remaining salt. Spoon the mixture into the terrine, spreading it gently over the red lentil layer. Spoon the remaining red lentil mixture over the green lentils and level the surface. Cover the terrine with lightly oiled foil, tented slightly to ensure that it does not touch the contents of the terrine.

Place the terrine in a roasting pan or dish, and pour in sufficient boiling water to come two thirds of the way up the side of the terrine. Bake the terrine until the centre of the lentil mixture is firm to the touch — about 1 hour. Remove the terrine from the water bath and allow it to cool completely.

Invert the terrine on to a flat surface and peel off the lining paper. Use a sharp, long-bladed knife to cut the terrine into slices, and serve it on a bed of lettuce leaves arranged on a large platter.

EDITOR'S NOTE: *To make this terrine easier to slice, chill it first in the refrigerator for at least 2 hours.*

Two-Lentil Terrine

Serves 6 as a main course
Working time: about 45 minutes
Total time: about 6 hours (includes cooling)

Calories **230**
Protein **17g**
Cholesterol **75mg**
Total fat **5g**
Saturated fat **2g**
Sodium **210mg**

200 g	red lentils, picked over and rinsed	7 oz
200 g	carrots, finely sliced	7 oz
1	orange, cut in half	1
100 g	green lentils, picked over and rinsed	3½ oz
20 g	dried ceps, rinsed thoroughly to remove all grit	⅔ oz
2 tbsp	low-sodium soy sauce or shoyu	2 tbsp
1	bay leaf, broken in half	1
1 tbsp	cider vinegar	1 tbsp
1 tsp	ground cumin	1 tsp
½ tsp	salt	½ tsp
	white pepper	
160 g	low-fat fromage frais	5½ oz
2	eggs	2
2 tbsp	finely chopped parsley	2 tbsp
1 tsp	finely chopped fresh thyme or ¼ tsp dried thyme	1 tsp
8	mint leaves, finely chopped	8
	lettuce leaves, for garnish	

Fennel and Lentil Pâté

Serves 10 as a first course
Working time: about 50 minutes
Total time: about 5 hours

Calories **100**
Protein **9g**
Cholesterol **0mg**
Total fat **1g**
Saturated fat **trace**
Sodium **225mg**

250 g	green lentils, picked over and rinsed	8 oz
1	large onion, chopped	1
2	garlic cloves, crushed	2
250 g	bulb fennel, trimmed and chopped, feathery tops reserved and chopped	8 oz
1 tsp	safflower oil	1 tsp
4 tbsp	plain low-fat yogurt	4 tbsp
1 tsp	mild chili powder	1 tsp
2 tsp	fresh lemon juice	2 tsp
1 tsp	salt	1 tsp
3 tbsp	chopped parsley	3 tbsp
	freshly ground black pepper	
1 tsp	dry mustard	1 tsp
4 tsp	powdered gelatine	4 tsp
4	egg whites	4
	lime slices, for garnish	
	fennel tops, for garnish	

Put the lentils in a heavy-bottomed saucepan with 60 cl (1 pint) of water. Bring the liquid to the boil, add half of the onion and garlic, cover the pan and reduce the heat. Simmer the lentils for 40 minutes, until they are tender. Turn them into a sieve set over a bowl and leave them to drain and cool.

Meanwhile, put the bulb fennel in another saucepan with water to cover, put the lid on the pan and bring the water to the boil. Reduce the heat and simmer the fennel for about 15 minutes, or until it is tender. Drain the fennel, reserving 2 tablespoons of the cooking liquid. Leave the fennel to cool.

Heat the safflower oil in a small, heavy frying pan and sauté the remaining onion and garlic until soft — about 5 minutes.

Purée the drained lentils in a food processor until smooth. Turn the lentil purée into a bowl and add the yogurt, chili powder, chopped fennel tops, half of the lemon juice and salt, 2 tablespoons of the chopped parsley and a generous grinding of black pepper. Mix the ingredients together well.

Rinse out the food processor. Purée the fennel and the sautéed onion and garlic until smooth. Transfer the

purée to a bowl; mix in the mustard, the remaining salt and lemon juice, and some black pepper.

Dissolve the gelatine in the reserved fennel-cooking water *(page 13)*. Thoroughly mix half of the gelatine solution into the lentil mixture and the other half, equally thoroughly, into the fennel purée.

Whisk the egg whites until they stand in stiff peaks. Using a metal tablespoon, stir 2 tablespoons of the whisked egg whites into each purée, to lighten the mixtures. Divide the remaining egg whites between the bowls and fold them in gently.

Line a 19 by 10 by 6 cm (7½ by 4 by 2½ inch) loaf tin with non-stick parchment paper *(page 34)*. Sprinkle the remaining chopped parsley evenly over the base of the tin; pour in half of the lentil mixture and smooth the surface. Place the tin in the refrigerator for 10 minutes, to firm up the lentil layer. Add the fennel mixture to the tin and spread it evenly over the lentil layer. Chill for another 10 minutes, to partially set the fennel mixture. Finally, add the rest of the lentil mixture and level the top. Chill for about 3 hours, until the pâté is firmly set.

Turn out the pâté on to a flat serving plate and peel off the lining paper. Serve the pâté sliced, garnished with lime slices and fennel tops.

Anchovy and Lentil Dip

Serves 6 as a first course
Working time: about 15 minutes
Total time: about 1 hour

Calories **180**			
Protein **13g**	250 g	red lentils, picked over and rinsed	8 oz
Cholesterol **10mg**	1 or 2	garlic cloves, finely chopped	1 or 2
Total fat **2g**	1	large onion, chopped	1
Saturated fat **trace**	60 cl	unsalted vegetable stock (recipe, page 10)	1 pint
Sodium **450mg**	60 g	anchovy fillets, soaked in a little milk for 15 minutes to reduce their saltiness	2 oz
	2 tbsp	fresh lemon juice	2 tbsp
	30 g	dry breadcrumbs	1 oz
		chives, for garnish	
		lemon slices, cut into pieces, for garnish	

Place the lentils, chopped garlic and onion, and the vegetable stock in a heavy-bottomed saucepan. Bring the stock to the boil and skim off any scum that rises to the surface of the liquid. Reduce the heat, cover the pan and cook the lentils until they are soft and have absorbed all the stock — about 30 minutes. If any stock remains at the end of this time, cook the lentils uncovered over medium heat, stirring constantly, until all the moisture has evaporated.

Pat the anchovies dry on paper towels and place them in a food processor or blender with the cooked lentils, the lemon juice and the breadcrumbs. Process the ingredients until they are smooth. Divide the mixture among six individual ramekins and leave it to cool. Just before serving, garnish each portion with a few chives and pieces of lemon.

SUGGESTED ACCOMPANIMENT: *bread sticks.*

Terrine of Carrots and Black Beans

Serves 6 as a main course
Working time: about 45 minutes
Total time: about 5 hours (includes soaking)

Calories **155**
Protein **15g**
Cholesterol **0mg**
Total fat **4g**
Saturated fat **2g**
Sodium **490mg**

125 g	dried black kidney beans, picked over	4 oz
1	onion, chopped	1
2	garlic cloves, chopped	2
2	fresh green chili peppers, seeded and chopped (caution, page 9)	2
½ tsp	salt	½ tsp
4	egg whites	4
500 g	carrots, sliced into rounds, plus one carrot cut lengthwise into strips with a vegetable peeler, soaked in iced water for 45 minutes and drained, for garnish	1 lb
1 tsp	paprika	1 tsp
250 g	low-fat cottage cheese	8 oz
1½ tbsp	freshly grated Parmesan cheese	1½ tbsp
2 tbsp	capers, rinsed and drained	2 tbsp
	salad leaves, for garnish	

Rinse the kidney beans under cold running water, then put them into a large saucepan with enough cold water to cover them by about 7.5 cm (3 inches). Discard any beans that float to the surface. Cover the pan, leaving the lid ajar, and slowly bring the liquid to the boil. Boil the beans for 2 minutes, then turn off the heat and leave them to soak, covered, for at least an hour. (Alternatively, soak the beans overnight in cold water.)

Rinse the beans and put them in a clean pan with enough cold water to cover them by about 7.5 cm (3 inches). Bring the water to the boil and boil the beans rapidly for 10 minutes. Drain and rinse them, and discard the water. Wash out the pan, replace the beans and cover them again by about 7.5 cm (3 inches) with water. Add the onion, garlic and chilies to the pan and bring the water to the boil. Cover the pan, reduce the heat and simmer the beans until they are tender — 45 minutes to 1 hour. Add more hot water during this time, if necessary. Drain the beans thoroughly and place them in a food processor. Add ¼ teaspoon of the salt and two of the egg whites, and process the mixture to a smooth purée. Set the mixture aside.

Simmer the sliced carrots in water until they are tender — about 15 minutes. Drain them, let them cool a little, then process them in a food processor with the paprika and the remaining salt and egg whites.

Preheat the oven to 220°C (425°F or Mark 7). Lightly oil a 22 by 12 by 6 cm (9 by 5 by 2½ inch) loaf tin.

Spoon the bean mixture into the tin and press it down with the back of the spoon to level it. Top the bean layer with the cottage cheese and spread it out evenly. Scatter on the Parmesan and the capers, and press them down lightly. Lastly, turn the carrot mixture into the tin and spread it evenly. Cover the terrine with foil and bake it for 50 minutes to 1 hour, or until a skewer inserted into the centre meets with little resistance. Allow the terrine to cool in the tin.

Turn out the terrine on to a flat serving platter and cut it into slices. Serve each portion garnished with a few salad leaves and carrot curls.

Indian Spiced Pâté

Serves 10 as a first course
Working time: about 20 minutes
Total time: about 3 hours (includes soaking)

Calories **125**	250 g	dried black-eyed peas, picked over	8 oz
Protein **6g**	2 tbsp	safflower oil	2 tbsp
Cholesterol **0mg**	1	large onion, finely chopped	1
Total fat **4g**	1	garlic clove, crushed	1
Saturated fat **trace**	1 ½ tbsp	black mustard seeds	1 ½ tbsp
Sodium **165mg**	1 tbsp	fennel seeds	1 tbsp
	½ tsp	chili powder	½ tsp
	½ tsp	ground coriander	½ tsp
	½ tsp	garam masala	½ tsp
	2 tbsp	tomato paste	2 tbsp
	1 tbsp	red wine vinegar	1 tbsp
	1 tsp	salt	1 tsp
		freshly ground black pepper	

Rinse the black-eyed peas under cold running water, then put them into a large saucepan and pour in enough cold water to cover them by about 7.5 cm (3 inches). Discard any peas that float to the surface. Cover the saucepan, leaving the lid ajar, and slowly bring the liquid to the boil. Boil the peas for 2 minutes, then turn off the heat and leave the peas to soak, covered, for at least 1 hour. (Alternatively, soak the peas overnight in cold water.)

Drain and rinse the peas and place them in a clean saucepan with enough cold water to cover them by about 7.5 cm (3 inches). Bring the water to the boil. Boil the peas for 10 minutes, then drain and rinse them again. Wash out the pan, replace the peas and cover them by about 7.5 cm (3 inches) with fresh water. Bring the water to the boil, reduce the heat and simmer the peas, covered, until they are tender — about 40 minutes. Check the water level in the pan from time to time and add more hot water if necessary. When they are cooked, drain the peas and reserve 6 tablespoons of the cooking water.

Heat the oil in a large, heavy-bottomed saucepan. Add the onion and garlic, and sauté them over medium heat until they are soft but not browned. Add the mustard seeds, fennel seeds, chili powder, ground coriander, garam masala and tomato paste to the pan. Stir the spices in well and continue frying for another 5 minutes. Mix in the vinegar and fry for a further minute.

Place the cooked peas in a food processor with the reserved cooking liquid, and process them until they are smooth. Stir them into the onion and spice mixture, together with the salt and some black pepper.

Turn the spiced pâté into a large bowl and allow it to cool before serving it.

SUGGESTED ACCOMPANIMENT: *hot pitta bread or toast.*

4 A terrine of sliced peaches suspended in layers of apple and blackberry jelly (recipe, page 126) provides a perfect harmony of sweet and tart flavours.

Terrines for Dessert

Light, refreshing and pleasing to the eye, the terrines in this chapter reflect a new and highly imaginative approach to the making of desserts. In this innovative style of cookery, spectacular sweets are created without undue reliance on the cream jug, the butter dish or the sugar bowl. The glorious desserts on the following pages are as healthy as they are glamorous, with little or no saturated fat, a modest calorie count, and all the life-sustaining nutrients that fresh fruit, nuts and low-fat dairy products supply.

The foundation for a number of these preparations is a mousse of whisked egg whites combined with yogurt or white cheese. The use of low-fat cheeses or yogurts as a base, instead of double cream or egg-yolk-laden custards, makes it possible to incorporate ingredients that would otherwise send fat and calorie counts soaring: the chocolate bavarois with its caramel sauce on page 117, for instance, becomes a permissible indulgence. Another foundation much used in this chapter is fruit, whether in the form of a purée or a clear jelly.

Fruit, indeed, is the chief source of inspiration for these terrines. Here are delicacies to celebrate the best of the market's offerings, whatever the time of year. The soft fruits of summer are put to good use in the strawberry cheese loaf *(page 120)* with its Cointreau-spiked sauce, and in the marbled blueberry dessert, with its garnish of lightly caramelized berries *(page 126)*. Yet there is no shortage of alternatives for winter, when dried and tropical fruits come into their own: the prune and almond terrine, with its mousse of yogurt, honey and brandy-soaked prunes *(page 114)* and the assemblage of exotic fruits in champagne jelly *(page 125)* are only two of many options.

A number of the moulds used for recipes in this chapter are first lined with either plastic film or parchment paper. This step will protect delicately flavoured ingredients from taking on any metallic taste if metal moulds are used, and — whatever the container — will make it easy to turn out the finished dish.

To exploit the vibrant colours and flavours of fresh fruit, the terrines on the following pages are best made on the day you intend to serve them. They should be assembled several hours in advance, cooled, chilled or set in the refrigerator or the freezer, as the recipe specifies, and served cold.

about 3 minutes. Remove the pan from the heat and add the softened gelatine; stir the liquid until the gelatine has fully dissolved. Strain the juice into a mixing bowl and leave it to cool. Chill it in the refrigerator until it has partially set — about 2 hours.

Using an electric beater, whisk the orange jelly until it is slightly foamy — 30 to 60 seconds — then whisk in the yogurt. Chill the mixture for a further 30 minutes, or until it is just on the point of setting. Stir the jelly lightly at this stage to eliminate any lumps.

Mix together the chopped walnuts, the breadcrumbs and the cinnamon. Line a 15 by 9 by 7 cm (6 by 3½ by 2¾ inch) loaf tin with plastic film, pulling the film as tight as possible and pressing it well into the corners of the tin. Spoon a quarter of the orange jelly mixture into the bottom of the tin and sprinkle a quarter of the walnut mixture on top in a thin, even layer. Repeat this process to create another three layers of each, finishing with the walnut mixture. Chill the assembly until it has set completely — about 3 hours.

To unmould the terrine, invert it on to a flat serving plate and carefully remove the plastic film. Decorate the terrine with a dusting of ground cinnamon along the centre and the reserved strips of orange rind. Serve the terrine cut into slices.

SUGGESTED ACCOMPANIMENT: *thick Greek yogurt.*

Orange and Walnut Layered Terrine

Serves 6
Working time: about 40 minutes
Total time: about 6 hours (includes chilling)

Calories **170**
Protein **6g**
Cholesterol **0mg**
Total fat **6g**
Saturated fat **1g**
Sodium **75mg**

60 g	crustless wholemeal bread	2 oz
4	oranges	4
1 tbsp	powdered gelatine	1 tbsp
60 g	caster sugar	2 oz
15 cl	plain low-fat yogurt	¼ pint
60 g	shelled walnuts, finely chopped	2 oz
½ tsp	ground cinnamon, plus a little extra for dusting	½ tsp

Preheat the oven to 170°C (325°F or Mark 3). Place the bread on a baking sheet and toast it in the oven for 25 minutes, or until it is crisp and dry. Allow the bread to cool, then place it in a polythene bag and use a rolling pin to crush it to fine crumbs.

Finely grate the rind of two of the oranges and set it aside. Using a vegetable peeler, pare short, wide strips of rind from the two remaining oranges. Place the strips of orange rind in a small, non-reactive saucepan, cover them with cold water and bring the water to the boil. Reduce the heat and simmer the strips for 5 minutes. Drain them and set them aside on paper towels until required.

Squeeze the juice from all four oranges. Put the orange juice and the finely grated rind in a small, non-reactive saucepan. Sprinkle the powdered gelatine over 2 tablespoons of water in a small bowl. Set it aside and leave it to soften for 5 minutes.

Add the sugar to the orange juice and stir the juice over medium heat until the sugar has dissolved —

Tropical Fruits Terrine with Passion Fruit Sauce

Serves 8
Working time: about 1 hour
Total time: about 6 hours

Calories **180**
Protein **6g**
Cholesterol **0mg**
Total fat **trace**
Saturated fat **trace**
Sodium **50mg**

1	mango, peeled, flesh cut into 1 cm (½ inch) wide strips	1
1	small papaya, peeled and seeded, flesh cut into 1 cm (½ inch) wide strips	1
1	kiwi fruit, peeled and cut lengthwise into thin slivers	1
15 cl	skimmed milk	¼ pint
1	vanilla pod	1
4 tsp	powdered gelatine	4 tsp
800 g	bananas	1 lb 10 oz
8 cl	fresh lime juice	3 fl oz
60 g	low-fat fromage frais	2 oz
1 tsp	caster sugar (optional)	1 tsp
Passion fruit sauce		
4 tsp	caster sugar	4 tsp
1	lime, grated rind only	1
4	passion fruits	4

Place the mango, papaya and kiwi fruit strips in a nylon sieve over a bowl, and leave them to drain. Heat the milk in a small, heavy-bottomed saucepan until it is just simmering, then remove it from the heat. Split the

vanilla pod lengthwise and add it to the milk. Cover the pan and set it aside for 30 minutes, to allow the milk to become infused with the vanilla flavour.

Remove the vanilla pod from the milk and scrape out all the seeds from inside it. Stir the seeds into the milk. Soften the gelatine in 2 tablespoons of water *(page 13, Step 1)*. Heat the milk to simmering point again and remove it from the heat. Add the softened gelatine and stir until it has dissolved completely. Set the vanilla-flavoured milk aside; if it starts to set, stand the saucepan in hot water.

Peel the bananas and cut them into chunks. Toss the chunks in the lime juice to prevent discoloration, then purée them with the lime juice in a food processor or blender. Add the vanilla-flavoured milk and the *fromage frais*, and process the mixture again until it is smooth. Taste the mixture, and add the sugar at this stage if you wish to sweeten it.

Dampen the insides of an 18 by 7.5 by 7.5 cm (7 by 3 by 3 inch) terrine with water. Spread a layer of the banana mousse about 5 mm (¼ inch) thick in the bottom of the terrine. Place the terrine in the refrigerator for about 15 minutes, to set the mousse. Spread a second layer of mousse in the terrine — this time about 1 cm (½ inch) thick. Arrange a selection of the fruit strips, lengthwise, on top of the mousse, in two or three lines; leave at least 1 cm (½ inch) between each line of fruit strips and make sure that no strips are touching the sides of the terrine. (Note down the position of fruit

varieties on a piece of paper so that you can make sure the arrangement differs between layers.) Gently press the strips down through the soft mousse to the set layer beneath and spread another 1 cm (½ inch) of mousse over the top. Tap the base of the terrine gently on the work surface, to eliminate any air bubbles, then return it to the refrigerator for 30 minutes, to set the new layers of mousse. Repeat this process twice more. Once the final layer of mousse has been added, chill the dessert for 3 hours, to set it firmly.

Meanwhile, prepare the passion fruit sauce. Bring 8 cl (3 fl oz) of water to the boil in a small, non-reactive pan. Add the sugar and lime rind and simmer, stirring occasionally, until the liquid has thickened slightly. Cut three of the passion fruits in half crosswise and spoon the pulp and seeds into the syrup. Simmer the sauce for a further 2 minutes. Remove the pan from the heat, cover it and leave the sauce to cool for 30 minutes. Chill it in the refrigerator until required.

Just before serving, press the passion fruit sauce through a fine nylon sieve. Halve the remaining passion fruit, spoon the pulp and seeds into the sauce and stir them in. Dip the base and sides of the terrine in hot water for 2 or 3 seconds and turn the dessert out on to a flat serving plate. Serve the terrine cut into slices, accompanied by the passion fruit sauce.

SUGGESTED ACCOMPANIMENTS: *Cape gooseberries, sliced star fruit, or some extra slices of any of the fruits featured in the dessert.*

Terrine of Prunes and Almonds

Serves 12
Working time: about 1 hour and 30 minutes
Total time: about 24 hours (includes marinating and chilling)

Calories **205**
Protein **8g**
Cholesterol **10mg**
Total fat **9g**
Saturated fat **3g**
Sodium **40mg**

2 tsp	Earl Grey tea leaves	2 tsp
500 g	ready-to-eat prunes	1 lb
10 cl	brandy	3½ fl oz
30 g	slivered almonds	1 oz
75 g	sugar	2½ oz
100 g	shelled almonds, 75 g (2½ oz) blanched, the remainder unskinned	3½ oz
30 cl	skimmed milk	½ pint
2 drops	pure almond extract	2 drops
2½ tbsp	powdered gelatine	2½ tbsp
10 cl	whipping cream	3½ fl oz
3	egg whites	3
2 tbsp	clear honey	2 tbsp
175 g	thick Greek yogurt	6 oz

Infuse the tea leaves in ¼ litre (8 fl oz) of boiling water for 5 minutes. Place the prunes in a saucepan and strain the tea over them. Bring the tea just to the boil, reduce the heat and simmer the prunes until they are tender — about 10 minutes. Allow the prunes to cool

in the tea, then drain and stone them, discarding the tea. Place the prunes in a bowl and pour 5 tablespoons of the brandy over them. Cover the bowl and leave the prunes to marinate for at least 12 hours.

When you are ready to make the terrine, drain the prunes and reserve the liquid. Select six firm prunes, slice them and set them aside until required. Purée the remaining prunes in a food processor or blender.

Place the slivered almonds in a dry, heavy frying pan and cook them over medium heat, stirring them from time to time, until they are golden-brown — about 5 minutes. Add 1 tablespoon of the sugar and continue cooking until the sugar caramelizes and coats the almonds — a further 1 to 2 minutes. As soon as the nuts have caramelized, remove them from the pan and spread them out on a sheet of lightly oiled greaseproof paper. Leave them to cool and harden, then place them in a plastic bag and crush them coarsely with a rolling pin.

Grind the blanched and unskinned almonds in a food processor. With the food processor running, gradually pour in 15 cl (¼ pint) of water. Pour in the milk, process again to mix, then pour the mixture into a small, heavy-bottomed saucepan. Bring the mixture to the boil and simmer it gently over very low heat for about 10 minutes. Allow the mixture to cool a little, then strain it through a fine nylon sieve, pressing down hard on the almonds to extract all the flavoured liquid; discard the solids in the sieve. Stir the almond extract and the remaining sugar into the liquid, then set it aside and leave it to cool slightly.

Dissolve 1 tablespoon of the gelatine in 2 tablespoons of water *(page 13)*. Stir the gelatine solution into the warm, almond-flavoured milk and set it aside until it is beginning to thicken — about 45 minutes. Whip the cream until it just holds its shape and fold it into the almond cream. Chill the mixture until it has almost set — about 20 minutes. Whisk two of the egg whites until they form soft peaks. Stir 1 tablespoon of the whites into the almond cream, then use a metal spoon to fold in the remainder. Fold in the sliced prunes and the crushed caramelized almonds.

Rinse a 30 by 7.5 by 7.5 cm (12 by 3 by 3 inch) tin with cold water; leave some water clinging to the insides of the tin. Pour in the almond mixture and chill it until it is firm — about 30 minutes.

Blend the honey and the yogurt into the puréed prunes. In a small bowl, add the remaining brandy to the reserved prune-soaking juices and dissolve the rest of the gelatine in this liquid, following the same method as before. Mix the gelatine solution thoroughly into the prune purée.

Whisk the remaining egg white until it forms soft peaks. Stir 1 tablespoon of the egg white into the prune purée, then use a metal spoon to fold in the rest. Spoon the mixture into the tin and chill it until it is set firmly — at least 4 hours.

Unmould the terrine on to a flat serving dish and serve it cut into slices.

Hazelnut Praline Block with Fresh Figs

Serves 16
Working time: about 30 minutes
Total time: about 4 hours (includes chilling)

Calories **135**
Protein **13g**
Cholesterol **trace**
Total fat **3g**
Saturated fat **1g**
Sodium **25mg**

125 g	shelled hazelnuts	4 oz
150 g	sugar	5 oz
7 tsp	powdered gelatine	7 tsp
1 kg	low-fat fromage frais	2 lb
1½ tbsp	brandy or Armagnac	1½ tbsp
5	fresh figs, tops sliced off	5

Preheat the oven to 180°C (350°F or Mark 4). Line a 25 by 10 by 10 cm (10 by 4 by 4 inch) terrine with non-stick parchment paper (page 34). Lightly oil a marble slab or a baking sheet.

Spread the hazelnuts out on a dry baking sheet and roast them in the oven for about 10 minutes, until they are evenly browned. Enfold them in a tea towel and roll them to and fro, then discard the loosened skins. Put the roasted nuts and 125 g (4 oz) of the sugar in a small, heavy-bottomed saucepan and stir them over low heat until the sugar has dissolved and turned a golden caramel colour. Pour the mixture on to the oiled slab or baking sheet and spread it out with a wooden spoon. Leave the praline to cool and harden for about 30 minutes.

Dissolve the gelatine in 3 tablespoons of water (page 13). Break the hazelnut praline into pieces and chop the pieces coarsely in a food processor. Scatter enough praline over the base of the prepared terrine to form a layer 1 cm (½ inch) deep. Process the remaining praline to a fine powder in the food processor. Add the remaining sugar, the fromage frais, the brandy and the dissolved gelatine. Process again until all the ingredients are smoothly combined.

Pour the praline cream into the terrine until it reaches a depth of 4 cm (1½ inches). Arrange the figs in a line down the centre of the terrine and pour on the remaining praline cream to cover the figs. Refrigerate the terrine for 2 to 3 hours, or until it has set firmly.

Dip the base and sides of the terrine in hot water for 2 or 3 seconds. Invert it on to a flat serving plate and peel off the lining paper. Dip a sharp, long-bladed knife in hot water, and use this to cut the terrine into slices.

Chestnut and Fig Terrine

Serves 12
Working time: about 1 hour and 10 minutes
Total time: about 5 hours and 40 minutes
(includes cooling and freezing)

Calories **280**
Protein **2g**
Cholesterol **0mg**
Total fat **12g**
Saturated fat **3g**
Sodium **110mg**

750 g	fresh chestnuts, or 350 g (12 oz) dried chestnuts, soaked overnight in cold water and drained thoroughly	1 ½ lb
6 tbsp	Marsala	6 tbsp
125 g	polyunsaturated margarine	4 oz
125 g	caster sugar	4 oz
175 g	semi-dried figs, chopped	6 oz
Chocolate coating		
60 g	plain chocolate, chopped	2 oz
2 tbsp	Marsala	2 tbsp
15 g	polyunsaturated margarine	½ oz

Cut a deep cross in the hull of each fresh chestnut. Drop the chestnuts into a saucepan of boiling water and parboil them for about 10 minutes to loosen their hulls. Remove the saucepan from the heat. Using a slotted spoon, lift the chestnuts out of the water a few at a time, and peel off the hulls and inner skins while the nuts are still hot. You should be left with about 500 g (1 lb) of peeled nuts.

Put the fresh or dried chestnuts into a saucepan and cover them with fresh cold water. Bring the water to the boil over medium heat, then reduce the heat to low and cook the chestnuts gently for 15 to 20 minutes, until they are tender. Drain the chestnuts and return them to the pan. Pour the Marsala over the nuts and continue to cook them gently for 5 to 10 minutes, until the Marsala has been completely absorbed and the nuts are very soft. Remove the pan from the heat and allow the nuts to cool for about 1 hour. Meanwhile, line a 19 by 9 by 5 cm (7½ by 3½ by 2 inch) loaf tin with non-stick parchment paper (page 34).

Put the cooled chestnuts into a food processor and process them to a smooth paste. Alternatively, pass them through a ricer or sieve. Using a wooden spoon, cream the margarine and sugar together in a mixing bowl until soft and fluffy. Beat in the chestnut purée, then fold in the chopped figs. Spoon the mixture into the prepared tin and smooth the surface with the back of the spoon. Freeze the terrine for 3 hours, or until it has frozen solid.

To make the coating, put the chocolate and Marsala in a small saucepan. Stir them over low heat until the chocolate melts and blends smoothly with the Marsala. Remove the pan from the heat and stir in the margarine. Allow the coating to cool — about 5 minutes — but do not let it set.

Cover a flat board with foil. Remove the terrine from the freezer and turn it out on to the board; carefully peel off the lining paper. Using a small metal spatula, quickly spread the chocolate coating evenly all over the terrine. Mark the surface roughly to create a pattern. Return the terrine to the freezer until the chocolate has set hard — about 15 minutes. Cover it with plastic film and keep it in the freezer until required.

Thirty minutes before serving the terrine, remove it from the freezer. Unwrap it, place it on a flat serving plate and put it in the refrigerator. To serve, cut the terrine into thin slices using a sharp, long-bladed knife.

EDITOR'S NOTE: *The terrine may be stored in the freezer for up to six months.*

Caramel and Chocolate Bavarois

Serves 12
Working time: about 1 hour and 40 minutes
Total time: about 8 hours (includes chilling)

Calories **190**			
Protein **8g**	175 g	granulated sugar	6 oz
Cholesterol **95mg**	1 litre	skimmed milk	1¾ pints
Total fat **8g**	4	eggs	4
Saturated fat **4g**	3 tbsp	powdered gelatine	3 tbsp
Sodium **90mg**	20 g	cocoa powder	¾ oz
	30 g	caster sugar	1 oz
	15 cl	double cream	¼ pint
	1	egg white	1

First make the caramel bavarois. Put half of the granulated sugar into a heavy-bottomed saucepan with 3 tablespoons of cold water. Stir them together over low heat until every granule of sugar has dissolved; brush down the sides of the pan from time to time with a pastry brush dipped in hot water. Bring the syrup to the boil over high heat and boil it rapidly until it has turned a rich golden colour. Remove the pan from the heat and pour in half of the milk. Set the pan over low heat for about 5 minutes, until the caramel has dissolved completely in the milk; stir the liquid occasionally during this time.

Meanwhile, lightly whisk two of the eggs together in a large bowl. Soften half of the gelatine in 3 tablespoons of cold water *(page 13, Step 1)*, and set the solution aside until it is needed.

Whisk the hot, but not boiling, caramel-flavoured milk into the whisked eggs. Set the bowl over a saucepan of gently simmering water and stir the mixture until it forms a smooth, thin custard — about 20 minutes. As soon as the custard is ready, pour it through a nylon sieve into a clean bowl. Add the softened gelatine solution and stir the mixture until the gelatine is completely dissolved. Set the caramel custard aside and leave it to cool, stirring it frequently to prevent a skin from forming.

To make the chocolate bavarois, blend the cocoa powder and half of the remaining milk together in a saucepan. Bring the mixture to the boil over medium heat, stirring continuously. Cook it gently for 1 to 2 minutes, then stir in the remaining milk. Continue to heat the milk until it is very hot but not boiling.

Meanwhile, in a large bowl, whisk the remaining two eggs and the caster sugar together. Using the same method as before, soften the remaining gelatine in 3 tablespoons of cold water.

Pour the hot milk on to the egg and sugar mixture. Set the bowl over a saucepan of gently simmering water and cook the chocolate custard in the same way as the caramel custard. When the chocolate custard is ready, pour it through a nylon sieve into a clean bowl. Add the softened gelatine and stir until it is completely dissolved. Allow the chocolate custard to cool, stirring it frequently to prevent a skin from forming. Place both the custards in the refrigerator until they begin to thicken — about 30 minutes.

Whisk the double cream and the egg white together until the mixture will hold soft peaks. Divide the cream mixture equally between the two custards and lightly whisk it in until evenly blended.

Wedge a 21 by 11 by 6 cm (8½ by 4½ by 2½ inch) non-reactive loaf tin on its side at a 45-degree angle in a large bowl of ice. Pour the caramel custard into the tin until it is level with one edge of the tin, forming a triangular cross section. Leave the tin in position until the custard has set firmly — about 30 minutes; alternatively, carefully transfer the bowl to the freezer for 10 to 15 minutes. Meanwhile, keep the chocolate custard at room temperature to prevent it from setting. If necessary, stand the bowl in warm water to soften the mixture, but do not let it become hot.

When the caramel custard has set, remove the tin from the bowl of ice and stand it flat on the work surface. Pour in the chocolate custard, then place the tin in the refrigerator to chill for 3 to 4 hours, until the chocolate custard has set firmly.

While the custard is chilling, make a caramel sauce. Put the remaining granulated sugar into a small, heavy-bottomed saucepan with 3 tablespoons of cold water, and make a rich golden caramel in the same way as before. Pour in 15 cl (¼ pint) of hot water, reduce the heat to low and leave the saucepan on the heat until the caramel has completely dissolved in the water, making a syrupy sauce. Allow the sauce to cool, then refrigerate it until required.

Unmould the bavarois on to a flat serving dish. Serve it sliced, with the caramel sauce.

Orange and Almond Terrine

Serves 12
Working time: about 30 minutes
Total time: about 2 hours and 30 minutes (includes chilling)

Calories **185**
Protein **18g**
Cholesterol **trace**
Total fat **6g**
Saturated fat **1g**
Sodium **30mg**

6	oranges	6
2 tbsp	powdered gelatine	2 tbsp
1 kg	low-fat fromage frais, at room temperature	2 lb
125 g	ground almonds	4 oz
60 g	caster sugar	2 oz
2 tbsp	Grand Marnier or other orange-flavoured liqueur	2 tbsp
	mint sprigs, for decoration	

Line the base of a 22 by 12 by 6 cm (9 by 5 by 2½ inch) non-reactive loaf tin with non-stick parchment paper.

Using a sharp knife, slice off the peel at both ends of the oranges. Stand each orange on one of its flat ends and cut off the remaining peel by slicing downwards in vertical strips; make sure you cut off all the pith when doing this. Working over a bowl to catch the juice, cut four of the oranges into segments by slicing between the flesh and membrane. Cut the orange segments in half crosswise and set them aside, with the juice, until required. Slice the remaining two oranges crosswise into thin rounds, then cut each round in half to make semicircles. Set the semicircles aside.

Dissolve the gelatine in 3 tablespoons of water *(page 13)*. Pour the juice from the oranges into a food processor or blender and add the *fromage · frais*, ground almonds, sugar, Grand Marnier and dissolved gelatine. Process the mixture until it is smooth.

Place a line of orange semicircles, slightly overlapping them, down the centre of the prepared tin. Reserve the rest for decoration. Stir the orange segments into the *fromage frais* mixture and spoon the mixture into the tin without disturbing the orange semicircles on the bottom. Refrigerate the terrine for 2 to 3 hours, or until it is firmly set.

To unmould the terrine, dip the base and sides of the tin in hot water for 2 or 3 seconds, then turn it out on to a serving plate. Slice the terrine with a sharp knife, and decorate each portion with a sprig of mint and one or two of the reserved orange semicircles.

Champagne and Melon Terrine

THIS TERRINE CAN BE SERVED EITHER AS A DESSERT OR AS A
FRESH AND UNUSUAL FIRST COURSE.

Serves 8
Working time: about 45 minutes
Total time: about 10 hours and 30 minutes (includes chilling)

Calories **180**
Protein **16g**
Cholesterol **trace**
Total fat **trace**
Saturated fat **trace**
Sodium **35mg**

3 tbsp	powdered gelatine	3 tbsp
¾ litre	dry champagne or sparkling white wine	1¼ pints
1	Charentais or Gallia melon (about 850 g/1¾ lb)	1
500 g	low-fat fromage frais	1 lb
30 g	caster sugar	1 oz
2.5 cm	piece fresh ginger root, peeled and finely chopped	1 inch
	mint sprigs, for decoration	

Dissolve 2 tablespoons of the gelatine in 4 tablespoons of water, following the instructions on page 13. Pour the champagne into a mixing bowl and gradually stir in the gelatine solution.

Line a 22 by 12 by 6 cm (9 by 5 by 2½ inch) loaf tin with champagne jelly as follows. Pour 15 cl (¼ pint) of the champagne and gelatine mixture into the tin and place the tin, on a tray, in the freezer. When the jelly has set — after 5 to 10 minutes — tilt the tin over on to one of its long sides and place a small weight under the rim of the tin to raise it a little. Pour another 8 cl (3 fl oz) of the jelly mixture into the tin and adjust the

position of the weight if necessary to ensure that the mixture just reaches the rim of the tin but does not flow out. Leave the jelly to set in the freezer for 5 to 10 minutes, then repeat the process to cover the other long side. Cover the two short sides of the tin in the same way, using about 6 cl (2 fl oz) of jelly mixture for each. When the jelly has set firmly, transfer the tin to the refrigerator while you prepare the melon.

Halve the melon, scoop out and discard the seeds and cut the melon into wedges; cut away and discard the skin. Using a sharp knife, cut enough flesh into very thin slices to line the base and sides of the loaf tin. Remove the tin from the refrigerator and, working quickly, arrange overlapping melon slices over the jelly-lined base and sides. (Do not worry about any slices that may stand proud of the rim; these can be trimmed off later.) Return the tin to the refrigerator while you make the filling.

Cut the remaining melon into small chunks. Dissolve the remaining gelatine in 1 tablespoon of water, using the same method as before. In a large bowl, mix together the *fromage frais*, melon chunks, sugar, ginger and the remaining champagne jelly mixture. Stir in the dissolved gelatine and chill the filling until it is on the point of setting — about 30 minutes. Spoon the filling into the lined tin and chill the terrine overnight.

Before unmoulding the terrine, trim any protruding melon slices that rise above the top of the tin. Dip the tin into boiling water for 2 or 3 seconds, then invert it on to a flat serving platter. Serve the terrine, either cut into slices or spooned into portions, garnished with sprigs of mint.

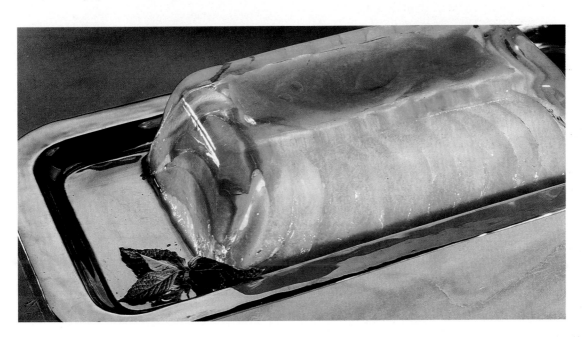

Strawberry Cheese Loaf

Serves 10
Working time: about 30 minutes
Total time: about 8 hours and 30 minutes (includes chilling)

Calories **130**
Protein **12g**
Cholesterol **10mg**
Total fat **2g**
Saturated fat **1g**
Sodium **240mg**

500 g	low-fat cottage cheese	1 lb
200 g	quark	7 oz
1 tsp	pure vanilla extract	1 tsp
45 g	caster sugar	1½ oz
2 tsp	powdered gelatine	2 tsp
1	egg white	1
850 g	fresh strawberries, six reserved for decoration, the remainder hulled	1¾ lb
2 tsp	redcurrant jelly	2 tsp
Strawberry-orange sauce		
250 g	strawberries, hulled	8 oz
30 g	caster sugar	1 oz
3 tbsp	fresh orange juice	3 tbsp
2 tbsp	Cointreau or other orange-flavoured liqueur	2 tbsp

Press the cottage cheese through a sieve into a mixing bowl. Beat in the quark, vanilla extract and sugar. Dissolve the gelatine in 2 tablespoons of water (page 13), then slowly pour it on to the cheese mixture, beating well all the time. Whisk the egg white until it forms soft peaks. Stir 1 tablespoon of the egg white into the cheese mixture, then use a metal spoon to fold in the remaining egg white.

Line an 18 by 10 by 7.5 cm (7 by 4 by 3 inch) loaf tin with a piece of dampened muslin. Spread a third of the cheese mixture in the base of the tin. Halve 13 of the hulled strawberries and arrange six halves, stalk ends down and cut sides against the muslin, along each long edge of the tin. Between these rows of strawberry halves, make a single layer of whole strawberries. Spoon half of the remaining cheese mixture over the strawberries, then lay another seven strawberry halves against the muslin on each long side of the tin — as before, but this time stalk ends up. Pack the remaining whole strawberries over the cheese mixture in an even layer and spread the last of the cheese mixture evenly on the top, pressing it down with the back of the spoon. Chill the terrine overnight, or until the cheese mixture is well set.

To make the sauce, purée the strawberries in a food processor or blender, and press the purée through a sieve into a small pan. Stir in the sugar, orange juice and Cointreau, and cook the sauce over low heat, stirring it gently, until the sugar has dissolved — about 2 minutes. Leave the sauce to cool.

Just before serving the dessert, slice all but a few of the reserved strawberries. Mix the redcurrant jelly with 1 tablespoon of water in a small saucepan over low heat. Unmould the dessert on to a flat serving dish and arrange the sliced strawberries on top. Brush them with the redcurrant glaze and decorate the dish with the remaining whole strawberries. Serve the terrine cut into slices, accompanied by the sauce.

EDITOR'S NOTE: *Once it has reached room temperature, this terrine becomes soft and difficult to slice. If you wish, return it to the refrigerator to firm it up once more before serving or, alternatively, spoon it into portions.*

Redcurrant and Passion Fruit Terrine with Vanilla Sauce

Serves 12
Working time: about 20 minutes
Total time: about 1 hour

Calories **70**	2	passion fruits	2
Protein **3g**	4	egg whites	4
Cholesterol **35mg**	90 g	caster sugar	3 oz
Total fat **1g**	125 g	redcurrants, picked over and stemmed	4 oz
Saturated fat **trace**		**Vanilla sauce**	
Sodium **35mg**			
	1 tbsp	cornflour	1 tbsp
	2	egg yolks	2
	½	vanilla pod, split lengthwise, seeds only scraped out and reserved	½
	1 tbsp	caster sugar	1 tbsp
	30 cl	skimmed milk	½ pint

Preheat the oven to 170°C (325°F or Mark 3). Following the instructions on page 34, line a 30 by 10 by 7 cm (12 by 4 by 2¾ inch) collapsible-sided tin with non-stick parchment paper.

Halve the passion fruits and spoon out the pulp and seeds into a small bowl. Whisk the egg whites in a mixing bowl until they form soft peaks. Whisk in the sugar in three batches, ensuring that the mixture is stiff and glossy each time before adding more sugar. Using a metal tablespoon, fold in the passion fruit pulp and seeds and the redcurrants. Spoon the mixture into the tin and level the surface with a spatula.

Stand the tin in a roasting pan and pour in boiling water to come half way up the side of the tin. Bake the terrine for 40 minutes, or until a fine skewer inserted into the centre comes out clean; watch the surface of the terrine while it is cooking, and cover it with a sheet of non-stick parchment paper if it appears to be browning too quickly. When the terrine is cooked, remove the tin from the water bath and gently invert it on to a flat serving plate. Carefully release the collapsible sides of the tin and lift it off. Peel off the lining paper and set the terrine aside to cool.

To prepare the sauce, whisk the cornflour and egg yolks together in a heatproof bowl. Combine the vanilla seeds and caster sugar, pressing down on the seeds with the back of a spoon to separate them and disperse them evenly in the sugar. Stir the sugar and vanilla seeds into the egg yolks. Heat the milk in a heavy-bottomed saucepan until it just reaches boiling point. Pour the milk on to the egg yolks and beat the mixture well with a wooden spoon. Pour it back into the pan through a sieve. Stir the vanilla sauce over low heat just until it thickens — do not allow it to boil. Pour the sauce into a bowl to cool; stir the sauce from time to time to prevent a skin from forming.

Transfer the vanilla sauce to a jug. Serve the terrine cut into slices, accompanied by the sauce.

SUGGESTED ACCOMPANIMENT: *fresh redcurrants, dipped in lightly whisked egg white and caster sugar.*

EDITOR'S NOTE: *This terrine can be kept in the refrigerator for up to 24 hours before it is served, but it should not be frozen. Raspberries, blueberries or sliced strawberries may all be used in place of redcurrants.*

Rice and Apricot Ring

Serves 8
Working time: about 1 hour and 10 minutes
Total time: about 3 hours and 30 minutes (includes chilling)

Calories **125**
Protein **6g**
Cholesterol **trace**
Total fat **1g**
Saturated fat **trace**
Sodium **60mg**

60 cl	skimmed milk	1 pint
60 g	round-grain rice, washed	2 oz
½ tsp	pure almond extract	½ tsp
5	large ripe apricots, peeled, halved and stoned, or 400 g (14 oz) canned apricot halves in fruit juice, drained	5
90 g	low-fat fromage frais	3 oz
1 tbsp	powdered gelatine	1 tbsp
2	egg whites	2
75 g	caster sugar	2½ oz
175 g	fresh raspberries	6 oz

Bring the milk to the boil in a heavy-bottomed saucepan. Reduce the heat to low and add the rice and the almond extract. Simmer the mixture, uncovered, until the rice has absorbed all the milk — about 50 minutes — stirring the mixture from time to time as it cooks.

If you are using fresh apricots, place them, cut side down, in a non-reactive saucepan and pour in 17.5 cl (6 fl oz) of boiling water. Simmer the fruit gently for 2 to 3 minutes, until it is just tender, then drain it.

Arrange eight apricot halves, skinned surfaces down, in the base of a 20 cm (8 inch) ring mould. Reserve the remaining apricot halves.

When the rice has absorbed the milk, remove it from the heat and allow it to cool slightly, then stir in the *fromage frais*. Dissolve the gelatine in 2 tablespoons of water *(page 13)* and stir it into the rice mixture. Whisk the egg whites until they stand in soft peaks. Whisk in 60 g (2 oz) of the sugar in three batches, ensuring that the mixture is stiff and glossy each time before adding further sugar. Stir a spoonful of the egg whites into the rice to lighten the mixture, then use a metal tablespoon to fold in the remainder of the egg whites. Spoon the mixture into the prepared ring mould, being careful not to disturb the apricot halves. Level the surface of the mixture and refrigerate the ring for at least 2 hours, or until set.

Meanwhile, put the raspberries in a non-reactive saucepan and add the remaining caster sugar. Heat the berries and sugar gently until the juice runs, then simmer the berries until they fall apart — 2 to 3 minutes. Allow them to cool. Purée the cooked raspberries with the reserved apricot halves in a food processor or blender. Press the purée through a fine nylon sieve to remove the pips.

To unmould the dessert, dip the base of the mould in hot water for 2 or 3 seconds, then turn the ring out on to a flat serving plate. Serve the dessert in slices, with the raspberry-apricot purée.

SUGGESTED ACCOMPANIMENT: *fresh raspberries, placed in the centre of the ring.*

EDITOR'S NOTE: *The ring may be stored in the refrigerator for up to four days but it should not be frozen.*

Moulded Chocolate Mousse with Orange-Caramel Sauce

Serves 8
Working time: about 25 minutes
Total time: about 3 hours and 25 minutes

Calories **210**
Protein **5g**
Cholesterol **5mg**
Total fat **7g**
Saturated fat **4g**
Sodium **50mg**

1 tbsp	powdered gelatine	1 tbsp
150 g	plain chocolate	5 oz
1 tbsp	dark rum (optional)	1 tbsp
250 g	thick Greek yogurt	8 oz
17.5 cl	plain low-fat yogurt	6 fl oz
1	orange, grated rind only	1
2	egg whites	2
1 tbsp	caster sugar	1 tbsp
2	satsumas, peeled and segmented, all pith removed	2
Orange-caramel sauce		
20 cl	fresh orange juice	7 fl oz
100 g	caster sugar	3½ oz
1 tsp	ground cinnamon	1 tsp

Line a 45 cl (¾ pint) decorative mould with plastic film, pulling the film as tight as possible and pressing it into the contours of the mould.

Dissolve the gelatine in 2 tablespoons of water *(page 13)*. Melt the chocolate, with the rum if you are using it, in a heatproof bowl set over a pan of simmering water; stir the chocolate until it is smooth. In a mixing bowl, whisk together the Greek yogurt and low-fat yogurt, then whisk in the melted chocolate, the orange rind, and finally the dissolved gelatine.

In a separate bowl, whisk the egg whites until they form soft peaks. Add the sugar and whisk again until the whites are stiff and glossy. Using a metal tablespoon, gently fold the whisked egg whites into the chocolate mixture, then turn the mixture into the prepared mould. Level the surface of the mousse and put it in the refrigerator to set — 3 to 4 hours.

To make the sauce, put 3 tablespoons of the orange juice in a heavy-bottomed pan with the sugar. Heat gently until the sugar has dissolved, then increase the heat and bring the liquid to the boil. Add the remaining orange juice to the pan (cover your hand with a towel when doing this, in case of splattering), and stir in the cinnamon. Boil the sauce for 5 minutes, to reduce it a little. Strain the sauce into a jug through a coffee filter paper or a layer of muslin, to remove the sediment. Allow the sauce to cool.

To serve the mousse, invert the mould on to a flat serving dish and carefully peel off the plastic film. Pour the orange-caramel sauce round the mousse, and arrange the satsuma segments along the top of the mousse and in the sauce.

Cassis, Peach and Raspberry Layered Pudding

Serves 8
Working time: about 35 minutes
Total time: about 5 hours (includes chilling)

Calories **160**
Protein **3g**
Cholesterol **0mg**
Total fat **0g**
Saturated fat **0g**
Sodium **5mg**

600 g	peaches, halved and stoned	1¼ lb
175 g	caster sugar	6 oz
4 tbsp	powdered gelatine	4 tbsp
350 g	fresh raspberries	12 oz
1 tbsp	cassis	1 tbsp
3	egg whites	3
Raspberry sauce		
250 g	fresh raspberries	8 oz
2 tbsp	gin	2 tbsp
1 tbsp	icing sugar	1 tbsp

Place the peaches in a small non-reactive saucepan with 15 cl (¼ pint) of water and half of the caster sugar. Poach them gently for a few minutes, to soften them. Drain the peaches, reserving the syrup, and set them aside to cool. Purée the peaches in a food processor or blender, and sieve the purée to remove any bits of skin. Put 3 tablespoons of the reserved poaching syrup in a small bowl and dissolve 2 tablespoons of the gelatine in this *(page 13)*. Stir the dissolved gelatine into the remaining poaching syrup, then stir in the peach purée. Set the mixture aside until it has partially set — about 40 minutes.

Meanwhile, purée 250 g (8 oz) of the raspberries in a food processor or blender and press the purée through a nylon sieve into a bowl. Stir the remaining 90 g (3 oz) of caster sugar into 4 tablespoons of water in a small pan, and heat gently to dissolve the sugar. Soften 1 tablespoon of the gelatine in 2 tablespoons of water *(page 13, Step 1)*. Add the softened gelatine to the hot sugar syrup and stir until it has dissolved fully, then mix it into the raspberry purée. Set the purée aside until it has partially set — about 25 minutes.

While the raspberry mixture is setting, stir the cassis into 30 cl (½ pint) of water. Place 3 tablespoons of this liquid in a small bowl and dissolve the remaining tablespoon of gelatine in it, as with the peach syrup *(page 13)*. Stir the dissolved gelatine thoroughly into the remaining cassis water.

Pour a thin layer of the cassis jelly mixture into the base of a 20 by 10 by 6 cm (8 by 4 by 2½ inch) non-reactive loaf tin, and leave it to set in the refrigerator for 10 minutes. When it has set, place the remaining raspberries on top of the jelly in an even layer. Pour the remaining cassis jelly mixture over the raspberries

and return the loaf tin to the refrigerator to set the jelly — about 15 minutes.

Whisk the egg whites until they form soft peaks. Using a metal tablespoon, fold one third of the egg whites into the partially set raspberry mixture and fold the remainder into the partially set peach mixture. Spoon half of the peach mixture into the tin and return it to the refrigerator to set — about 30 minutes. When the peach layer has set, spoon in the raspberry mixture and refrigerate it until set — about 30 minutes. Finally, add the remaining peach mixture and thoroughly chill the pudding again to set the top layer — about 2 hours.

To make the sauce, purée the raspberries in a food processor or blender until smooth. Press the purée through a nylon sieve into a bowl, then beat the gin and icing sugar into the sieved purée.

To unmould the pudding, dip the base and sides of the tin in hot water for 2 or 3 seconds, then turn it out on to a serving plate. Serve the pudding cut into slices, accompanied by the raspberry sauce.

EDITOR'S NOTE: *If the peaches are very ripe, they may be puréed without first being poached.*

Exotic Fruits in Champagne Jelly

Serves 8
Working time: about 1 hour and 30 minutes
Total time: about 5 hours and 30 minutes
(includes chilling)

Calories **165**
Protein **6g**
Cholesterol **0mg**
Total fat **0g**
Saturated fat **0g**
Sodium **10mg**

3 tbsp	powdered gelatine	3 tbsp
45 cl	dry champagne or good-quality sparkling white wine	¾ pint
60 g	sugar	2 oz
1	small ripe mango, peeled, stoned and cut into strips	1
1	small star fruit, thinly sliced crosswise	1
300 g	lychees, skinned, stoned and quartered	10 oz
175 g	kumquats, thinly sliced crosswise, slices seeded	6 oz
1	small papaya, peeled, seeded and thinly sliced	1
500 g	water melon, peeled, seeded and thinly sliced	1 lb

Soften the gelatine in 6 tablespoons of water *(page 13, Step 1)*. Pour 30 cl (½ pint) of the champagne into a saucepan, add the sugar and stir well. Heat them gently until the sugar has dissolved. Remove the pan from the heat and add the softened gelatine; stir the liquid until the gelatine has completely dissolved.

Leave the jelly mixture to cool to room temperature.

When the jelly has cooled, stir in the remaining champagne and spoon a little of the mixture into a 22 by 12 by 6 cm (9 by 5 by 2½ inch) loaf tin, covering the bottom with a thin layer. Chill the tin until the jelly has set — about 10 minutes. Arrange a few pieces of mango, star fruit, lychee and kumquat in an attractive pattern on top of the jelly. Spoon a little more jelly over this first layer of fruit and chill for another 10 minutes, until set. Continue layering the fruit in the tin — either using a variety of fruits in each layer or creating layers of each individual fruit — and coat each layer with a little of the champagne jelly. Chill the mould for 10 minutes between each layer, to set the jelly. When the tin is filled with fruit and jelly, chill it for at least 3 hours to ensure that the jelly is well set.

To unmould the chilled jelly, dip the base and sides of the tin in hot water for 2 or 3 seconds, then invert it on to a flat serving platter. To serve, cut the jelly into slices with a sharp knife.

SUGGESTED ACCOMPANIMENT: *thin dessert biscuits.*

EDITOR'S NOTE: *For the most attractive result, select small fruits and arrange the best pieces in the first layer at the base of the tin. The selection of fruits may be varied to take advantage of what is in season, but avoid using pineapple and kiwi fruit as they contain enzymes that inhibit the setting power of gelatine.*

will need about 45 cl (¾ pint) of purée; make up the quantity with water if necessary.

Pour 15 cl (¼ pint) of cold water into a non-reactive saucepan with the remaining caster sugar. Stir them together over medium heat until the sugar dissolves. Bring the solution to the boil and boil it rapidly for 1 minute. Reduce the heat to low and stir in the kirsch, then add the sliced peaches and poach them gently for 2 to 3 minutes, until they have softened. Using a slotted spoon, transfer the peaches from the syrup to a wire rack lined with paper towels. Set the rack aside and leave the peaches to drain and cool.

Dissolve 1½ tablespoons of the gelatine in 3 tablespoons of water (page 13). Stir the hot gelatine solution into the apple purée.

Pour one third of the apple purée into the bottom of a 21 by 11 by 6 cm (8½ by 4½ by 2½ inch) non-reactive loaf tin. Place the tin in the refrigerator for 30 to 40 minutes, or until the apple purée has set. Keep the remaining apple purée at room temperature during this time, to prevent it from setting.

Meanwhile, dissolve the remaining gelatine in 3 tablespoons of water as before, and stir the solution into the blackberry purée.

Arrange half of the peach slices evenly over the set apple purée, then carefully pour in the blackberry purée. Return the tin to the refrigerator for 30 to 40 minutes, or until the blackberry purée has set.

Place the remaining peach slices evenly over the set blackberry purée, and carefully spoon in the remaining apple purée. Refrigerate the terrine for 3 hours, or overnight, to set it firmly.

Unmould the terrine on to a flat serving plate, and serve it cut into slices.

EDITOR'S NOTE: *The syrup in which the peaches were poached may be reserved for poaching fruits on another occasion; it will keep in the refrigerator for about three weeks.*

Peach, Apple and Blackberry Terrine

Serves 12
Working time: about 1 hour and 20 minutes
Total time: about 6 hours (includes chilling)

Calories **120**
Protein **3g**
Cholesterol **0mg**
Total fat **0g**
Saturated fat **0g**
Sodium **5mg**

1 kg	cooking apples, peeled, quartered, cored and sliced	2 lb
½	lemon, juice only	½
150 g	caster sugar	5 oz
500 g	fresh or frozen blackberries	1 lb
2 tbsp	kirsch	2 tbsp
3	large peaches, peeled, stoned and sliced	3
2½ tbsp	powdered gelatine	2½ tbsp

Put the apples, lemon juice and 60 g (2 oz) of the sugar into a non-reactive, heavy-bottomed saucepan. Cover the saucepan and cook the ingredients over low heat for 15 to 20 minutes, stirring frequently, until the apples are soft and fluffy.

Meanwhile, put the blackberries into another non-reactive, heavy-bottomed saucepan with 60 g (2 oz) of the remaining sugar. Cover the saucepan and cook the blackberries over low heat for 8 to 10 minutes, until they have softened.

Purée the apples and their juice in a food processor, or pass them through a nylon sieve into a heatproof measuring jug. You should have about 60 cl (1 pint) of purée; if necessary, make up the quantity with apple juice. Press the blackberries and their juice through a nylon sieve into another heatproof measuring jug. You

Marbled Blueberry Dessert

Serves 12
Working time: about 35 minutes
Total time: about 3 hours (includes chilling)

Calories **105**
Protein **7g**
Cholesterol **5mg**
Total fat **2g**
Saturated fat **1g**
Sodium **40mg**

90 g	fresh blueberries, stemmed and picked over	3 oz
150 g	caster sugar	5 oz
400 g	thick Greek yogurt	14 oz
175 g	low-fat fromage frais	6 oz
8 tsp	powdered gelatine	8 tsp
4	egg whites	4

Line an 18 by 7.5 by 7.5 cm (7 by 3 by 3 inch) loaf tin with plastic film, pulling the film as tight as possible and pressing it well into the corners.

Place the blueberries in a small, non-reactive saucepan with 1 tablespoon of water and 30 g (1 oz) of the caster sugar. Cover the pan and cook the fruit gently over low heat for 4 to 5 minutes, to soften the blueberries. Remove the pan from the heat and allow the berries to cool in the syrup.

Put the Greek yogurt and *fromage frais* in a mixing bowl. Dissolve the gelatine in 8 cl (3 fl oz) of water *(page 13)*, then whisk all but 1 tablespoon of the gelatine solution into the yogurt and *fromage frais* mixture. Stir the remaining tablespoon of gelatine into the cooled blueberries. In a bowl, whisk the egg whites until they form soft peaks, then whisk in the remaining sugar a little at a time, ensuring that the mixture is stiff and glossy after each addition of sugar. Using a metal tablespoon, gently fold the whisked egg whites into the yogurt and *fromage frais* mixture.

Spoon alternate layers of the yogurt and *fromage frais* mixture and the blueberries into the prepared loaf tin. Plunge a skewer into the mixture and draw it back and forth along the length of the tin a few times, to marble the filling. Level the surface of the filling with a spatula and refrigerate the dessert for 2 to 3 hours, until it has set firmly.

To unmould the dessert, invert the tin on to a flat serving plate and remove the plastic film. Serve the dessert cut into slices.

SUGGESTED ACCOMPANIMENT: *a bowl of soft summer fruits, with a light caramel poured over the top.*

EDITOR'S NOTE: *Prepare a light caramel for the soft fruit accompaniment with 90 g (3 oz) of sugar and 3 tablespoons of water, following the method described in the recipe for the caramel and chocolate bavarois on page 117.*

5 *Thinly pounded chicken breasts wrapped in spinach leaves (recipe, opposite) reveal a green-flecked, basil-scented mousseline when sliced.*

Microwaved Terrines and Pâtés

All the particular virtues and benefits of microwave cookery come to the fore in the making of terrines and pâtés. The microwave oven reduces much of the time, effort (and washing up) required for the most labour-intensive preparations, making it possible to produce delicacies worthy of a banqueting table in a matter of minutes. Its ability to preserve and, indeed, intensify, the full flavour and colour of fresh vegetables and fish, all within the briefest possible cooking time, makes the microwave oven an ideal medium for the repertoire of light, healthy dishes shown on the following pages.

Only 9 minutes are required to cook the aubergine for the Middle Eastern style pâté on page 137, and it is unnecessary to salt the vegetable in advance to purge its acrid juices: the microwave process eradicates any bitterness while the vegetable cooks. Garlic-lovers will appreciate the ease with which the aromatic cloves are softened and mellowed to provide the foundation for a creamy pâté *(page 136)*. Where visual appeal is important, colours remain bright and true: the trout and asparagus terrine on page 138, for instance, displays a delicate interplay of pink and green.

Sauces thicken smoothly, with no need for constant stirring. Gelatinous stocks, made in advance and held in the refrigerator, can be melted down rapidly in the microwave oven for use in jellied dishes. Delicate meats such as chicken livers can be cooked gently and thoroughly in only a few minutes to provide the starting point for a warm, port-spiked pâté *(page 131)*.

Microwave cookery takes place at such high speeds that mixtures in small, individual serving dishes seem to finish cooking almost before they have started. To avoid the risk of their contents boiling over, do not leave them unattended even for a few moments; microwave oven timers may often not be reliable for cooking times under 60 seconds.

When recipes call for a food to be covered with plastic film, be sure that only film labelled microwave-safe is used. If you are placing film over a dish that contains any amount of liquid, prevent any potentially dangerous accumulation of steam by pulling back a corner of the film.

The recipes in this chapter have been tested in 650-watt and 700-watt microwave ovens. The term "high" is used to indicate 100 per cent power, "medium high" 70 per cent power and "defrost" 30 per cent power. In calculating cooking times, remember that food will continue to cook for a few minutes after its removal from the microwave oven.

Chicken Ballotines

Serves 8 as a first course
Working time: about 45 minutes
Total time: about 3 hours (includes chilling)

Calories **155**
Protein **23g**
Cholesterol **55mg**
Total fat **7g**
Saturated fat **3g**
Sodium **180mg**

4	boneless chicken breasts, skinned (about 150 g/5 oz each)	4
1 tbsp	crème fraîche	1 tbsp
1 tbsp	low-fat fromage frais	1 tbsp
½ tsp	salt	½ tsp
⅛ tsp	white pepper	⅛ tsp
12	large spinach leaves, washed and stemmed, blanched in boiling water for 30 seconds, drained and spread out on paper towels to dry	12
	mixed salad leaves, for garnish	
Mixed herb pesto		
15 g	pine-nuts	½ oz
30 g	fresh basil leaves	1 oz
30 g	parsley leaves	1 oz
1 tbsp	freshly grated Parmesan cheese	1 tbsp
1 tbsp	virgin olive oil	1 tbsp

Lay the chicken breasts skinned side down on a board. With a small knife, open out the two flaps of flesh on the inner side of the breasts, taking care not to sever the flaps. Place the opened-out breasts between two sheets of plastic film or greaseproof paper. Using a wooden rolling pin or a meat mallet, beat the breasts out as thinly as possible, without tearing the meat. Trim off the edges from each chicken breast to form a rectangle measuring about 12 by 11 cm (5 by 4½ inches). Set the flattened breasts aside and reserve the trimmings for use in the filling.

To make the mixed herb pesto, grind the pine-nuts to a coarse powder in a food processor or blender, then add the basil, parsley, Parmesan and oil. Process the mixture briefly until just smooth. Transfer the pesto to a bowl and wash out the food processor.

Place the reserved chicken trimmings in the food processor together with the *crème fraîche, fromage frais,* half of the salt and the white pepper, and blend the mixture to a smooth paste. Add the pesto and process until the filling is well mixed.

Place three large spinach leaves, vein side up, on a square of plastic film. Overlap the leaves to form a square slightly larger than a flattened chicken breast. Place one of the chicken breasts on top of the spinach, sprinkle it with a little of the remaining salt, and spoon on a quarter of the pesto filling, shaping it into a cylinder along the length of the piece of chicken. ▶

With the aid of the plastic film, roll up the chicken breast round the filling, ensuring that the spinach leaf encloses the chicken completely. Seal the plastic film tightly round the roll, twisting the ends firmly and tucking them underneath. Repeat with the remaining chicken breasts, then place the four rolls in the refrigerator to chill for at least 1 hour.

Arrange the chilled rolls in a single layer in a shallow dish, and puncture the plastic film wrapping in several places. Microwave the rolls on high for 4 minutes, giving the dish a quarter turn after every minute. Turn and rearrange the chicken rolls and microwave them on high for a further minute.

Leave the chicken, still wrapped in film, to cool, then chill it thoroughly in the refrigerator, keeping the rolls wrapped in film until required. Unwrap the chicken rolls, cut them into slices and serve them garnished with the mixed salad leaves.

Cucumber Timbales

Serves 6 as a first course
Working time: about 25 minutes
Total time: about 1 hour and 25 minutes
(includes chilling)

Calories **170**
Protein **11g**
Cholesterol **trace**
Total fat **trace**
Saturated fat **trace**
Sodium **185mg**

3 tsp	powdered gelatine	3 tsp
15 g	cornflour, mixed with 3 tbsp cold water	½ oz
15 cl	skimmed milk	¼ pint
1	cucumber (about 500 g/1 lb), 12 thin slices reserved for garnish, the rest finely chopped	1
3 tbsp	chopped mint, plus six mint sprigs for garnish	3 tbsp
2	garlic cloves, crushed	2
250 g	low-fat fromage frais	8 oz
2 tbsp	fresh lemon juice	2 tbsp
¼ tsp	salt	¼ tsp
	white pepper	

Sprinkle the gelatine over 3 tablespoons of water in a small bowl, then leave it to soften for 2 minutes. Microwave the solution on high for 30 seconds; stir to dissolve the granules.

In a large bowl, whisk the cornflour mixture into the milk. Heat the milk on high for 1½ to 2 minutes, whisking several times, until the sauce has thickened. Beat the gelatine mixture and the chopped cucumber into the sauce. Add the chopped mint, garlic, *fromage frais*, lemon juice, salt and some pepper, and mix well.

Rinse six small, rounded ramekins in cold water. Spoon the cucumber mixture into the ramekins and refrigerate them for at least 1 hour. Unmould the timbales on to individual plates and serve them garnished with the reserved cucumber slices and the mint sprigs.

SUGGESTED ACCOMPANIMENT: *warm pitta bread.*

Chopped Chicken Livers

LIVER IS A RICH SOURCE OF VITAMINS BUT HAS A RELATIVELY
HIGH CHOLESTEROL CONTENT, WHICH SHOULD BE TAKEN INTO
ACCOUNT WHEN PLANNING THE REST OF THE DAY'S MENU.

Serves 8 as a first course
Working time: about 10 minutes
Total time: about 1 hour and 30 minutes

Calories **85**
Protein **7g**
Cholesterol **110mg**
Total fat **4g**
Saturated fat **1g**
Sodium **120mg**

125 g	shallots, chopped	4 oz
1	garlic clove, crushed	1
1 tbsp	virgin olive oil	1 tbsp
250 g	chicken livers, soaked in skimmed milk to cover for 30 minutes, drained and patted dry with paper towels	8 oz
3 tbsp	port or red wine	3 tbsp
60 g	fresh granary or wholemeal breadcrumbs	2 oz
¼ tsp	salt	¼ tsp
	freshly ground black pepper	

Place the shallots and the garlic in a bowl and stir in the olive oil. Cover the bowl with plastic film, pull back one corner of the film, and cook the shallots and garlic on high for 3 minutes.

Add the chicken livers and the port to the bowl, re-cover it with plastic film, again pulling back one corner, and cook the mixture on high for a further 5 minutes. Allow the livers to cool slightly, then place all the cooked ingredients, together with the breadcrumbs, salt and some black pepper, in a food processor or blender and process to form a coarse pâté. Pile the pâté on to a serving plate.

SUGGESTED ACCOMPANIMENTS: *toast; gherkins.*

Smoked Cod Brandade

BRANDADE IS A FRENCH DISH OF SALT COD CREAMED
WITH OLIVE OIL, MASHED POTATO AND CREAM, THEN
FLAVOURED WITH GARLIC TO PRODUCE A LIGHT, FRAGRANT
PASTE. THIS MODERN VERSION REDUCES THE FAT AND SALT
CONTENT CONSIDERABLY

Serves 6 as a first course
Working (and total) time: about 25 minutes

Calories **150**
Protein **8g**
Cholesterol **20mg**
Total fat **8g**
Saturated fat **1g**
Sodium **465mg**

250 g	smoked cod fillet, skinned	8 oz
12.5 cl	skimmed milk	4 fl oz
1	bay leaf	1
350 g	potatoes, scrubbed, skins pricked	12 oz
1	large garlic clove	1
	white pepper	
3 tbsp	virgin olive oil	3 tbsp

Place the cod, milk and bay leaf in a shallow dish.
Cover the dish with a lid or plastic film, leaving one
corner open, and microwave on high for 4 minutes.
Leave the cod to stand while you cook the potatoes.

Place the potatoes on a double layer of paper
towels in the microwave oven and cook them on high
for 10 minutes, turning and rearranging them once
during cooking. They should feel soft in the centre
when pierced with a skewer; if they still feel firm, cook
them for a further 2 minutes. Set the potatoes aside.

Drain the cod, discarding the bay leaf; reserve the
cooking liquid. Break the fish into chunks, removing
any bones, and place it in a food processor. Process
the fish in bursts, scraping down the sides of the bowl
as necessary, until it is very finely shredded.

Peel and quarter the potatoes, then add them to the
fish in the food processor. Again using short bursts of
power, process the potato and fish to a coarse purée.
Add half to two thirds of the fish-cooking liquid and
process briefly until well mixed. Use the flat blade of a
knife or a pestle and mortar to crush the garlic, then
add it to the brandade, together with some pepper.
With the food processor running, slowly pour in the oil
through the feeder funnel. Stop the motor and check
the consistency of the mixture: it should be light and
soft. If it is too stiff, add more of the cooking liquid. Put
the brandade into a microwave-proof serving bowl.

Cover the bowl with plastic film, leaving one corner
open, and microwave the brandade on medium low for
2 minutes, to warm it through. Serve immediately.

SUGGESTED ACCOMPANIMENT: *cracker biscuits or a selection
of fresh new vegetables.*

EDITOR'S NOTE: *This dish may be made in advance and
warmed through on high for 3 minutes just before serving.
Fluff it up with a fork once or twice during this time.*

Spiced Tomato Rice Mould

Serves 6 as a first course
Working time: about 20 minutes
Total time: about 2 hours (includes cooling)

Calories **235**
Protein **5g**
Cholesterol **0mg**
Total fat **6g**
Saturated fat **1g**
Sodium **10mg**

1	large onion, roughly chopped	1
750 g	tomatoes, quartered	1 ½ lb
1	large sweet red pepper, roughly chopped	1
12.5 cl	dry white wine	4 fl oz
2 tbsp	virgin olive oil	2 tbsp
¼ tsp	cayenne pepper	¼ tsp
1 tbsp	paprika	1 tbsp
	bouquet garni	
250 g	Italian round-grain rice	8 oz
3 tbsp	finely chopped parsley	3 tbsp
	cherry tomatoes, for garnish (optional)	
	sweet yellow or red pepper slices, for garnish (optional)	

Put the onion, tomatoes and chopped sweet pepper in a large bowl with the wine, oil, cayenne pepper, paprika and bouquet garni. Cover the bowl with plastic film, pulling back one corner, and cook on high for 12 to 14 minutes, until the vegetables are soft.

Remove the bouquet garni and rub the remaining ingredients through a sieve into a large bowl. Stir the rice into the resulting purée, cover with plastic film, again pulling back one corner, and cook on high for 10 minutes, stirring twice. Cook on defrost for about 10 minutes more, stirring twice; the rice should have absorbed all the liquid. Add the parsley and blend well.

Lightly oil six 9 cm (3½ inch) diameter brioche moulds. Spoon the spiced rice into the moulds, packing it down with the back of the spoon and smoothing the surface. Leave to cool and set for about 1 hour.

To serve, turn out the rice moulds on to individual plates. Garnish, if you like, with cherry tomatoes and sweet pepper slices.

Paupiettes of Sole in Aspic

Serves 4 as a first course
Working time: about 30 minutes
Total time: about 2 hours (includes chilling)

Calories **110**
Protein **19g**
Cholesterol **40mg**
Total fat **3g**
Saturated fat **1g**
Sodium **190mg**

4	small lemon sole fillets (about 300 g/10 oz), skinned	4
1 tbsp	fresh lemon juice	1 tbsp
⅛ tsp	salt	⅛ tsp
	freshly ground black pepper	
90 g	white crab meat, picked over and flaked	3 oz
2 tbsp	thick Greek yogurt	2 tbsp
1 ½ tsp	chopped fresh tarragon	1 ½ tsp
3 tbsp	dry white wine or dry vermouth	3 tbsp
45 cl	vegetable aspic (recipe, page 13), melted	¾ pint
	dill or tarragon sprigs, for garnish (optional)	
Tarragon-yogurt sauce		
15 cl	plain low-fat yogurt	¼ pint
½ tsp	grated lemon rind	½ tsp
1 tbsp	fresh lemon juice	1 tbsp
1 ½ tsp	chopped fresh tarragon	1 ½ tsp

Lay the fillets of sole on a flat surface, skinned side up, and trim them to form neat, even-sized rectangles; reserve the trimmings. Sprinkle the fillets with the lemon juice and season them with the salt and some black pepper. Chop the sole trimmings and mix them with the crab meat, Greek yogurt and chopped tarragon. Place one quarter of the crab mixture in a mound at the thick end of each fillet, then carefully roll up the fish from head to tail, keeping the filling central.

Place the paupiettes in the centre of a shallow dish so that they almost touch each other. Pour the wine over them and cover the dish loosely with plastic film, leaving a corner open. Microwave the paupiettes on high for 2 minutes, rearranging them after 1 minute to ensure that they cook evenly. Set the fish aside, still covered, to cool completely. Drain the cooled paupiettes thoroughly and chill them in the refrigerator for at least 1 hour.

Spoon a very thin layer of the vegetable aspic into the base of four small, round moulds or ramekins and refrigerate them until the aspic is set — about 10 minutes. Place one paupiette, standing on end, in each dish, then pour in the remaining aspic to cover the paupiettes completely. Chill until the aspic is set — about 30 minutes.

To make the tarragon-yogurt sauce, mix the low-fat yogurt, lemon rind, lemon juice and chopped tarragon in a small bowl. Carefully unmould the jellied paupiettes on to four small serving plates. Spoon a little of the sauce on to each plate and serve at once, garnished with sprigs of dill or tarragon.

Monkfish and Prawn Terrine

Serves 8 as a first course
Working time: about 20 minutes
Total time: about 1 hour and 30 minutes (includes chilling)

Calories **95**
Protein **20g**
Cholesterol **75mg**
Total fat **2g**
Saturated fat **trace**
Sodium **450mg**

3 tsp	powdered gelatine	3 tsp
500 g	monkfish or other firm white fish fillets, skinned, cut into 1cm (½ inch) cubes	1 lb
60 g	watercress, washed, thick stems discarded, chopped	2 oz
150 g	low-fat soft cheese	5 oz
⅛ tsp	salt	⅛ tsp
	freshly ground black pepper	
2 tbsp	fresh lemon juice	2 tbsp
2 tbsp	chopped parsley, plus small parsley sprigs for garnish	2 tbsp
2	egg whites	2
125 g	peeled cooked prawns	4 oz
8 cl	vegetable aspic (page 13), melted	3 fl oz
4	lemon slices, halved, for garnish	4
8	whole cooked prawns, for garnish (optional)	8

Sprinkle the gelatine over 3 tablespoons of water in a small bowl, and leave it to soften for 2 minutes. Heat it on high for 30 seconds, then stir to dissolve the granules. Set the gelatine aside to cool.

Place the fish in a shallow dish and sprinkle over 1 tablespoon of water. Cover the dish with plastic film, leaving one corner open, and microwave on medium high until the fish is just firm — about 4 minutes. Leave the fish to cool, still covered, then drain off any cooking liquid and pat the fish dry on paper towels.

Place the watercress, soft cheese, salt, a little black pepper, the lemon juice and half of the chopped parsley in a bowl and stir well. Stir the cooled gelatine solution into the watercress mixture.

In a mixing bowl, whisk the egg whites until they form soft peaks. Gently stir 1 tablespoon of the whites into the watercress mixture, then use a metal spoon to fold in the remaining whites. Leave the mixture until it is just beginning to set — about 20 minutes — then gently stir in the fish and half of the peeled prawns.

Lightly grease an 18 by 8 by 6 cm (7 by 3½ by 2½ inch) loaf tin. Place the remaining peeled prawns in the bottom of the tin, pour on the aspic and refrigerate the tin for 10 minutes, until the aspic is partially set. Sprinkle the remaining chopped parsley evenly over the aspic, then carefully pour the watercress, fish and prawn mixture into the tin and chill until the terrine is set — about 1 hour. Unmould and slice the terrine, and serve it garnished with parsley sprigs, lemon slices and, if you like, with whole cooked prawns.

Garlic Pâté

Serves 4 as a first course
Working time: about 15 minutes
Total time: about 20 minutes

Calories **140**
Protein **8g**
Cholesterol **trace**
Total fat **6g**
Saturated fat **2g**
Sodium **350mg**

18	large garlic cloves	18
75 g	fresh wholemeal breadcrumbs	2½ oz
175 g	low-fat soft cheese	6 oz
⅛ tsp	salt	⅛ tsp
	freshly ground black pepper	
1 tbsp	virgin olive oil	1 tbsp

Peel and quarter the garlic cloves. Place the pieces in a small bowl and add just enough cold water to cover them. Microwave the garlic on medium high for 3½ minutes. Drain the garlic and discard the water.

Place the garlic in a food processor or blender with half of the breadcrumbs, and blend for a few seconds. Add the remaining breadcrumbs, the low-fat soft cheese, the salt and a generous amount of black pepper, and continue to process until smooth. With the machine running, slowly dribble in the olive oil.

To serve, transfer the pâté to a serving bowl and gently smooth the surface.

SUGGESTED ACCOMPANIMENTS: *an assortment of crisp, colourful raw vegetables; chunks of French bread.*

Aubergine Pâté

Serves 6 as a first course
Working time: about 8 minutes
Total time: about 50 minutes

Calories **60**
Protein **2g**
Cholesterol **trace**
Total fat **4g**
Saturated fat **1g**
Sodium **75mg**

3	large aubergines (about 1.5 kg/3 lb)	3
4 tbsp	fresh lemon juice	4 tbsp
6 tbsp	plain low-fat yogurt	6 tbsp
3 tbsp	tahini	3 tbsp
1/8 tsp	salt	1/8 tsp
2	garlic cloves, finely chopped	2
	paprika, for garnish	

Prick the aubergines in several places with a skewer or the tip of a sharp knife, and place them in the microwave oven on a double thickness of paper towels. Microwave the aubergines on high for about 9 minutes, turning them over half way through the cooking time. When cooked, the aubergines should be soft right through. Set them aside until they have cooled enough to handle. Cut each aubergine in half and scoop out the soft flesh, then set the flesh aside in a bowl to cool completely — about 30 minutes.

Purée the aubergine flesh in a food processor or blender, together with the lemon juice, yogurt, tahini, salt and garlic. Transfer the purée to a bowl and sprinkle it with paprika before serving.

SUGGESTED ACCOMPANIMENT: *wholemeal bread.*

Trout and Asparagus Terrine

Serves 6 as a main course
Working time: about 30 minutes
Total time: about 3 hours and 40 minutes (includes chilling)

Calories **120**
Protein **18g**
Cholesterol **trace**
Total fat **4g**
Saturated fat **1g**
Sodium **300mg**

250 g	asparagus spears, trimmed and peeled	8 oz
2	trout (about 250 g/8 oz each), cleaned, filleted and skinned	2
½	lemon, juice only	½
1 tbsp	powdered gelatine	1 tbsp
12.5 cl	dry white wine	4 fl oz
350 g	low-fat soft cheese	12 oz
4	spring onions, finely chopped	4
1 tbsp	chopped parsley	1 tbsp
2	egg whites	2
	fresh chervil leaves, for garnish	
	lemon wedges, for garnish	

Place the asparagus spears in a large, shallow bowl, tips towards the centre. Pour in 15 cl (¼ pint) of water and cover the bowl with plastic film, pulling one corner back a little. Cook on high for 4 minutes. Leave the asparagus to cool, still covered.

Cut each trout fillet into three long strips. Lay the strips flat on a plate and sprinkle them with the lemon juice. Cover the plate loosely with plastic film and cook the fillets on high for 3½ minutes. Uncover the plate and leave the fish to cool.

Line the base of a 18 by 7.5 by 7.5 cm (7 by 3 by 3 inch) loaf tin with greaseproof paper or plastic film. In a small bowl, sprinkle the gelatine over the white wine and leave it to soften for 2 minutes. Heat the mixture on high for 30 seconds, then stir to dissolve the granules. Leave the mixture to cool. Beat the cheese until it is soft and creamy. Add the spring onions and parsley, and whisk in the wine and gelatine mixture. Whisk the egg whites until they are just stiff, then fold them into the cheese mixture.

Pour a little of the cheese mixture into the base of the loaf tin, and top it with a third of the asparagus, laid lengthwise. Pour in a little more cheese and top with trout strips. Continue building up the terrine, alternating the cheese mixture with asparagus and trout strips, and finishing with a thin layer of cheese mixture. Refrigerate the terrine for at least 3 hours.

To serve the terrine, turn it out on to a flat serving platter and cut it into slices. Garnish the slices with chervil leaves and wedges of lemon.

SUGGESTED ACCOMPANIMENT: *boiled new potatoes garnished with cut chives.*

Parslied Duck

Serves 6 as a main course
Working time: about 30 minutes
Total time: about 9 hours (includes marinating and chilling)

Calories **235**
Protein **27g**
Cholesterol **110mg**
Total fat **10g**
Saturated fat **2g**
Sodium **160mg**

2 kg	duck, cut into four pieces, skinned	4 lb
45 g	flat-leaf parsley, stems reserved, leaves finely chopped, plus two large leaves for garnish	1½ oz
1	lemon, thinly pared rind only	1
10	black peppercorns	10
60 cl	dry cider or dry white wine	1 pint
1 tbsp	powdered gelatine	1 tbsp

Place the duck pieces in a large bowl and add the parsley stems, lemon rind, peppercorns and cider. Cover the bowl with a lid or plastic film and leave the duck to marinate for 2 to 3 hours, turning once.

Place the duck, still in its marinade, in the microwave; if it is covered with plastic film, pull back one corner. Cook the duck on high for 10 minutes, then cook it on defrost for a further 30 minutes, turning the pieces once after 15 minutes, until the juices run clear when a thigh is pierced with a skewer. Transfer the duck pieces to a plate. Strain the cooking juices through a sieve lined with a paper towel and allow them to cool. Chill this stock for at least 3 hours, then discard the fat that has risen to the top.

Remove the duck meat from the bones, cut the meat into small dice and place it in a large bowl together with the chopped parsley leaves. Cover the bowl and set it aside in a cool place.

Put four tablespoons of the defatted stock into a small bowl, sprinkle over the gelatine and leave it to soften for 2 minutes. Heat the stock and gelatine on high for 30 seconds, then stir to dissolve the granules. Pour the gelatine into the remaining stock and leave it until it is just beginning to thicken — about 30 minutes. Reserve 4 tablespoons of the stock and add the remainder to the duck and parsley, mixing well. Pour the duck and stock mixture into a 60 cl (1 pint) serving dish, and refrigerate for 10 minutes until it is just beginning to set. Pour the reserved stock over the duck, garnish with the parsley leaves and return the dish to the refrigerator until set completely — at least 2 hours.

SUGGESTED ACCOMPANIMENTS: *green beans; crusty bread.*

Glossary

Acidulated water: a dilute solution of lemon juice in water, used to keep certain vegetables and fruits from discolouring after they are peeled.

Bain marie: see Water bath.

Balsamic vinegar: a mild, intensely fragrant wine-based vinegar made in northern Italy; traditionally it is aged in wooden casks.

Bouquet garni: several herbs — the classic three are parsley, thyme and bay leaf — tied together or wrapped in muslin and used to flavour a stock, sauce, braise or stew. The bouquet garni is removed and discarded at the end of the cooking time.

Bok choy (also called Chinese chard): a sweet-tasting cruciferous vegetable that grows in a celery-like bunch and has smooth white stalks and wide, dark-green leaves.

Calorie (or kilocalorie): a precise measure of the energy food supplies when it is broken down for use in the body.

Capers: the pickled flower buds of the caper plant, a shrub native to the Mediterranean. Capers are preserved sometimes in vinegar, sometimes in salt; they should be rinsed before use.

Caramelize: to heat sugar, or a food that is naturally rich in sugar such as fruit, until the sugar turns brown and syrupy.

Cassis: a blackcurrant-flavoured liqueur.

Caul: a weblike fatty membrane that surrounds a pig's stomach. When wrapped round a savoury filling, it melts during cooking and moistens the mixture.

Cayenne pepper: a fiery powder ground from the seeds and pods of red peppers. Used in small amounts to heighten other flavours.

Ceps (also called porcini): wild mushrooms with a pungent, earthy flavour that survives drying or long cooking. Dried ceps should be soaked in warm water before they are used.

Chanterelle mushroom (also called girolle): a variety of wild mushroom that is trumpet-shaped and yellow-orange in colour. Chanterelles are available fresh or dried; dried chanterelles should be soaked in warm water before use.

Chicory: a small, cigar-shaped vegetable, composed of many tightly wrapped white to pale-yellow leaves. Can be cooked, or eaten raw in salads.

Chiffonade: a leafy vegetable sliced into thin shreds.

Chili peppers: hot or mild red, yellow or green members of the pepper family. Fresh or dried, most chili peppers contain volatile oils that can irritate the skin and eyes; they must be handled carefully (see caution, page 9).

Chili powder: a peppery red powder made from ground dried chili peppers. It is available in various strengths from mild to hot.

Chinese five-spice powder: see Five-spice powder.

Cholesterol: a waxlike substance manufactured in the human body and also found in foods of animal origin. Although a certain amount of cholesterol is necessary for proper body functioning, an excess can accumulate in the arteries, contributing to heart disease. See also Monounsaturated fats; Polyunsaturated fats; Saturated fats.

Cod: a salt-water fish, normally weighing between 3 and 7.5 kg (6 and 15 lb), which is caught all year round in the Atlantic and Pacific. Its lean, white flesh flakes easily when cooked.

Coral: the edible roe of the scallop, lobster or crab.

Cornflour: a starchy white powder made from corn kernels and used as a thickening agent. Like arrowroot, it is transparent when cooked and makes a more efficient thickener than flour.

Cottage cheese: a low-fat soft cheese with a mild flavour and a non-uniform texture. It is made from skimmed milk but the cottage cheese used in this book has added cream to give it a fat content of 4 per cent.

Court-bouillon: a flavoured liquid used for poaching fish or shellfish. It may contain aromatic vegetables, herbs, wine or milk.

Crab: a crustacean with five pairs of jointed legs, the first of which have pincers. It is often sold cooked because of the high perishability of raw crab. A dressed crab is a ready-to-eat cooked crab that has had its viscera, gills, legs and tail flap removed. The meat is then arranged in the body shell; usually, the brown meat and white meat are kept separate.

Crème fraîche: a slightly ripened, sharp-tasting French double cream containing about 35 per cent fat.

Curly endive: a curly leafed green with a bitter taste similar to chicory. The lighter leaves are sweeter and more tender than the dark green ones.

Cumin: the aromatic seeds of an umbelliferous plant similar to fennel, used whole or powdered as a spice, especially in Indian and Latin American dishes. Toasting gives it a nutty flavour.

Debeard: to remove the fibrous threads from a mussel. These threads, called the beard, are produced by the mussel to attach itself to stationary objects.

Devein: to remove the intestinal vein that runs along the outer curve of a prawn. To devein a prawn, peel it first, then make a shallow cut along the line of the vein and scrape out the vein with the tip of the knife.

Dublin Bay prawn (also called Norway lobster, scampi or langoustine): a large crustacean found in the Atlantic, Mediterranean and Adriatic. The meat, mainly in the tail, is firm and sweet.

Eel: an Atlantic fish that resembles a snake, with firm, rich flesh and a mild flavour. They are generally skinned before they are cooked.

Fennel: a herb (also called wild fennel) whose feathery leaves and dried seeds have a mild anise flavour and are much used for flavouring. Its vegetable relative, the bulb — or Florence — fennel (also called finocchio) can be cooked, or eaten raw in salads.

Five-spice powder: a pungent blend of ground Sichuan pepper, star anise, cassia, cloves and fennel seeds; available in Asian food shops.

Fromage frais: a soft cheese made from skimmed milk. The fromage frais used in this book has a small amount of added cream and a 1 per cent fat content.

Garam masala: an aromatic mixture of ground spices used in Indian cookery. It usually contains coriander, cumin, cloves, ginger and cinnamon.

Gelatine: a virtually tasteless protein, available in powdered form or in sheets. Dissolved gelatine is used to firm liquid mixtures so they can be moulded.

Ginger: the spicy, buff-coloured rhizome, or rootlike stem, of the ginger plant, used as a seasoning either fresh or dried and powdered.

Haddock: a silvery-grey member of the cod family, with lean, delicately flavoured flesh. The average weight of a haddock is 1 to 2.5 kg (2 to 5 lb).

Hazelnut: the fruit of a shrublike tree found primarily in Turkey, Italy and Spain, and in the United States. Filberts, which are cultivated, have a stronger flavour than hazelnuts, which grow wild. Both are prized by bakers and sweetmakers.

Horn of plenty: a wild mushroom, sometimes known as a trompette, with a pale grey exterior and a delicate flavour. It is occasionally available fresh, but is more often sold dried; the dried form should be soaked in warm water before use.

Julienne: the French term for vegetables or other food cut into strips.

Juniper berries: the berries of the juniper tree, used as the key flavouring in gin as well as in pork dishes and sauerkraut. Whole berries should be removed from a dish before it is served.

Kirsch: a clear cherry brandy distilled from small black cherries grown in Switzerland, Germany and the Alsace region of France.

Lemon sole: not a true sole, this flat fish is an important food fish in Britain and France.

Mace: the aril, or covering, that encases the nutmeg seed. It is often sold ready ground.

Macerate: to soften a food by soaking instead of cooking, usually in an aromatic or spiced liquid.

Madeira: a fortified wine, often used in cooking, that is produced on the island of Madeira. There are four classes of Madeira, ranging from sweet to dry in flavour and brown to gold in colour.

Mange-tout: flat green pea pods eaten whole, with only stems and strings removed.

Marinade: a mixture of aromatic ingredients in which meat or vegetables are allowed to stand before cooking to enrich their flavour. Some marinades will tenderize meat, but they do not penetrate deeply.

Marsala: a dark, Sicilian dessert wine with a caramelized flavour.

Monkfish (also called angler-fish): an Atlantic fish with a scaleless, thick-skinned body and a large head; only the tail portion is edible. Although the monkfish weighs on average 3.5 to 7.5 kg (8 to 15 lb), some specimens grow as large as 22 kg (50 lb).

Monounsaturated fats: one of the three types of fats found in foods. Monounsaturated fats are believed not to raise the level of cholesterol in the blood.

Morel: a brown fungus with a pitted conical cap. It is usually sold dried and should be soaked in warm water and very carefully cleaned of all grit before use.

Mullet, grey: silvery blue-grey fish found in the Atlantic and Mediterranean. The firm yet delicate flesh is rather like a mackerel but less rich. In the eastern Mediterranean, the roe is used to make taramasalata.

Mullet, red: a small fish, weighing between 175 g and 500 g (6 oz and 1 lb). The liver is greatly prized.

Mussel: a bivalve mollusc with bluish-black shells found along Atlantic and Pacific coasts as well as in the Mediterranean. The mussel's sweet flesh varies from beige to orange-yellow in colour when cooked.

Non-reactive pan: a cooking vessel whose surface does not chemically react with food. Materials used include stainless steel, enamel, glass and some alloys. Untreated cast iron and aluminium may react with acids, producing discoloration or a peculiar taste.

Nori: paper-like dark green or black sheets of dried seaweed, often used in Japanese cuisine as a flavouring or as wrappers for rice and vegetables.

Olive oil: any of various grades of oil extracted from olives. Extra virgin olive oil has a full, fruity flavour and very low acidity. Pure olive oil, a processed blend of olive oils, has the lightest taste and highest acidity. For salad dressings, virgin and extra virgin olive oils are preferred. Store in a cool, dark place.

Oyster mushroom: a variety of wild mushroom, now cultivated. They are stronger tasting than button mushrooms, and pale brown, gold and grey varieties are available.

Papaya (also called pawpaw): a fruit native to Central America. The colour of the skin ranges from green to orange, and the flesh from pale yellow to salmon. When ripe, the fruit is sweet and enjoyed raw, but unripe papayas may be eaten cooked as a vegetable.

Paprika: a slightly sweet, spicy, bright-red powder produced by grinding dried red peppers. The best type of paprika is Hungarian.

Parchment paper: a reusable paper treated with silicone to produce a non-stick surface. It is used to line loaf tins and baking sheets.

Passion fruit: a juicy, fragrant, egg-shaped tropical fruit with wrinkled skin, yellow flesh and many small black seeds. The seeds are edible; the skin is not.

Peppercorns: the berries of the pepper vine picked at various stages of ripeness and then dried. Black, white, pink and green peppercorns are available.

Pesto: a paste made by pounding basil, garlic, pine-nuts and salt with olive oil. It can be bought ready made from delicatessens and supermarkets. In Italian, *pesto* simply means "pounded".

Pine-nuts: seeds from the cone of the stone pine, a tree native to the Mediterranean. Pine-nuts are used in pesto and other sauces; their buttery flavour can be heightened by light toasting.

Pistachio nuts: prized for their flavour and green colour, pistachios must be shelled and boiled for a few minutes before their skins can be removed.

Poach: to cook gently in simmering liquid.

Polyunsaturated fats: one of the three types of fats found in foods. They exist in abundance in such vegetable oils as safflower, sunflower, corn and soya bean. Polyunsaturated fats lower the level of cholesterol in the blood.

Prawn: a crustacean that lives in cold and warm waters in all parts of the world, called prawn or shrimp (or both) depending on local preference and size. Prawns and shrimps can be cooked in or out of the shell. They are moderately high in cholesterol but very low in fat. See also Devein and Dublin Bay prawn.

Quark: a type of soft cheese with a mild, clean, slightly acid flavour; usually very low in fat, but smoother varieties have added cream.

Quatre épices: a blend of ground spices often used in French cuisine, consisting of white pepper — which gives it its predominantly peppery taste — cloves, nutmeg and ginger.

Radicchio: a purplish-red Italian chicory with a chewy texture and slightly bitter taste.

Ramekin: a small, round, straight-sided glass or porcelain mould, used to bake a single serving of food.

Recommended Daily Amount (RDA): the average daily amount of an essential nutrient as recommended for groups of healthy people by the UK Department of Health and Social Security.

Red lollo lettuce: a red-tinged, frilly lettuce.

Reduce: to boil down a liquid in order to concentrate its flavour and thicken its consistency.

Rice vinegar: a mild, fragrant vinegar less assertive than cider vinegar or distilled white vinegar; available in dark, light, seasoned and sweetened varieties.

Ricotta: soft, mild, white Italian cheese, made from cow's or sheep's milk. Full-fat ricotta has a fat content of 20 to 30 per cent, but the low-fat ricotta used in this book has a fat content of only about 8 per cent.

Roe: refers primarily to fish eggs, but edible roe is also found in scallops, crabs and lobsters.

Safflower oil: a vegetable oil that contains a high proportion of polyunsaturated fats.

Saffron: the dried, yellowish-red stigmas (or threads) of the saffron crocus, which yield a powerful yellow colour as well as a pungent flavour. Powdered saffron may be substituted for threads but has less flavour.

Salmon: a sea fish, the salmon can weigh 3 to 13 kg (7 to 30 lb). Much of the commercial supply is farm raised and is often cut into steaks and cutlets. Baltic salmon has paler pink flesh than Atlantic salmon, and a higher fat content.

Saturated fats: one of the three types of fats found in foods. They exist in abundance in animal products and coconut and palm oils; they raise the level of cholesterol in the blood. Because high blood-cholesterol levels may cause heart disease, saturated fat consumption should be restricted to less than 15 per cent of the calories provided by the daily diet.

Savoy cabbage: a variety of round cabbage with a mild flavour and crisp, crinkly leaves.

Scallop: a bivalve mollusc found throughout the world. The white nut of meat and the orange roe, or coral, are eaten. Tiny queen scallops are a different species from the familiar larger scallops known in France as *coquilles Saint-Jacques*.

Sea bass: a fish with firm, lean flesh, the sea bass is found in the Atlantic.

Sesame seeds: small, nutty-tasting seeds used frequently, either raw or toasted, in Middle Eastern and Indian cookery. They are also used to make an oil with a nutty, smoky aroma.

Shallot: a refined cousin of the onion, with a subtle flavour and papery, red-brown skin.

Shiitake mushroom: a variety of mushroom, originally grown only in Japan, sold fresh or dried. The dried form should be soaked and stemmed before use.

Sichuan pepper (also called Chinese, Japanese or anise pepper): a dried shrub berry with a tart, aromatic flavour less piquant than black pepper.

Skimmed milk: milk from which almost all the fat has been removed.

Sodium: a nutrient essential to maintaining the proper balance of fluids in the body. In most diets, a major source of the element is table salt, made up of 40 per cent sodium. Excess sodium may contribute to high blood pressure, which increases the risk of heart disease. One teaspoon (5.5 g) of salt, with 2,132 milligrams of sodium, contains just over the maximum daily amount recommended by the World Health Organization.

Soft cheese: any soft, spreadable cheese with a high moisture content and a mild, slightly acidic flavour. The low-fat soft cheese used in this book has a fat content of 8 per cent.

Soy sauce: a savoury, salty brown liquid made from fermented soya beans and available in both light and dark versions. One teaspoon of ordinary soy sauce contains 1,030 milligrams of sodium; lower-sodium variations, such as naturally fermented shoyu, may contain half that amount.

Squab: a young pigeon, weighing from 250 to 500 g (8 oz to 1 lb) when sold. Domestic pigeons reared for the table have paler flesh and a more mellow taste than wild pigeons.

Squid: a shell-less mollusc of the cephalopod family found in the Atlantic and Mediterranean. The two main varieties are short-finned and long-finned squid. Eighty per cent of the squid is edible. If it is bought whole, the pen, beak, ink sac and gonads should be removed before eating. Squid is high in cholesterol.

Star anise: a woody, star-shaped spice, similar in flavour to anise. Ground star anise is a component of five-spice powder.

Stock: a savoury liquid made by simmering aromatic vegetables, herbs and spices, and usually meat bones and trimmings, in water. Stock forms a flavour-rich base for sauces.

Sun-dried tomatoes: tomatoes that have been dried in the open air to concentrate their flavour; some are then packed in oil.

Swiss chard: a plant native to the Mediterranean, with large, spinach-like leaves on the ends of broad, white stalks. Both leaves and stalks may be used.

Tabasco sauce: a hot, unsweetened chili sauce.

Timbale: a creamy mixture of vegetables or meat baked in a mould. The term, French for "kettledrum", also denotes a drum-shaped baking dish.

Tomato paste: concentrated tomato purée, available in cans and tubes, used in sauces and soups.

Total fat: an individual's daily intake of polyunsaturated, monounsaturated and saturated fats. Nutritionists recommend that fats constitute no more than 35 per cent of a person's total calorie intake. The term as used in the nutrient analyses in this book refers to all the sources of fat in a recipe.

Trout, rainbow: a freshwater fish, with an average weight of 250 to 500 g (8 oz to 1 lb). Most of the commercial supply is farm raised. The flesh is soft and rich in flavour.

Trout, sea (also called salmon trout): the same species as the brown river trout; the flesh is pale pink and moist with an excellent flavour and texture.

Tuna: refers to several varieties of fish, found in both the Atlantic and the Pacific; some tuna can weigh as much as 675 kg (1,500 lb). The flesh is dense, full-flavoured and oily; it can be white, as in long-finned or albacore tuna, or light brown, as in bigeye and skipjack tuna. Bluefin has a dark, nearly red flesh.

Turmeric: a yellow spice from a plant related to ginger, used as a colouring agent and occasionally as a substitute for saffron. Turmeric has a musty odour and a slightly bitter flavour.

Vine leaves: the tender, lightly flavoured leaves of the grapevine, used in many ethnic cuisines as wrappers for savoury mixtures. Preserved vine leaves, usually packed in brine, should be rinsed before use.

Virgin olive oil: see Olive oil.

Water bath (also called bain marie): a large pan partially filled with hot water and placed in a preheated oven as a cooking vessel for foods in smaller containers. The combination of ambient hot water and air serves to cook the food slowly and evenly.

Whiting: a member of the cod family, whiting is caught in the North Sea and the Atlantic. The flesh is delicate and sweet.

Wholemeal flour: wheat flour which contains the whole of the wheat grain with nothing added or taken away. It is nutritionally valuable as a source of dietary fibre and is higher in B vitamins than white flour.

Yeast: a micro-organism which feeds on sugars and starches to produce carbon dioxide and thus leaven breads and pastries. Yeast can be bought either fresh or dried; fresh yeast will keep for up to six weeks in a refrigerator.

Yogurt: a smooth-textured, semi-solid cultured milk product made with varying percentages of fat. Yogurt can be substituted for soured cream in cooking, or combined with soured cream to produce a sauce or topping lower in fat and calories than soured cream alone. Thick Greek-style strained yogurt is another alternative to soured cream. This contains 10 per cent fat, as compared to 18 per cent in soured cream.

Index

Picture Credits

Cover: Chris Knaggs. 4: John Elliott, except bottom left, Chris Knaggs. 5: David Johnson. 6: Chris Knaggs. 12-16: John Elliott. 17: David Johnson. 18: Chris Knaggs. 19-20: John Elliott. 21: David Johnson. 22: Chris Knaggs. 23: David Johnson. 24: Andrew Whittuck. 26: John Elliott. 27: Chris Knaggs. 29: John Elliott. 30: Andrew Whittuck. 31: Chris Knaggs. 33: Andrew Whittuck. 34: Chris Knaggs. 35: Andrew Williams. 36: John Elliott. 37: Andrew Whittuck. 39: John Elliott. 40: David Johnson. 41: Andrew Whittuck. 43: Chris Knaggs. 44: David Johnson. 45-46: John Elliott. 47: David Johnson. 48: Andrew Whittuck. 49: John Elliott. 50: Andrew Whittuck. 51: Chris Knaggs. 52: David Johnson. 53: Andrew Whittuck. 54-55: James Murphy. 56: John Elliott. 57: David Johnson. 58: James Murphy. 59: Andrew Whittuck. 60-61: John Elliott. 63: Andrew Williams. 64: David Johnson. 65-66: John Elliott. 67-68: David Johnson. 69: John Elliott. 70: Chris Knaggs. 71: John Elliott. 72: David Johnson. 73: Chris Knaggs. 74-75: John Elliott. 76: David Johnson. 77: Andrew Williams. 79: John Elliott. 80: David Johnson. 81: Andrew Whittuck. 82: Chris Knaggs. 83: David Johnson. 84-85: James Murphy. 86: Chris Knaggs. 87-89: John Elliott. 90: (top) David Johnson; (bottom) Taran Z Photography. 91: John

Elliott. 92: Andrew Whittuck. 93: Andrew Williams. 94: John Elliott. 95: David Johnson. 96-97: John Elliott. 98: Chris Knaggs. 99: Andrew Williams. 101: David Johnson. 102: Chris Knaggs. 103: John Elliott. 104-105: David Johnson. 106: John Elliott. 107: David Johnson. 108: Andrew Williams. 109-112: Chris Knaggs. 113: Andrew Whittuck. 114-115: David Johnson. 116-119: John Elliott. 120: David Johnson. 121: Andrew Whittuck. 122: Chris Knaggs. 123: John Elliott. 124: Andrew Whittuck. 125: David Johnson. 126: John Elliott. 127: Andrew Whittuck. 128-130: Chris Knaggs. 131: David Johnson. 132: John Elliott. 133-135: David Johnson. 136: Chris Knaggs. 137: Andrew Whittuck. 138: Chris Knaggs. 139: David Johnson.

Props: The editors wish to thank the following outlets and manufacturers; all are based in London unless otherwise stated. Cover: cloth, Ewart Liddell; plate, Villeroy & Boch. 14-15: marble, W.E. Grant & Co. (Marble) Ltd.; plate, Mappin & Webb Silversmiths. 16: china, Royal Worcester, Worcester; cutlery, Mappin & Webb Silversmiths. 18: plate and dish, David Winkley, The Craftsmen Potters Shop. 19: china, Hutschenreuther (U.K.) Ltd. 39: cloth, Ewart Liddell; plate, Royal Worcester, Worcester. 44: cloth, Ewart

Liddell; silver, Mappin & Webb Silversmiths. 50: cloth, Ewart Liddell; china, Royal Worcester, Worcester. 53: plate, Villeroy & Boch. 60: china, Hutschenreuther (U.K.) Ltd. 61: silver, Mappin & Webb Silversmiths. 64: plates, Villeroy & Boch. 65: platter, Hutschenreuther (U.K.) Ltd. 66: marble, W.E. Grant & Co. (Marble) Ltd. 67: china, Royal Worcester, Worcester. 68: formica, Formica, Newcastle, Tyne and Wear. 69: plate, Royal Worcester, Worcester. 70: platter, Villeroy & Boch. 74: silver, Mappin & Webb Silversmiths. 82: plate, Hutschenreuther (U.K.) Ltd. 84-85: marble, W.E. Grant & Co. (Marble) Ltd.; plate, Chinacraft. 98: platter, Villeroy & Boch. 99: plate, Royal Worcester, Worcester. 101: dark marble, W.E. Grant & Co. (Marble) Ltd. 102: formica, Formica, Newcastle, Tyne and Wear. 114: marble, W.E. Grant & Co. (Marble) Ltd. 116: cakeslice, Mappin & Webb Silversmiths. 117: cloth, Ewart Liddell. 120: cloth, Ewart Liddell; platter, Hutschenreuther (U.K.) Ltd. 121: china, Royal Worcester, Worcester. 123: plate, Royal Worcester, Worcester. 124: linen, Ewart Liddell; china, Hutschenreuther (U.K.) Ltd. 128: cloth, Ewart Liddell; plate, Augarten Gesellschaft MBH, Augarten, Austria. 135: plate, Royal Worcester, Worcester. 138: plate, Rosenthal (London) Ltd.

Acknowledgements

The index for this book was prepared by Myra Clark, London. The editors also wish to thank: Rachel Andrew, London; Steve Ashton, London; Paul van Biene, London; René Bloom, London; Maureen Burrows, London; Sean Davis, London; Jonathan Driver, London; Ellen Galford, Edinburgh; Jamie Griffiths, London; Bridget Jones, Guildford, Surrey; Jim Murray, London; Sharp Electronics (UK) Ltd, London; Jane Stevenson, London; Toshiba (UK) Ltd, London; Ian Watson, London.

Colour separations by Fotolitomec, S.N.C., Milan, Italy
Typesetting by G. Beard and Son Ltd, Brighton, Sussex, England
Printed in Italy by New Interlitho S.p.A. - Milan